Keynes for the Twenty-First Century

Also by Mathew Forstater:

Little Book of Big Ideas: Economics. ABC Books & Audio/BBC Audio, 2007.

Co-editor, *Post Keynesian Macroeconomics: Essays in Honour of Ingrid Rima.* Routledge, 2007.

Co-editor, *Money, Financial Instability and Stabilization Policy.* Edward Elgar, 2006.

Co-editor, *Contemporary Post Keynesian Analysis.* Edward Elgar, 2005.

Co-editor, *Full Employment and Price Stability: The Macroeconomic Vision of William S. Vickrey.* Edward Elgar, 2004.

Co-editor, *Reinventing Functional Finance: Transformational Growth and Full Employment.* Edward Elgar, 2003.

Also by L. Randall Wray:

Co-editor, *Money, Financial Instability and Stabilization Policy.* Edward Elgar, 2006.

El Papel Dinero Hoy: La Clave del Pleno Empleo y la Estabilidad de Precios, Spanish-language edition of *Understanding Modern Money: The Key to Full Employment and Price Stability.* Translated by Guillermina Free. Universidad Nacional Autónoma de México, Mexico, D.F., 2006.

Co-editor, *Contemporary Post Keynesian Analysis.* Edward Elgar, 2005.

Editor, *Credit and State Theories of Money: The Contributions of A. Mitchell Innes.* Edward Elgar, 2004.

Trabalho e Moeda Hoje: A Chave Para o Pleno Emprego e a Estabilidade dos Preços, Portuguese-language edition of *Understanding Modern Money: The Key to Full Employment and Price Stability.* Editora UFRJ/Contraponto, 2003.

Understanding Modern Money: The Key to Full Employment and Price Stability. Edward Elgar, 1998, reprinted 2003.

Money and Credit in Capitalist Economies: The Endogenous Money Approach. Edward Elgar, 1990.

Keynes for the Twenty-First Century

The Continuing Relevance of *The General Theory*

Edited by Mathew Forstater and L. Randall Wray

palgrave
macmillan

KEYNES FOR THE TWENTY-FIRST CENTURY

First published in 2008 by
PALGRAVE MACMILLAN™
175 Fifth Avenue, New York, N.Y. 10010 and
Houndmills, Basingstoke, Hampshire, England RG21 6XS.
Companies and representatives throughout the world.

PALGRAVE MACMILLAN is the global academic imprint of the Palgrave Macmillan division of St. Martin's Press, LLC and of Palgrave Macmillan Ltd. Macmillan® is a registered trademark in the United States, United Kingdom and other countries. Palgrave is a registered trademark in the European Union and other countries.

ISBN-13: 978-0-230-60581-7
ISBN-10: 0-230-60581-8

Library of Congress Cataloging-in-Publication Data

Keynes for the twenty-first century / edited by Mathew Forstater, L. Randall Wray.
p. cm.
Includes bibliographical references and index.
ISBN 0-230-60581-8
1. Keynesian economics. I. Forstater, Mathew, 1961– II. Wray, L. Randall, 1953–
HB99.7.K3954 2008
330.15'6--dc22 2007039407

A catalogue record of the book is available from the British Library.

Design by Scribe Inc.

First edition: April 2008

10 9 8 7 6 5 4 3 2 1

Printed in the United States of America.

Contents

Preface

This volume is an outgrowth of the Ninth International Post Keynesian Conference, which was held September 15–18, 2006, in Kansas City, Missouri.

The conference was co-sponsored by the *Journal of Post Keynesian Economics*, the Center for Full Employment and Price Stability of the University of Missouri–Kansas City (UMKC), and the Economics Department of UMKC.

The 2006 conference was especially significant, for it was a commemoration of several significant anniversaries: publication of *The General Theory of Employment, Interest and Money* (1936), passage of the Employment Act (1946), establishment of the IMF and the World Bank (1946), the death of Keynes (1946), and passage of the Freedom Budget (1966). Thus, it was most fitting for Post Keynesians to take note of progress, or lack of it, over the last seventy years.

Attending the conference were nearly two hundred academic economists, policymakers, graduate students, and dignitaries, representing twenty countries. There were thirty-three concurrent sessions on Friday, Saturday, and Sunday. Noted Post Keynesian figures gave addresses at the Saturday banquet and at Monday's Keynote Session. These presentations are collected in this volume, along with those of other well-known Post Keynesian scholars who were unable to attend.

The papers collected in this volume demonstrate a crucial point: Assessing the importance of Keynes's work shows that it is not a mere exercise in the history of economic thought but, rather, that there is a continuing theoretical and practical significance of *The General Theory* and his other works. While at most economics departments today Keynes's writings have been removed from the syllabi, at UMKC's interdisciplinary and heterodox economics program, Keynes's contributions remain central to understanding the workings of modern capitalist economies. It is our contention that the papers contained herein reveal just such a continuing—and even increasing—significance of Keynes for contemporary political economy.

ACKNOWLEDGMENTS

The editors recognize and thank all of the participants of the Ninth International Post Keynesian Conference, particularly those who made the Monday Keynote Session such a success.

The organization of such an extensive conference is a lengthy and time-consuming affair, and there are many people who should be recognized for their vital contributions to the planning and implementation process:

- The members of the organizing committee—Bob Brazelton, Paul and Louise Davidson, Charles Goodhart, Geoff Harcourt, Jan Kregel, Dennis Merrill, Warren Mosler, Claudio Sardoni, and Robert Skidelsky—who were instrumental in shaping the Keynote Session
- Michael Devine and Ray Geselbracht of the Harry S. Truman Library and Museum for financial support
- Jim Sturgeon, representing the UMKC Department of Economics, for extending a warm welcome to conference attendees
- Warren Mosler, for his organization of the highly entertaining roast of Paul Davidson and (in a more serious vein) his essential financial support of the conference and other CFEPS activities
- Troy Nash, City Councilman of Kansas City, Missouri, for his originality and hospitality in bestowing on Paul and Louise Davidson the keys to the city
- Geoff Harcourt, for delivering the UMKC Bernardin Haskell lecture following the conference; also, for his memorable post-dinner poetry reading during the conference
- Edward Elgar Publishing, Palgrave Macmillan, and Worth Publishers for their participation and support
- Pavlina Tcherneva, who laid the groundwork for the conference by coordinating the initial planning and months of preparation
- Charlene Heinen, who took over from Pavlina shortly before the conference and handled a host of final details
- Fred Lee, who was extremely helpful in publicizing the conference
- Kelly Pinkham, who assisted with the keynote-recognition ceremonies and managed speaker transport and on-site supplies
- The UMKC graduate students who most ably assisted with a myriad of tasks, both before and during the conference: Karol Gil-Vasquez, Ergun Meric, Gerald J. B. Mupingo, Michael Murray, Gianluca Rossi, Alla Semenova, Natalia Speer, and Heather Starzynski

Finally, we are grateful to those who were responsible for preparation of the volume: Charlene Heinen, who edited the papers, assembled the final manuscript, and responded to the publisher's queries; John F. Henry, who was a resource on publication issues; and Tae-Hee Jo, who provided valuable technical assistance.

Contributors

W. Robert Brazelton is Emeritus Professor of Economics at the University of Missouri–Kansas City, with an expertise in Institutional and Post Keynesian macroanalysis, the works of Leon H. Keyserling of the Truman Council of Economic Advisors, and comparative European systems.

Luiz Carlos Bresser-Pereira is Emeritus Professor of Economics and Political Theory at Getulio Vargas Foundation, São Paulo, Brazil, and editor of the *Brazilian Journal of Political Economy*.

William A. Darity Jr. is Arts and Sciences Professor of Public Policy Studies, Economics, and African and African American Studies at Duke University, Durham, North Carolina.

Robert Dimand is Professor of Economics at Brock University, St. Catherines, Ontario, Canada, and has held a Chancellor's Chair for Research Excellence. He is the author of *Origins of the Keynesian Revolution*, co-author of volume 1 of *A History of Game Theory*, co-editor of *A Biographical Dictionary of Women Economists*, and editor of the ten-volume work, *The Origins of Macroeconomics*.

Mathew Forstater is Associate Professor of Economics and Black Studies at the University of Missouri–Kansas City and Director of the Center for Full Employment and Price Stability, UMKC.

James K. Galbraith holds the Lloyd M. Bentsen Jr. Chair in Government/Business Relations at the Lyndon B. Johnson School of Public Affairs, The University of Texas at Austin. He is a Senior Scholar with the Levy Economics Institute and Chair of the Board of Economists for Peace and Security.

Charles A. E. Goodhart is Professor Emeritus of Banking and Finance at the London School of Economics and Political Science and Program Director, Regulation and Financial Stability, Financial Markets Group Research Centre, LSE, London, UK. He has also been Chief Adviser to the Bank of England and a member of the Advisory Committee of the Hong Kong Exchange Fund.

G. C. Harcourt is Emeritus Reader in the History of Economic Theory at the University of Cambridge, UK; Emeritus Fellow at Jesus College, Cambridge, UK; and Professor Emeritus at the University of Adelaide, Australia.

Jan Kregel is Distinguished Research Professor at the Center for Full Employment and Price Stability, University of Missouri–Kansas City; Professor of Finance and Development at Tallinn University of Technology, Tallinn, Estonia; and Senior Scholar at the Levy Economics Institute of Bard College, Annandale-on-Hudson, New York.

Axel Leijonhufvud is Professor Emeritus at the University of California–Los Angeles; former Chairman of the Department of Economics at UCLA; and Professor of Monetary Theory and Policy at the University of Trento, Italy.

Julio López is Professor of Economics at the Universidad Nacional Autónoma de México, Mexico City, Mexico.

Maria Cristina Marcuzzo is Professor and Director of the Department of Economics at the University of Rome "La Sapienza," Italy. She is co-author of *Ricardo and the Gold Standard* (Macmillan, 1991), co-editor of and author in *The Economics of Joan Robinson* (Routledge, 1996), and co-editor of and author in *Economists in Cambridge* (Routledge, 2005).

Basil Moore studied economics at the University of Toronto and at The Johns Hopkins University. From 1958 to 2003, he was Professor of Economics at Wesleyan University and, since 2003, has been Professor Extraordinary at Stellenbosch University, Stellenbosch, South Africa. He has authored nearly one hundred articles and four books: *Shaking the Invisible Hand: Complexity, Endogenous Money and Exogenous Interest Rates*; *Horizontalists and Verticalists: The Macroeconomics of Credit Money; An Introduction to Modern Economic Theory*; and *An Introduction to the Theory of Finance: Assetholder Behavior under Uncertainty*.

Robert Skidelsky is former Professor of Political Economy at the University of Warwick, England; the author of *The World after Communism* and a prize-winning biography of John Maynard Keynes; and a fellow of the British Academy in both the History and the Economics sections.

L. Randall Wray is Professor of Economics at the University of Missouri–Kansas City; Research Director of the Center for Full Employment and Price Stability, UMKC; and Senior Scholar at the Jerome Levy Economics Institute of Bard College, Annandale-on-Hudson, New York.

Introduction
The Continuing Legacy of John Maynard Keynes

L. Randall Wray

WHAT IS THE ENDURING LEGACY OF KEYNES? Among mainstream economists there isn't much of interest—sticky wages and the (now discredited) notion of fine-tuning through fiscal policy. As Kregel argues in this volume, the most charitable orthodox interpretations contend that, at best, *The General Theory* applies only to the special case of the deflationary conditions of a deep slump. In the modern, globalized economy, the mostly unfettered market relegates Keynesian policy to the historical dustbin. It will be clear to readers of this volume, however, that there is an alternative perspective. To varying degrees, the authors of the following chapters still find much relevance in Keynes's writing.

Central Propositions of *The General Theory*

In my view, the central proposition of *The General Theory* can be simply stated as follows: *Entrepreneurs produce what they expect to sell, and there is no reason to presume that the sum of these production decisions is consistent with the full employment level of output either in the short run or in the long run*. Moreover, this proposition holds regardless of market structure—even where competition is perfect and wages are flexible. It holds even if expectations are always fulfilled, and in a stable economic environment. In other words, Keynes (1964) did not rely on sticky wages, monopoly power, disappointed expectations, or economic instability to explain unemployment. While each of these conditions could certainly make matters worse, he wanted to explain the possibility of equilibrium with unemployment even under the conditions most favorable to orthodoxy.

Keynes's central proposition draws focus to the entrepreneurial decision: Each firm produces what it expects to sell. As Kregel makes clear, that decision is based on a comparison between the costs incurred to produce now against the proceeds expected to be received in the future. The implication of beginning analysis with the production decision marks the critical difference between the Keynesian approach and neoclassical economics (which begins with allocations of consumption through time to maximize utility). A decision to produce is simultaneously a decision to employ and to provide incomes to workers. It probably also commits the firm to a stream of payments over some time period. Production will not be undertaken unless the proceeds expected to be received on future dates exceed by a sufficient margin the costs incurred today and into the future. Both the costs and the revenues accrue in the form of money. If the comparison of estimated costs and expected revenues is deemed unfavorable, production is not undertaken and income is not generated. There is no reason to believe that the result of all of these individual production decisions will be full employment of labor resources.

Keynes required only three conditions to ensure the possibility of equilibrium with unemployment: historical time, autonomous spending, and existence of a nonproducible store of value. With historical time, the past is more or less known but cannot be changed; decisions taken today depend on outcomes that depend in part on past decisions as well as on outcomes expected in the future; and the future cannot be known now. (In his chapter, Harcourt quotes Robinson on the definition of post-Keynesian economics: "It applies to an economic theory or method of analysis which takes account of the difference between the future and the past.") Each of these considerations represents an important deviation from most orthodox analysis. Mistakes cannot be easily eliminated through "recontracting"; hysteresis and cumulative causation are pervasive phenomena; decisions must be taken without the possibility of knowing with certainty what the future might bring. At least a portion of spending depends on expectations of the future rather than on today's income—allowing individual spending to be less than, equal to, or greater than income (that is, some spending is autonomous of income). Both income and spending are in monetary terms; income received but not spent means—in the first instance, at least—accumulation of money balances. Returning specifically to the entrepreneurial decision, an alternative to producing is to accumulate (again, at least initially) money balances. When entrepreneurs' expectations about revenues from production are low, they will prefer to hold money. As Kregel explains in his chapter, Hayek had argued that the market would automatically operate to ensure a quick return to the full employment level of production because labor would be diverted to produce gold to satisfy the preference for accumulation of money over production of other commodities. Keynes's response was that gold is not money; rather, money is an asset with "special properties": nearly zero carrying costs, elasticity of substitution, and elasticity of production. The last characteristic means that, when the demand for money rises, labor is not diverted to its production. So long as there is at least one asset that is not produced by labor, it can become a bottomless sink of purchasing power, overturning Say's Law and subverting any market forces to return the system to full employment.

As mentioned, Keynes did not need to assume that expectations had been disappointed, causing production to temporarily fall below the full employment level. Indeed, after publication of *The General Theory*, he argued that he could have assumed that expectations are always fulfilled and still obtained the same results (Keynes 1973). All that is necessary is that entrepreneurs cannot be sure that their expectations *will be* fulfilled. It is the uncertainty that generates a preference for liquid assets and thus a barrier to achieving full employment. Nor does the outcome require instability. Some of Keynes's best known passages (especially those in chapter 12) do refer to "whirlwinds of speculation" and other examples of instability; however, as Kregel (1976, 1997) has argued, Keynes's favorite explanation of equilibrium with unemployment utilized a static model in which expectations—both short-run and long-run—are held constant, uninfluenced by outcome. Again, firms produce only what they expect to sell at a profit, and it is not necessary for them to have been disappointed or to be subject to unstable economic forces in order for the sum of their individual production decisions to leave some labor resources unutilized.

Keynes (1973) famously remarked that no one in a neoclassical model would hold money because there could be no value to holding a riskless (hence, low-return) asset. This was later confirmed by Hahn, who lamented that there is no room for money in any rigorous orthodox model. In this volume, Goodhart insists that the possibility of default is central to any analysis of a money-using economy. As decisions made today about production commit entrepreneurs to payments in the future, there is the possibility that they will not be able to meet contractual terms. However, orthodox models explicitly rule out default, implying that all IOUs are risk-free, thereby eliminating any need for the monitoring services provided by financial institutions. Not only is there no room for money in these models, there is also no need for banks or other financial intermediaries. Financial instability is also ruled out, not—as in Keynes—because instability is unnecessary to demonstrate the desired results, but because absence of the possibility of default requires perfect foresight or complete and perfect markets so that all outcomes can be hedged. As Goodhart concludes, these mainstream macro models cannot incorporate the real-world features that Keynes included: animal spirits and degree of confidence, market psychology, liquidity preference, or even a consumption function relating spending to income (since all agents are equally creditworthy). By contrast, the basic Keynesian model is easily extended to account for heterogeneous credit ratings, to allow default to affect expectations, and to include "contagions" and other repercussions set off by default of one large economic entity on its commitments. The best example of such extensions is, of course, the work of the late Hyman Minsky (1986).

Keynes (1964) had addressed stability issues when he argued that, if wages were flexible, then market forces set off by unemployment would move the economy further from full employment due to effects on aggregate demand, profits, and expectations. This is why he argued that one condition for stability is a degree of wage stickiness in terms of money. (Incredibly, this argument has been misinterpreted to mean that sticky wages cause unemployment—a point almost directly opposite to Keynes's conclusion.) Minsky and others have carried this further by arguing that, if the economy ever were to achieve full employment, this would generate destabilizing forces restoring unemployment. There is, of course, the Marxian-Kaleckian political economy argument that full employment emboldens workers, sparking a capitalist reaction to restore a disciplining reserve army of the unemployed. However, more directly related to Keynes's analysis is Minsky's argument that the main instability experienced in a modern capitalist economy is a tendency toward explosive euphoria. High aggregate demand and profits that can be associated with full employment raise expectations and encourage increasingly risky ventures, based on commitments of future revenues that will not be realized. A snowball of defaults then leads to a Fisher-type debt deflation and high unemployment unless there are "circuit breakers" that intervene to stop the market forces. The main circuit breakers, according to Minsky, are Big Bank (central bank) intervention as lender of last resort and Big Government countercyclical budget deficits.

Keynes's Impact on Policy

Keynes's impact on postwar policy was at least as great as his impact on theory and is taken up by most of the chapters of this volume, particularly those by Bresser-Pereira, Darity, Dimand, Galbraith, Kregel, Leijonhufvud, López, Moore, and Skidelsky. Of course, it is questionable whether much of the policy that was called Keynesian really had strong roots in Keynes's *General Theory*. Still, the influences of Keynes's work on domestic fiscal and monetary policy, on the international financial system, and on development policy—especially in Latin America—cannot be denied. If we take the central message of *The General Theory* as the proposition that entrepreneurial production decisions cannot be expected to generate equilibrium at full employment, then the obvious policy response is to use government to try to raise production beyond the level "ground out" by market forces. Unfortunately, "Keynesian" policy was eventually reduced to overly simplistic metaphors such as "pump-priming" and "fine-tuning" that would keep aggregate demand at just the right level to maintain full employment. It is now commonplace to claim that Keynesian policy was tried, but failed.

In practice, postwar policy usually consisted of measures to promote saving and investment. The first was wholly inconsistent with Keynes, based instead on the neoclassical loanable funds view that saving "finances" investment; the second was based on a multiplier view that, while somewhat consistent with Keynes's explication of the determination of the equilibrium level of output, relied on overly simplistic views of entrepreneurial expectation formation while ignoring important stability questions. First, there are the Harrod-Domar concerns that, unfortunately, have been reduced to growth theory's "knife-edge" problem. The more useful interpretation of their work is that there is no reason to believe that the demand (or multiplier) effect of investment will be sufficient to absorb the additional capacity generated by the supply effect of investment. There are several related avenues of research, ranging from the Hansen stagnation thesis, to a Keynesian "disproportionalities" argument (adopted by Keyserling—see the chapter by Brazelton—among others) that such gross policy measures would generate the wrong mix of productive capacity relative to demand, to the Vatter and Walker view that sustaining adequate rates of growth through time would require continuous growth of the government sector relative to growth of the private sector (see Wray, forthcoming)

Second, attempting to maintain full employment by stimulating private investment would shift the distribution of income toward owners of capital, worsening inequality and thereby lowering society's propensity to consume—one of the problems addressed by Keynes in chapter 24 of *The General Theory*. As Harcourt and others in this volume note, one of the main areas addressed by Post Keynesians has been distribution theory and the implications of heterogeneous saving rates on distribution. Further, work based on Kalecki's profit equation shows how higher investment rates generate higher profit rates and shift the distribution of income toward entrepreneurs and away from workers. There are also two kinds of sectoral issues raised. A high investment strategy will tend to favor capital-intensive industries, shifting the distribution of income toward higher-paid and unionized workers. The sectoral balances approach implicitly adopted by Minsky in his earliest work, and developed in detail by Wynne Godley, carries the Kalecki analysis further by examining the implications for financial balances implied by spending growth. For example, an expansion led by private-sector deficit spending (with firms borrowing to finance investment in excess of internal income flows) requires that either the government or the external sector (or both) will record equivalent surpluses (a government budget surplus, a capital account surplus, or both). This then raises sustainability issues, as private debt will grow faster than private-sector income.

Third, Minsky's financial instability hypothesis raises related concerns. Over the course of an economic boom that is led by investment spending, private firms stretch liquidity (income flows are leveraged by debt, and the ratio of safe assets to liabilities falls) and this leads to increasingly fragile financial positions. This happens at both the micro level and the level of the economy as a whole. According to Minsky's famous exposition, speculative and Ponzi positions replace hedge positions, and the economy becomes increasingly vulnerable to any one of several possible triggers that can set off a financial crisis and increase the potential for a Fisher-type debt deflation: an unexpected default that snowballs; rising interest rates (perhaps at the hands of a central bank that fears inflation) or tightening credit terms that close access to credit; and realized profits that are lower than expected—which then lowers expectations and investment, leading to even lower profits through the Kalecki relation. When the financial fragility hypothesis is combined with the Godley sectoral balances approach, it is apparent that the government budget plays an important role in cooling a boom: Rapid growth of income moves the government budget toward balance and even to a surplus, which destroys profits. The mostly unrecognized flip side of a government-sector surplus is a private-sector deficit (holding the foreign balance constant), so "improvement" of government balances must mean by identity that nongovernment balances become more precarious. (Followers of the work of Minsky and Godley were thus amused by orthodox reactions to the Clinton-era budget surpluses and by their predictions that all federal government debt would be eliminated over the subsequent decade and a half. It was no surprise that the Clinton surpluses killed the boom and morphed into budget deficits.) By the same token, the budget automatically moves toward larger deficits in a slump, maintaining profit flows and strengthening private balance sheets that accumulate net wealth in the form of safe government bonds.

Finally, growth led by investment can have both inflationary and exchange-rate implications. Of course, orthodoxy claims that inflation is mostly demand-driven: If expansionary fiscal or monetary policy raises demand above the full employment level (defined variously as the natural rate or the NAIRU), inflation results. By contrast, Keynes argued that "semi-inflation" can arise long before full employment is reached; he defined as "true inflation" the type of inflation considered by orthodoxy. Keynes's followers argue that much or even most of the real-world experience with inflation occurs in conditions of insufficient aggregate demand. There are a number of explanations, ranging from bottlenecks and other structural problems to unionized labor and oligopoly pricing of output. For these reasons, an increase of aggregate demand—especially if induced by rising investment—can be associated with inflation long before full employment is achieved. In addition, an increase of aggregate demand can worsen the trade balance, depreciate the currency, and cause pass-through inflation even in the presence of widespread unemployment (see Bresser-Pereira, this volume). Some emphasize the impact of tight money policy, which can have a perverse effect on inflation as high interest rates raise costs and thus prices (see Moore and Brazelton, this volume). While in orthodox stories it is excessive government spending (or loose monetary policy) that causes inflation, in the Post Keynesian view an increase of demand due to private investment spending might actually be more inflationary than an increase attributed to government spending. In an exposition similar to that used by Kalecki to explain the source of profits, Minsky (1986) argued that the aggregate markup of the price of consumption goods is a function of the amount of consumption spending in excess of the wage bill in the consumption sector. Because investment generates a wage bill in the investment sector, most of which will be spent on consumer goods, investment growth relative to consumption increases the markup and the overall price level. Hence, the alternative approach to the explanation of distribution and price determination can explain inflation with unemployment—the stagflation problem that could not be explained by the neoclassical synthesis (see Kregel, this volume).

Keynes and Development

In his chapter, Julio López highlights the importance of Keynes's approach to analysis of the development process (as do Bresser-Pereira and, to a lesser extent, Galbraith). As López says, Keynesianism dominated Latin American thinking through the 1970s, and it is making something of a comeback as the neoliberal Washington Consensus is thrown off. Bresser-Pereira sees the failed neoliberal policy that was promulgated over the past two decades as little more than a thinly disguised effort to maintain U.S. hegemony over Latin America. As López explains, Keynesian theory had to be adapted to the Latin American case, where growth was mostly fueled by exports, not by investment. The Latin American structuralist approach adopted industrial policy that included protection of domestic industries and that favored import substitution. Both López and Bresser-Pereira reject the orthodox dichotomy of market versus government in favor of a planned and mixed economy.

Bresser-Pereira's very interesting chapter calls for a new developmentalism that retains some features of structuralism while recognizing the changed environment created by globalization. Modern capitalism is intensely nationalistic, and a development strategy requires state involvement to put firms in a position to compete internationally. Industry in many of the larger developing nations is already mature, so protectionism only impedes productivity growth and generates inferior products that cannot compete. Hence, Bresser-Pereira advocates economies that are open to trade, although capital controls could be required to stabilize exchange rates. A flexible but managed exchange rate is called for to dampen currency appreciation that would make exports uncompetitive.

The new developmentalism rejects the notion that low inflation is the overriding goal of policy and instead advocates policy geared toward maintaining moderate interest rates. Inflation arises due not to loose monetary policy but rather to inappropriate indexing of prices and incomes paid by government, to exchange-rate crises, and to fiscal imbalance. Bresser-Pereira has long argued that Brazil's high-inflation episode was not caused by budget deficits but rather that high inflation caused budget deficits; further, he has argued that eliminating indexing of government payments could brake the inflationary spiral. While a sovereign nation does not need to balance its budget, Bresser-Pereira does call for better management of fiscal policy, including elimination of indexing, use of longer-maturity debt, and maintenance of a small outstanding debt stock. Both Bresser-Pereira and López point the way to formulation of a Keynesian alternative to the neoliberal orthodox reliance on free trade and small government.

Keynes and Monetary Policy

Turning to Keynes's approach to monetary policy, several of the chapters of this volume renew Keynes's call for low interest rates. This is justified for several reasons. Keynes argued for euthanasia of the rentier—the functionless coupon clipper who earns a return without taking risk. Not only does a low–interest-rate policy improve equity (eliminating an unjustified return) and reduce inequality (in his chapter, Galbraith cites his father's axiom: People who have money to lend have more money than people who do not have money to lend), but it also lowers the bar so that—as Keynes put it—average luck and ability are sufficient to ensure a good probability of success. Others justify lower interest rates on the argument that this encourages investment, although there are the caveats raised above about the wisdom of a growth-through-investment strategy. As mentioned, Moore and others argue that interest is a cost, so lower rates allow lower prices, and, because interest is a rate that is compounded, a lower interest rate allows slower growth of prices and wages.

Keynes did not simply call for cyclically lower rates (for example, in recession to encourage recovery) but rather for permanently lower rates. I would go further than some of Keynes's followers and call for setting the overnight interbank lending rate at zero and leaving it there forever. In other words, monetary policy should not be used as a countercyclical force. As Brazelton argues (following Keyserling), the central bank should be used instead to promote financial stability, imposing quantity controls during a speculative boom and intervening as lender of last resort in a bust.

Keynes and the International Monetary System

There remains some controversy over Keynes's preferred reform of the international monetary system. Paul Davidson has revived and modified Keynes's (1980) famous Bancor plan, arguing for a return to fixed exchange rates based on a new international reserve currency, with a reflux mechanism to eliminate any incentive to accumulate international reserves. This would remove the bias inherent in a gold standard—mercantilist nations want to accumulate gold reserves to protect their exchange rates. The modern equivalent finds the major exporters accumulating vast dollar reserves while using domestic austerity to ensure a continued trade surplus. Hence, Davidson's plan would punish the surplus nations and put in place conditions that would allow the deficit nations to increase exports. Along these lines, Moore (in this volume and 2004) advocates currency unions and even dollarization by small nations with weak currencies. Eliminating exchange-rate movements is believed to promote domestic stability.

On the other hand, Keynes's advocacy of the Bancor plan can be seen as a pragmatic response by the UK to the hegemonic position the United States would enjoy after WWII. In Keynes's previous work (1976, 1980), he clearly rejected fixed exchange rates (especially those based on metallic standards). While he did not call for a "free float," he did advocate flexible but managed exchange rates—the position Bresser-Pereira seems to adopt. Goodhart (1998) also rejects fixed exchange rates and currency unions; he sees the experiment with the Euro as dangerous because it requires the individual nations to give up sovereignty over their currency—a topic to which I will return in a moment. I have argued that floating the currency allows for domestic policy space. Under a fixed exchange-rate system, only those nations that manage to accumulate an unassailable international reserve have the freedom to use domestic monetary (interest rate) policy and fiscal policy to achieve full employment—another topic I will turn to below. For this reason, a floating rate system is necessary to provide more domestic policy independence.

Keynes and the Nature of Money

Elsewhere (Wray 1990, 1998, 2006), I have dealt with Keynes's theoretical approach to money, a topic also addressed by Goodhart and Kregel in this volume. While the textbook "money supply and demand" approach is based on chapters 13 and 15 of *The General Theory*, the more revolutionary ideas of Keynes are contained in chapter 17 of *The General Theory*, in the *Treatise on Money*, and in his mostly unpublished writings on ancient monies. Keynes (1914, 1976) closely followed the approach of Innes (1913, 1914) and Knapp (1973), integrating what has been called a "creditary" (or, credit money) approach and a "chartalist" (or, state money) approach (Wray 2004). As Goodhart argues (1998; see also 2005), even if there have been examples of a "commodity money" (for example, a full-bodied gold coin, the nominal value of which is determined by the value of its gold content), modern money is a credit money denominated in a state-chosen unit of account. Innes insisted that even the state's own currency is a credit money, not a commodity money or a fiat money. A gold coin is simply a government IOU that happens to be stamped on gold. Only if the government's creditworthiness is called into question does the value of a government's IOU fall to the value of the embodied precious metal. While the nominal value of a coin is determined by the state, the value is not maintained by mere "proclamation" (or fiat). Rather, as both Kregel and Goodhart emphasize, the value of government currency is maintained by acceptance in payments that must be made to the state—today, primarily tax payments. The logical sequence is that the state first imposes a tax, denominated in the state money; it then can emit its currency (an IOU) denominated in that same unit as it spends (and lends); finally, the holders of the state's IOU can retire their tax and other monetary obligations by delivering the state's IOU.

Innes argues that this "reflux" of IOUs back to their issuer is the fundamental law of credit: A creditor (one holding an IOU) must be able to return an IOU to its issuer for credit. In the same manner, one holding a claim on a bank can deliver the bank IOU in payments made to the bank (for example, to pay down a bank loan). Refusal by the issuer to accept the IOU at its nominal value is a default—the subject of Goodhart's chapter. The position of the sovereign state is different from that of other debtors because the sovereign state first *imposes* a liability (what Kregel jokingly refers to as the original sin of taxation) on subjects or citizens (whether these are "self-imposed" by the electorate is irrelevant; all that is important is that the individual taxpayer is not free to choose to avoid paying tax liabilities—as Kregel says, neither death nor taxes can be avoided), and then issues "that which is necessary to pay taxes" ("twin-topt" in Wray 1998). Only an entity with something like sovereign power is able to ensure acceptability of its IOUs by first imposing liabilities. We return to Goodhart's claim that any theory of a capitalist economy that uses money must allow for heterogeneous credit risk. The state money approach explains why the state's IOUs are special, attributing sovereign power to the state.

This leads to a revised view of the nature of government finance. Because the government spends its IOUs into circulation, it does not need to use income or borrowing in order to spend. When taxes are paid, refluxed government IOUs are "redeemed," that is, eliminated. When government spending (IOU emissions) exceeds tax payments (redemptions), the nongovernment sector accumulates net claims on government. For a variety of reasons, the nongovernment sector normally wishes to run a positive balance against the government, which allows accumulation of net (or outside) wealth in the form of government IOUs. One of the important reasons is that the financial system uses government IOUs as the reserve for clearing accounts, holding a reserve of them against issued private liabilities. In this sense, private IOUs leverage government IOUs.

It is this relation that allows the central bank to implement monetary policy, maintaining positive overnight interest rates by keeping financial institutions "hungry" on the margin for more reserves. From this perspective, government sales of bonds are not a borrowing operation but rather a part of monetary policy management. When the quantity of banking system reserves is too high, banks offer the excess in the overnight interbank lending market; but if there is an aggregate excess, these offers place downward pressure on the overnight rate, triggering a sale of government bonds by the central bank or treasury. (In practice, there is a division of labor, such that the central bank operates in the open market to manage interest rates on a day-to-day basis while the treasury operates in the new-issue market to facilitate monetary policy over the longer run. So long as the treasury maintains a more-or-less constant deposit at its central bank, it is helping the central bank to hit its interest rate target by minimizing the reserve effects of fiscal operations. See Wray 1998; Bell 2000; Bell and Wray 2003.) When banks are short of reserves, bidding in the overnight market drives rates above the central bank target, triggering open market purchases by the central bank or bond redemption by the treasury.

For this reason, the notion of a government budget constraint is rejected. While the government can choose to constrain its spending through balanced-budget laws or rules governing operating procedure, it does not really face a financial constraint. This does not mean that its spending should rise without limit, for it will eventually face real resource constraints. The question is not one of government solvency but one of the appropriate share of resources that ought to go to government—and hence, the inflation threshold for government spending. Abba Lerner long ago got it correct with his "functional finance" approach to the budget: What matters is whether the budget is at the right level to achieve the public purpose, not whether the sums of revenues and spending happen to be matched over a time span determined by movements of celestial objects (Wray 1998).

Keynes and Globalization

Some of the chapters in this volume also invite a revised view of globalization. Many of those following Keynes do not necessarily reject the mainstream view that more freedom to trade across borders results in net benefits. According to Skidelsky, however, Keynes was rather skeptical of the advantages of trade, arguing that it tends to lead to excessive specialization that lowers the quality of life—a sentiment that surely would be shared by the Latin American structuralists, who saw a strong trend toward deteriorating terms of trade for those countries that specialized in primary commodity exports (see López, this volume). Still, Bresser-Pereira argues that protectionism for industry today is particularly unwise for all but the very largest nations, because production cannot be undertaken on the scale necessary to achieve production efficiency. It has long been recognized that part of the reason for America's phenomenal economic growth in the nineteenth century was the scale of the market, something that European integration has sought to replicate.

Critics of the neoliberal free trade ideology, however, emphasize the negative impacts that the opening of economies has had on wages and thus on living standards of workers in the developed nations. Both Skidelsky and Galbraith also mention some negative impacts that the orientation toward global markets has had on Russia and China. High wages in the export centers of China fuel migration of rural workers to the cities, where many end up unemployed. Skidelsky believes that Keynes would have advocated greater public infrastructure investment outside the boom areas. According to Skidelsky, President Putin has embraced neoliberalism and sound finance, using a budget surplus to accumulate foreign securities. This makes little sense in a country that operates with a depressed economy well below capacity. Keynesian policy, again, would focus on raising domestic income and increasing spending on public infrastructure.

In his very interesting chapter, Galbraith argues that greater wage convergence across countries is not only inevitable but also desirable. Immigration, both legal and illegal, will continue so long as wage differentials across developed and developing nations remain wide. Galbraith cleverly argues that the wage differential contributes to high unemployment, as workers from poorer nations abandon the certainty of low wages at home for the chance of high wages in the rich nations. Imposing more labor market flexibility in the rich nations cannot be the solution to unemployment, because there is a nearly infinite supply of low-wage labor willing to take jobs even at wages much below those common in the rich nations. Thus, Galbraith updates Keynes's skepticism over the ability of wage flexibility to resolve unemployment problems. Convergence of wages, together with greater demand stimulus in each country, is seen by Galbraith as the only path to full employment—what he terms a Global Keynesian strategy.

Keynes and Full Employment Policy

While I endorse Galbraith's policy recommendations, I doubt they would generate true full employment—defined either in the Beveridge way (more vacancies than job seekers) or as a job for anyone willing to work. As several of the authors of this volume discuss (particularly Skidelsky and Brazelton, but also implied in the chapter by Darity), demand stimulus alone will not ensure that all who want to work will find jobs in the private sector. As discussed in Skidelsky's chapter, Keynes argued that much of the observed unemployment in the 1920s was structural; Minsky updated this observation in the 1960s, arguing that any dynamic capitalist economy will be eliminating the need for some skills while creating new skill requirements at a pace much faster than the gestation period for a worker (perhaps sixteen years in the early twentieth century, but twenty-five or thirty years today in technologically advanced nations). For this reason, there would always be a structural mismatch.

There are also more nefarious reasons that some are left behind by discriminating employers, such as the lingering effects of the legacy of slavery addressed by Darity. Even at the peak of economic booms, blacks in America experience unemployment rates that are so high that the boom would be called a depression if whites had similar unemployment rates. This is due in part to continuing overt racial discrimination and also to the legacy of racism in that blacks come to the labor market less prepared to compete. For this reason, pump-priming demand stimulus will create bottlenecks for the types of labor desired by the private sector long before unemployment is eliminated for those deemed less desirable. Galbraith calls for administered prices to dampen inflation pressure, a policy I do not believe is up to the task of delivering full employment with stable wages and prices, even if price control policy is still a good idea. I am skeptical that most of the U.S. joblessness today is due to insufficient aggregate demand; as Minsky argued about U.S. unemployment in the 1960s and Keynes argued about UK unemployment in the 1920s, a very large part is structural and requires directed employment programs.

Kregel provides a brief summary of an alternative path to full employment, although it could be seen as a supplement to Galbraith's proposal for Global Keynesianism. Like Kregel, I advocate a government job guarantee—what Minsky and others called an employer of last resort (ELR) program—that offers an infinitely elastic demand for labor at a wage set by government (Wray 1998, 2007). This wage ideally should be set at the locally determined living wage and hence would vary across countries, depending on national living standards. Over time, there could be convergence toward an international ELR wage, in congruence with the policy advocated by Galbraith. However, unlike Galbraith's proposal, ELR would guarantee a job to anyone, regardless of skills, education, gender, race, ethnicity, national origin, and so on. Performance standards would be enforced, so that only those willing to work would be allowed to participate—this is not meant to be a welfare program or to necessarily replace welfare. Neither is it workfare—a punitive program that forces individuals to meet means-tested criteria and then to work for welfare; participation would not be means-tested and it would be purely voluntary. Work would be designed to be productive, providing socially valuable output and services, such as public infrastructure development and maintenance, public services for youth and aged persons, environmental and public space enhancement, and so on. America's New Deal programs, Argentina's *Jefes* program, and India's long-running Maharashtra job guarantee program can serve as useful models for further development of such programs. As Minsky argued in 1965, only a national program of direct job creation can ensure continuous full employment of all those who want to work (Wray 2007).

Minsky argued that ELR can achieve full employment without many of the detrimental effects of trying to achieve full employment through aggregate demand stimulus alone (Wray 2007). For the reasons discussed above, Minsky advocated a high consumption strategy rather than a high investment strategy. ELR directly provides income to those who need it most, and most of this income will go to consumption. Full employment is achieved without relying on finance of inherently risky private investment spending and, hence, is not necessarily associated with rising financial fragility. While higher consumption associated with full employment will probably raise the expectations of entrepreneurs, stimulating production and investment, there is an automatic stabilizing feature: As the economy expands, ELR employment and government spending decline because workers are drawn out of the program and into the private sector; thus, the expansion will increase tax revenues even as government spending falls, reducing fiscal stimulus in a countercyclical manner. Further, ELR will not have the same impact on income distribution that an investment-led expansion would have, nor would it be as inflationary. Minsky argued that, because ELR can be used to lower private-sector costs (for example, through provision of public infrastructure), it tends to raise both demand and supply, mitigating inflationary pressures.

However, as Kregel discusses, the most important price-stabilizing feature of ELR is the wage anchor. ELR can be analyzed like a commodity buffer stock program—which stabilizes the price of the buffer stock commodity. The ELR wage is simply a price floor, which by itself cannot pressure wages since it catches only workers who fail to find a higher paying job elsewhere. Some critics have argued that worker behavior will change with ELR in place without the labor-disciplining effects of a reserve army of the unemployed. However, ELR provides a reserve army of the *employed* (private employers can always recruit from the pool of employed workers)—a much more effective reserve army as workers remain employed, demonstrating their availability to work while maintaining and even improving their skills and training.

Galbraith briefly notes that immigration raises issues for rich nations implementing ELR programs. If a U.S. ELR program offered jobs to all regardless of immigration status (as it ideally should do), this could encourage more immigration because the ELR wage would almost certainly exceed the wage most workers south of the border could earn at home. The best solution would be to simultaneously create ELR programs throughout Latin America to resolve the unemployment problems there while reducing emigration to the United States. Galbraith's argument that wage differentials could still draw immigrants to the United States is certainly true, but the flow would be much diminished if jobs were available in all nations. Finally, Kregel has argued elsewhere that ELR should be part of a strategy of development, because it can be used to upgrade skills, provide needed infrastructure and public services, reduce excessive migration to urban centers (as jobs can be provided wherever people live), and integrate marginalized populations. Again, the *Jefes* program provides a particularly useful model that generated such benefits. Hence, implementation of ELR in poor and in rich nations can be used to reduce immigration, eliminate unemployment, and further the development process—to eventually close wage and standard-of-living gaps internationally.

Keynes as Political Economist

Many of the contributors to this volume have focused on policy, strategy, and pragmatic approaches to real-world problems. As López mentions, Keynes was a *political* economist. Marcuzzo examines the role played by Keynes in negotiations to protect the interests of Britain. While he may not have been a *successful* negotiator, he was an eloquent persuader. An overriding theme in his work is that the appeal to self-interest as an effective means of achieving the social purpose had to be rejected. What is variously called the managed economy or mixed economy is necessary. Further, he rejected any argument that the economist should avoid ethical and moral questions. As Marcuzzo (this volume) puts it, "His message was to change the environment within which individuals operate so that moral and rational motives become the spring of action of the collective as a whole." His theoretical approach still provides the basis for a range of policy proposals to solve economic problems and to advance the public interest while providing space for the individual initiative necessary for a successful capitalist economy.

References

Bell, Stephanie. 2000. Do taxes and bonds finance government spending? *Journal of Economic Issues* 34 (3): 603–20.

Bell, Stephanie, and L. Randall Wray. 2003. Fiscal impacts on reserves and the independence of the Fed. *Journal of Post Keynesian Economics* 25 (2): 263–71.

Brazelton, W. Robert. 2008. Leon H. Keyserling, American Keynesian: Theory, policy, and practice. In *Keynes for the twenty-first century: The continuing relevance of* The general theory, ed. Mathew Forstater and L. Randall Wray. New York: Palgrave Macmillan.

Bresser-Pereira, Luiz Carlos. 2008. Macroeconomics of stagnation and new developmentalism in Latin America. In *Keynes for the twenty-first century: The continuing relevance of* The general theory, ed. Mathew Forstater and L. Randall Wray. New York: Palgrave Macmillan.

Darity, William, Jr. 2008. African American reparations, Keynes, and the transfer problem. In *Keynes for the twenty-first century: The continuing relevance of* The general theory, ed. Mathew Forstater and L. Randall Wray. New York: Palgrave Macmillan.

Dimand, Robert W. 2008. How Keynes came to Canada: Mabel Timlin and Keynesian economics. In *Keynes for the twenty-first century: The continuing relevance of* The general theory, ed. Mathew Forstater and L. Randall Wray. New York: Palgrave Macmillan.

Galbraith, James K. 2008. Keynes and globalization. In *Keynes for the twenty-first century: The continuing relevance of* The general theory, ed. Mathew Forstater and L. Randall Wray. New York: Palgrave Macmillan.

Goodhart, C. A. E. 1998. Two concepts of money: Implications for the analysis of optimal currency areas. *European Journal of Political Economy* 14 (3): 407–32.

———. 2005. Review of *Credit and state theories of money: The contributions of A. Mitchell Innes, History of Political Economy* 37 (4): 759–61.

———. 2008. Money and default. In *Keynes for the twenty-first century: The continuing relevance of* The general theory, ed. Mathew Forstater and L. Randall Wray. New York: Palgrave Macmillan.

Harcourt, G. C. 2008. The structure of post-Keynesian economics: The core contributions of the pioneers. In *Keynes for the twenty-first century: The continuing relevance of* The general theory, ed. Mathew Forstater and L. Randall Wray. New York: Palgrave Macmillan.

Innes, A. Mitchell. 1913. What is money? *Banking Law Journal* 30 (5): 377–408. Repr. in Wray 2004.

———. 1914. The credit theory of money. *Banking Law Journal* 31 (2): 151–68. Repr. in Wray 2004.

Keynes, J. M. 1914. What is money? Review article in *Economic Journal* 24 (95): 419–21.

———. 1964 (1936). *The general theory of employment, interest and money*. New York: Harcourt Brace Jovanovich.

———. 1973. *The collected writings of John Maynard Keynes*. Ed. D. E. Moggridge. Vol. 14, *The General Theory and after: Part II: Defence and development*. London: MacMillan, for the Royal Economic Society.

———. 1976 (1930). *A treatise on money*. Vols. 1 and 2. New York: Harcourt, Brace.

———. 1980. *The collected writings of John Maynard Keynes*. Ed. D. E. Moggridge. Vol. 25, *Activities 1940–1944: Shaping the post-war world: The clearing union*. London: Macmillan.

Knapp, Georg Friedrich. 1924. *The state theory of money*. Repr., Clifton, NY: Augustus M. Kelley, 1973.

Kregel, Jan. 1976. Economic methodology in the face of uncertainty: The modeling methods of Keynes and the Post Keynesians. *The Economic Journal* 86 (342): 209–25.

———. 1997. The theory of value, expectations and chapter 17 of *The general theory*. In *A 'second edition' of* The general theory, ed. G. C. Harcourt and P. A. Riach, vol. 1. London and New York: Routledge, 261–82.

———. 2008. The continuing policy relevance of Keynes's *General theory*. In *Keynes for the twenty-first century: The continuing relevance of* The general theory, ed. Mathew Forstater and L. Randall Wray. New York: Palgrave Macmillan.

Leijonhufvud, Axel. 2008. Moving on: Where to? In *Keynes for the twenty-first century: The continuing relevance of* The general theory, ed. Mathew Forstater and L. Randall Wray. New York: Palgrave Macmillan.

López G., Julio. 2008. Keynes in Latin America and Latin American Keynesianism. In *Keynes for the twenty-first century: The continuing relevance of* The general theory, ed. Mathew Forstater and L. Randall Wray. New York: Palgrave Macmillan.

Marcuzzo, Maria Cristina. 2008. Keynes and persuasion. In *Keynes for the twenty-first century: The continuing relevance of* The general theory, ed. Mathew Forstater and L. Randall Wray. New York: Palgrave Macmillan.

Minsky, Hyman P. 1963. Discussion. *American Economic Review* 53 (2): 412.

———. 1986. *Stabilizing an unstable economy*. New Haven and London: Yale University Press.

Moore, Basil. 2004. A global currency for a global economy. *Journal of Post Keynesian Economics* 26 (4): 631–53.

———. 2008. Targeting inflation *and* full employment in South Africa: A critique of inflation targeting in developing economies. In *Keynes for the twenty-first century: The continuing relevance of* The general theory, ed. Mathew Forstater and L. Randall Wray. New York: Palgrave Macmillan.

Skidelsky, Robert. 2008. The origins of Keynesian economics and some applications to restructuring and globalization. In *Keynes for the twenty-first century: The continuing relevance of* The general theory, ed. Mathew Forstater and L. Randall Wray. New York: Palgrave Macmillan.

Wray, L. Randall. 1990. *Money and credit in capitalist economies: The endogenous money approach*. Aldershot, UK: Edward Elgar.

———. 1998. *Understanding modern money: The key to full employment and price stability*. Cheltenham, UK: Edward Elgar.

———, ed. 2004. *Credit and state theories of money: The contributions of A. Mitchell Innes*. Cheltenham, UK: Edward Elgar.

———. 2006. Keynes's approach to money: An assessment after 70 years. *Atlantic Economics Journal* 34 (2): 183–93.

———. 2007. The employer of last resort programme: Could it work for developing countries? Monograph, *Economic and Labour Market Papers*, no. 5, International Labour Office, Geneva (August).

———. Forthcoming. Demand constraints and big government. *Journal of Economic Issues,* March 2008.

Part I

The Keynesian Revolution

Development, Introduction, and Legacy

CHAPTER 1

KEYNES AND PERSUASION

MARIA CRISTINA MARCUZZO*

> Brilliant man as [Keynes] is, he is too brilliant to be persuasive with us Americans. Many Americans admire him. . . . But, rightly or wrongly, how many trust him? How many will accept his sales talk? No one.
>
> —R. Leffingwell, August 31, 1945[1]

> May it never fall to my lot to have to persuade anyone to do what I want, with so few cards in my hands.
>
> —Maynard to Florence Keynes, November 21, 1945; quoted in Skidelsky 2000, 248

I. INTRODUCTION

IN THIS CHAPTER, I examine the central role persuasion—in the two-way sense of persuading and of being persuaded—played in Keynes's work, for it is crucial to an understanding of his behavior in all of his multifarious endeavors. In the process of both elaborating and transmitting ideas, persuasion calls for ability in reasoning, the gift of arousing passions, and a particular flair in personal relationships—qualities that Keynes possessed to the utmost degree. But why was persuasion so important for him? Biography played a part, insofar as Keynes was embedded in the *milieu* of the highly educated British class, for which clubs, debating societies, and learned fellowships represented the bulk of social life. More fundamentally, however, persuasion was essential to his conception of

* I am grateful to Nario Naldi, Annalisa Rosselli, Eleonora Sanfilippo, Anna Simonazzi, and Giordano Sivini for comments and suggestions. The usual disclaimers apply.

economics as a method of molding ideas and opinions in an exchange with others, as he explained in a celebrated passage of *The General Theory of Employment, Interest and Money*: "It is astonishing what foolish things one can temporarily believe *if one thinks too long alone*, particularly in economics (along with the other moral sciences), where it is often impossible to bring one's ideas to a conclusive test either formal or experimental" (*CWK* 7, xxiii; emphasis added).

Keynes formed his ideas in the process of submitting them to others, and we have ample evidence of his style of work and reasoning intertwined in close personal relations. In order to be convinced himself and to persuade another of an argument, Keynes needed to engage in exchanges that had a strong emotional side (affection, trust, respect), affording a "meeting of minds" (one of Keynes's favorite expressions) that for him was conducive to fruitful interaction. In a collective work in which, by reviewing the correspondence, we examined extensively Keynes's relationship with his closer fellow economists, we concluded that "the group of Keynes's correspondents . . . seems to have been an extended community, membership of which depended not so much or not only on academic performance as on the capacity to encapsulate and convey understanding through discussion" (Marcuzzo and Rosselli 2005a, 9).

We found several examples of Keynes's style of working by forming and refining his argument vis-à-vis his interlocutors, with an ample range of cases in which the "meeting of minds" was thwarted, intermittent, or wholly successful. In the drafting of his two major books, *Treatise on Money* and *The General Theory*, his former students Denis Robertson and Richard Kahn played essential roles as critics and collaborators.[2]

In his activities as policy adviser, Keynes was in constant contact with ministers, civil servants, officers, politicians, bankers, and opinion makers. The extraordinary number of his correspondents testifies to the compelling need he felt to be keyed in with opinions and points of view coming from different quarters and the fundamental importance he attached to it. Those to be convinced, like those by whom he was convinced, were the well-intentioned and well-disposed, since he held that a particular state of mind was a prerequisite for persuasion to be successful.

In the preface to *Essays in Persuasion* (1931), Keynes attributed his failure in influencing "the course of events in time" to the "overwhelming weight of contemporary sentiment and opinion" (*CWK* 9, xvii). In the aftermath of the First World War, he compared the advice and unheeded premonitions contained in those essays to "the croakings of a Cassandra," emitted by someone who is "desperately anxious to convince his audience in time" (*CWK* 9, xviii).

In this chapter, I address the question of just how adept Keynes was at tuning in to "contemporary sentiment and opinion" and convincing his opponents when he was personally engaged in steering the wheel of history. I will look, in particular, into Keynes's success in reaping the fruits of persuasion as a negotiator in his missions to the United States in the 1940s, when he bore the responsibility of protecting his country's interests and shaping the new economic order emerging from the ruins of the Second World War while being confronted with the power of conflicting interests and the clash of cultures. In section 2, I give a brief overview of the purpose and scope of Keynes's missions to the United States; in section 3, I attempt an assessment of his achievements and shortcomings in the light of the literature; in section 4, I take a closer look at three of Keynes's *tours de force* in the art of persuasion, drawing some tentative conclusions in the final section.

2. Keynes's Six Treasury Missions

Keynes carried out six missions to the United States on behalf of the British Treasury between May 1941 and March 1946 (Table 1.1); they add up to a year of his life—now coming to an end—spent outside his usual space and *milieu* whose boundaries were Cambridge, London, and Tilton.

Keynes had joined the Treasury in June 1940, in an unofficial position; he simply had a room there, was available for consultation, and drew no salary. In the autumn of 1940, Great Britain was facing its first dramatic ordeal: France had fallen, Britain was fighting the war alone, and the country's reserves were rapidly falling. Orders were placed for aircraft and tanks from the United States, although the British Treasury had

Table 1.1 Keynes's Six Missions to the United States

I.	May–July 1941
II.	September–October 1943
III.	June–August 1944
IV.	October–December 1944
V.	September–December 1945
VI.	March 1946

no financial resources left to pay for them. It was only with the re-election of Franklin Roosevelt in November and his announcement two weeks later that he was prepared to offer American aid to the British that the "worst financial perils" (Harrod 1951, 504) seemed to be over. This marked the beginning of Anglo-American reciprocal involvement in financing the Second World War effort, in which Keynes played a major role.

In the first mission, between May and July 1941, Keynes was to assist the British Treasury in application of the Lend-Lease Act, the U.S. program providing supplies to Britain "not in exchange for money but acknowledged by some 'consideration' to be negotiated later" (Moggridge 1992, 652). Keynes was to assist in resolving some of the issues related to the scope and application of Lend-Lease, such as the financing of expenditures already incurred by Great Britain before 1941 and the liquidation of British assets overseas, which the Americans insisted upon as a condition for aid. In fact, the main purpose of Keynes's mission was to secure American financial help to increase Britain's reserves, which by then had slumped to a critical level.[3]

In the second mission, between September and October 1943, Keynes was entrusted with the task of preliminary discussions on what was known as Article VII of the Lend-Lease agreement, that is, the terms ("consideration") under which aid was being given. The conditions required by the Americans amounted to Britain giving up her imperial preference system, in force of which the reciprocal tariff concessions between Britain and the Dominions implied *de facto* discrimination against products of countries outside the British Empire.

The third mission, between June and August 1944, was intended to finalize the criteria for the establishment of the International Monetary Fund and the International Bank for Reconstruction and Development, and to link these criteria with principles to be incorporated in a commercial treaty that would see an end to both the imperial preference and the U.S. tariff systems. The Bretton Woods Conference (July 1–22), with 730 delegates from 44 countries (Skidelsky 2000, 446) witnessing the keen confrontation between the British and the American views, was the major arena for these antagonistic events.

In the fourth mission, between October and December 1944, Keynes's task was to negotiate an extension of Lend-Lease for the period between the collapse of Germany and the end of the Japanese war, known as Stage II. At stake, too, was Britain's plan to resume its basic export activities in order to boost its reserves; to this, the State Department was opposed, and it renewed its assault on imperial discrimination against American trade interests.

In the fifth mission, between September and December 1945, Keynes led the British delegation to negotiate the loan Britain desperately needed, given that Lend-Lease had been abruptly suspended as a result of Japan's surrender in August. The postwar international scenario involved negotiating financial and commercial arrangements for Great Britain and its relationship with both the United States and the Empire.

During the sixth mission, in March 1946, Keynes was involved in the final details of the design of the International Monetary Fund and the World Bank, whose inaugural meeting was held in Savannah, Georgia, and where, again, he did his best to oppose the American approach to the location and governance of the two institutions. Keynes died four weeks after he returned to Britain, on April 21.

Keynes's negotiating skills and abilities during his Treasury missions to the United States have been scrutinized in the literature under various aspects[4] and with diverging conclusions; the overall assessment by Keynes's two major biographers are a striking example of these differences.

According to Skidelsky: "Keynes could never understand that American and British interests were not identical, attributing differences to deficiencies in the American political system, and thus *over relying on logic and eloquence* to overcome them" (Skidelsky 2000, 117; emphasis added). The point being made is that Keynes's logic and eloquence were powerless, since British and American interests could not be reconciled, and, indeed, his reliance on the art of persuasion actually impaired his negotiating capability.

On the other hand, Moggridge, while stressing that, on overseas issues, Keynes "became the dominant force in the Treasury, determining grand strategy and a high proportion of the tactics" (Moggridge 1992, 663), does not arrive at the same conclusions as Skidelsky. His only critical remark refers to the unfortunate negotiation on the 1945 loan, but, unlike Skidelsky,[5] he places greater blame on the Treasury than on Keynes.[6] Pressnell (2003, 603), for his part, argues that, in 1945, due to "his possible overconfidence," Keynes "underestimated the determination of the Americans."[7]

In the next section, we briefly review Keynes's successes and failures during these six missions, not so much to measure his negotiating skills as to delineate the background necessary for evaluation of his strategy of persuasion.

3. Envoy or Negotiator?

Lionel Robbins, who joined Keynes on three of the U.S. missions, wrote: "He was not always a good *negotiator*. . . . But as an *envoy* he was supreme" (quoted in Skidelsky 2000, 110). According to the *Oxford Dictionary*, an envoy is "a messenger, especially one sent on a special mission," while a negotiator is "someone who confers in order to come to an agreement." Robbins's distinction seems, therefore, to suggest that Keynes showed greater ability in voicing the British point of view than in sealing agreements favoring British interests. Robbins's position appears closer to Skidelsky's than to Moggridge's, and it prompts a closer examination of Keynes's behavior during these six missions.

As we have seen, the purpose of the first mission was to make Britain not entirely dependent on Lend-Lease but to grant it financial and economic freedom of action; the means to achieve this was to increase the level of its gold and dollar reserves without stripping it of much of its foreign assets. On May 16, 1941, Keynes presented his plan, whereby the U.S. Treasury was to refund Great Britain one-third of the advances already paid on contracts outstanding before Lend-Lease and to employ Lend-Lease to eliminate Britain's current deficit with the United States. The proposal was firmly rejected by the U.S. Secretary of State, Henry Morgenthau, and Keynes was forced to change strategy; thus, while still endeavoring to put as many U.S. imports as possible on Lend-Lease, he proposed a commercial loan against collateral of British-owned activities. The U.S. Treasury accepted, on the condition that it receive a daily report on the Bank of England's level of reserves, which were not allowed to rise above a given figure.

As far as "consideration" was concerned, Keynes was confronted with two opposite views of what the United States should get in exchange for Lend-Lease: The U.S. Treasury, by controlling Britain's reserves, aimed to render the country financially dependent on the United States; the State Department, on the other hand, aimed to dismantle the imperial preference system.[8]

Keynes had initially presented a draft in which reference was made to reducing trade barriers and trade discrimination in pursuit of a "free and healthy" flow of trade (*CWK* 23, 128–40), but it was vetoed in London by the Chancellor of the Exchequer, Kinsley Woods. Keynes then reluctantly drafted a second proposal, following Churchill's and Woods' guidelines, in which Britain's postwar commitments to changing its trade policy were deliberately left vague and undefined (*CWK* 13, 162–65). Eventually, the initiative was taken by the State Department, which produced a draft in which Article VII invoked measures that "shall provide against discrimination in either the United States of America or the United Kingdom against the importation of any produce originating in the other country" (*CWK* 23, 174). Against Keynes's protestation that no trade concessions should be made before the financial arrangements were cleared, the door was thus thrown wide open to American control over Britain's balance of payments.

Discussion of Article VII was the core issue of Keynes's second mission, which, in fact, revolved around the future of the international monetary system. Keynes went to America with the hope of reaching a compromise between Harry White's plan (Stabilization Fund) and his own (Clearing Union), which were simultaneously published in Washington and New York on April 7, 1943. Each was the product of different visions of the banking function of the new institution and expressions of the contrasting interests of the United States and Great Britain.[9] Most of the negotiations were conducted in a series of eight meetings of the Anglo-American delegations in September 1943, and the balance turned out to be very much on the side of the U.S. proposals, which eventually prevailed. Skidelsky argues that, in those meetings, "the British proposed, the Americans disposed" (2000, 310), while Moggridge maintains that those discussions were "fruitful," since, "of points where there was an Anglo-American difference, six were solved, while another seven would be solved in the months that followed" (Moggridge 1992, 728).[10] The Joint Statement by Experts, signed in Washington on October 13, 1943, embodied the agreement that had been so laboriously reached. On May 23, 1944, Keynes defended it in the House of Lords.

The third mission was almost entirely taken up with the preparation for and subsequent proceedings of the Bretton Woods Conference. Keynes, as usual, was bargaining hard to get the Americans to agree with the British point of view over the delicate issues of postwar sterling convertibility and of eligibility for and terms of borrowing from the international bank. Once more, the results were mixed.

About the conference, Kahn aptly wrote, "An appreciation of the development of Keynes's attitude presents the difficulty that while Keynes was obviously fighting a rearguard action, constantly being forced to yield ground to the Americans, he was claiming from time to time that his concessions on points to which he had attached importance were not after all of serious consequence. He was terrified of failing to secure agreement with the Americans, and, at the same time, he had to maintain the *morale* of the U.K. Delegation, of officials and Ministers in London, of the Bank of England—and of himself" (Kahn 1976, 14).

The Final Act, which Keynes came to accept on the last day of the conference, was to be ratified by the governments involved. It was obvious that alterations would have been almost impossible to make. As Moggridge points out, "The only alternative to rejecting the whole agreement was to join the new institutions and seek an amendment or an interpretation from the Executive Directors, after the organisation came into operation" (1992, 748). How to persuade Parliament and how to pave the way to "interpretations" favorable to his vision of the working of the fund became one of Keynes's main concerns in the following months.

The central issue in the fourth mission was the checks America was imposing on Britain's gold and foreign exchange reserves, which the UK was intent on holding against the sterling balances of various countries (mainly India and the Middle East) accumulating in London as a result of the heavy military expenses incurred by Britain in those parts of the world. As Keynes was at pains to explain to Morgenthau: "For five years we, and we alone, have been responsible for practically the whole cash outgoings for the war over the vast territories from North Africa to Burma" (*CWK* 23, 166).

The United States insisted that, if British reserves rose above a given level, it was proof that Lend-Lease was excessive. Keynes's position, on the contrary, was that an increase in dollar reserves resulting from U.S. financial help was the only way to offset the growth of the sterling liabilities accumulated.

The fifth mission was undoubtedly a dramatic experience that took a heavy toll on Keynes's health and well-being. The Lend-Lease program had been canceled a fortnight before, after Japan's surrender, and it was really a case of going back to Washington begging for help. The strategy envisaged by Keynes for this goal was based on points and principles set out in a memorandum of March 18, 1945. The Americans were to be persuaded to share, as an act of justice, the burden of war sacrifices disproportionately incurred by Great Britain.[11] An American grant in the form of a "free gift" would allow Britain to return to normal peace conditions in production and consumption and would ease its way into multilateralism in international trade and payments. Without financial aid by the United States—the direst prospect, which Keynes dubbed Starvation Corner—Great Britain would plunge into severe economic recession and rationing, and it would be forced to rely on commercial and financial bilateralism with the same countries with which it had incurred a huge level of indebtedness.[12] The middle ground, which Keynes dubbed Temptation, was a loan on more or less commercial terms, which would have, however, placed a crippling burden on Great Britain, preventing it from fully exploiting the gains from free trade and full employment policies.[13] However, the reasons for rejecting Temptation went beyond Britain's ability to pay, since, in Keynes's view, it was "not as the result of some statistical calculation about what we may be able to manage, that the mind revolts from accepting the counsels of Temptation. The fundamental reasons for rejection are incommensurable in terms of cash" (*CWK* 24, 278). It was a matter of principles and of preservation of Britain's financial independence and hegemony in the postwar international order.

By the end of November 1945, the negotiations had come to a dead end, with Whitehall resisting those concessions that Keynes himself had originally advised rejecting but now no longer could be. At the last minute, the British Government decided to send A. T. K. Grant[14] and E. Bridges[15] to carry out what eventually amounted to capitulation to the terms imposed by the U.S. delegation. It was left to Keynes to defend the loan and the Bretton Woods agreements in the House of Lords on December 18, 1945, in a speech that Skidelsky describes as "the most courageous and skilful public speech of his life" (2000, 448).

The last mission was the shortest—less than four weeks—during which Keynes again had to give in to the American delegation on many important institutional features of the fund and the bank, such as its location, governance, and even remuneration of its appointed managers and directors. According to Kahn, "The Savannah Conference . . . had in a brutal manner revealed—especially . . . to Keynes—that the Americans were not going to prove so easy to deal with as, over a short phase of a few months, Keynes may conceivably have become lulled into believing" (Kahn 1976, 9).

When it came to reporting to the Chancellor of the Exchequer the results of his last mission, Keynes was apparently bewildered as to what to do. According to Kahn, he was persuaded to change the tone, if not the substance, of the memorandum he had drafted on the *Queen Mary* on the return trip, by two traveling companions[16] who were scared that it "might have resulted in a revolt in favour of withdrawal by the UK from the IMF" (Kahn 1976, 28). Moggridge disputes the importance of the episode, arguing that it simply shows that, while Keynes "was obviously disappointed with the results of Savannah" (Moggridge 1992, 834), he would never have suggested withdrawal. Skidelsky dismisses Kahn's interpretation, that "anything Keynes wrote was bound to have a decisive effect on the policy of the British government," as "symptomatic of the veneration in which Keynes was held for many years after his death, which was far from being complete while he was still alive" (Skidelsky 2000, 469).

There is no consensus in the literature on how far and to what extent Keynes's art of persuasion was constrained by circumstances or, rather, was jeopardized by his scarce negotiating skills. It is a matter that cannot be settled by any evidence, but we can nevertheless try to get a better idea of his style of rhetoric and strategy of communication by looking more closely into three of the most striking of his *tours de force* in persuasion.

4. The Rhetoric of Responsibility

If judged against the declared objectives, Keynes's missions can hardly be described as successful. However, in all contemporary records, as in most of the subsequent literature, Keynes is portrayed as a master in eloquence[17] and superb in his overall and far-reaching vision, with a full understanding of the minute details and implications of the arrangements that were being negotiated and displaying real rhetorical skill in pleading the British case, although there are reservations about his handling of the American opponents. Moreover, when it came to persuading the Treasury or the House of Lords to accept what he had negotiated, there is almost unanimous consensus that Keynes's art was unrivaled.

Keynes's eloquence won the day in three notable instances: defending the Joint Statement by Experts[18] with the Treasury[19] and in Parliament in April–May 1944, bringing Whitehall around to his strategy for Stage III in a memorandum of March–May 1945,[20] and pledging acceptance of the loan and the Bretton Woods agreements in the House of Lords in December 1946.

The logic of his defense of the Joint Statement rested on the necessary connection between Britain's domestic policy and its external position: the importance of avoiding the interwar experience with beggar-my-neighbor measures, which had resulted in unemployment and disruption of trade. As Keynes stated in the House of Lords on May 16, 1944, "The policy of full employment to which His Majesty's Government are committed would be immensely easier in practice if we could have a concerted policy with other countries, and if we all moved altogether and did not allow what is sometimes called the export of unemployment from one country to another" (*CWK* 26, 4–5).

In his speech to the House of Lords of May 23, 1944, Keynes's rhetorical pledge to the Lords to endorse the Joint Statement by Experts rested on two pillars. The first was to argue that it was a case of "a voluntary undertaking, genuinely offered in the spirit both of a good neighbour and, I should add, of enlightened self-interest, not to allow a repetition of a chain of events which between the wars did more than any other single factor to destroy the world's economic balance and to prepare a seed-bed for foul growths" (*CWK* 26, 4).

The second, and more important, pillar was that there was no viable choice: "What alternative is open to us which gives comparable aid, or better, more hopeful opportunities for the future? I have considerable confidence that something very like this plan will be in fact adopted, if only on account of the plain demerits of the alternative of rejection" (*CWK* 26, 15).

A year later, addressing again the alternatives facing Great Britain in the postwar period in a memorandum written between March and May 1945, Keynes bluntly depicted a bleak scenario, in which he insisted that an appeal to justice was the first and the best option. His approach was commented upon extensively by Bob Brand,[21] who was at the time one of Keynes's most important interlocutors and correspondents on Anglo-American relationships. Brand's reaction and Keynes's response are worth quoting at length: "What you propose the United States should do, is, taken as a whole, something like Justice to us, and that as for the part we assign to the United States we ask it from her not because it is just but because she is rich and well able to do so, and because it is very much in her interest. My point in saying all this is that I doubt whether it will be wise to stress to the American people that what we propose is not only Justice to us, but for them" (R. H. Brand to J. M. Keynes, April 5, 1945, in *CWK* 24, 307).

To which Keynes reacted, "You must remember that the present document is primarily addressed to critical members of the Cabinet here and is putting the case primarily from our point of view. I contemplate that a different sort of paper would be prepared and used for U.S.A. . . . One should give more attention to emphasising the advantages to U.S.A than I have given in this paper as compared with the advantage to the UK" (J. M. Keynes to R. H. Brand, April 24, 1945, in *CWK* 24, 312–13).

Here Keynes's persuasion strategy relied on two levers. The first was selecting the arguments that would appeal to the self-interest of the party that he was addressing at the time. The second was searching for a framework in which each side's interests could be made to coincide as parts of the same general interest. As he explained to Wilfrid Eady,[22] who was also unconvinced of Keynes's strategy in negotiating postwar American financial assistance: "[The appeal to Justice] is wider conception about the way in which the financial consequences of the war should be liquidated" (J. M. Keynes to W. Eady, June 13, 1945, in *CWK* 24, 360).

Keynes's appeal to justice to persuade the Americans to share the burden of the cost of the war was a rhetorical device to present as a mutual interest that which, in the minds of the two parties involved in defending the U.S. and U.K. viewpoints, appeared to be conflicting interests. The substantive reason for putting forward his proposal of a "free gift" from the United States stemmed, however, from a firm belief that settling the British external debt by the application of a strictly commercial point of view, as the Americans were determined to do, would have a worldwide deflationary effect. This position is similar to the one Keynes took with regard to German reparations in the aftermath of the First World War. Ironically, the Marshall Plan, which the Americans introduced after the end of the war to inflate the European economy, was a Keynesian remedy; but, to American politicians, it had the virtue of not being geared to British interests. The literature is divided on this issue. Skidelsky endorses the view that Keynes was fighting against the U.S. intention to destroy Britain as a great power, while American economic historian Brad DeLong rejects the idea that Britain could ever have remained a great power, no matter how much Keynes might have been able to extract in terms of financial aid from the United States.[23]

Finally, we come to Keynes's address to the House of Lords on December 18, 1945 (*CWK* 24, 605–28), delivered barely twenty-four hours after he had disembarked from the *Queen Elizabeth* at Southampton to seek Parliamentary ratification of the loan and the Bretton Woods agreements. Here his persuasion strategy was geared to appealing to a sense of responsibility. While conceding "to his regret that this is not an interest free loan," Keynes expressed sympathy for his American negotiators and their difficulties, arguing that relying on a sterling area bloc was not a viable alternative to Anglo-American collaboration, and he enumerated all of the advantages that multilateralism held for Great Britain in terms of short-term recovery and long-term growth.

However, he also recanted his strategy of appealing to a sense of justice, devised in March 1944: "In no phase of human experience does the past operate so directly and arithmetically as we were trying to contend. Men's sympathies and less calculated impulses are drawn from their memories of comradeship, but their contemporary acts are generally directed towards influencing the future and not towards pensioning the past. . . . We soon discovered, therefore, that it was not our past performance or our present weakness but our future prospects of recovery and our intention to face the world boldly that we had to demonstrate" (*CWK* 24, 610–11).

Skidelsky argues that "the *magic* of Keynes's words is still potent more than half a century later" (Skidelsky 2000, 449; emphasis added). Moggridge describes Keynes's speech as "a *powerful*, frank description of the arrangements" (Moggridge 1992, 816; emphasis added). The choice of adjectives reflects the contrasting evaluation of his two biographers, the former stressing the eloquence, the latter the logic, of Keynes's defense of his own doings. Harrod (1951, 618) takes a middle course, describing the address as a "graceful and persuasive speech . . . compounded of penetrating analysis, tact and sagacity."

Once again, we see here different evaluations of Keynes's role in the various agreements that sealed the final act in Anglo-American financial negotiations during the Second World War. Skidelsky, together with Robbins, takes the view that Keynes was more a "master of words" (in Harrod's definition) than a successful negotiator, while Moggridge, together with Kahn, presents him as painfully aware that this was the best the British could achieve against the Americans' refusal to consider the alternative option.

5. Conclusions

Success in persuasion requires the thorough grasp of public feelings and sentiment which, by the end of his life, Keynes had fully acquired, above all in the context of his intellectual and political milieu. In the 1940s he was no longer—as in the 1920s—an outcast on the political scene. He was the most influential advisor to the Treasury, a director of the Bank of England, and a member of the House of Lords addressing his peers. He knew the right strings to pull, and he pulled them. It was not only his prestige at stake but the postwar economic and political system he had helped design.

By assuming responsibility for what had been achieved, Keynes forced Parliament and the Government—by then accustomed to the idea that he was one of them—to share in it. A similar point was made by Harrod in his comment on the speech of December 18, 1945, when he asked what lay behind Keynes's success in persuasion in this particular instance: "The speech in December 1945 was excellent, but no more excellent than his utterances for twenty-seven long years. Were the mighty ones in the land merely indifferent to wisdom, or were they incapable of detecting it, except when it was adorned with a coronet?" (Harrod 1951, 618).

Keynes's appeal to overcome self-interest as the sole guide to action and to transcend situations that take the form of zero-sum games was made in the context of both internal and external economic problems. As far as full-employment policy was concerned, he endeavored to persuade his "countrymen and the world at large to change their traditional doctrines and, by taking better thought, to remove the curse of unemployment" (*CWK* 26, 16). In the case of postwar international economics, he fought to persuade governments that "only by a more comprehensive settlement, which attempts to offer everyone what is reasonable, and so far as we can make it fair, [can] the financial consequences of the war . . . be liquidated" (*CWK* 24, 291–92).

His persuasion strategy was not always successful, but to the extent that it was—as the experience of employment policies and international financial stability in the postwar years has amply shown it to have been—much was gained in terms of creation and allocation of resources.

Robbins (1932) claimed that arguments pertaining to ethics and political philosophy should be banned from economics. His message was that, while moral sciences deal with what ought to be, economics is concerned with what is. Keynes fought for the opposite view, for investigation "into problems which seek to bring about defined or desired end states (or solutions) and clarify values" (see Marcuzzo 2004). His message was to change the environment within which individuals operate, so that moral and rational motives become the spring of action of the collective as a whole (*CWK* 17, 453). The role of persuasion was precisely that of inducing behavior to conform to goals that were attainable only by moving beyond individualistic motivation or utilitarian calculation. Zero-sum games were more the results of a vision of society and of a conception of economics based on the principle of scarcity and self-interest than on a true representation of reality.

As Skidelsky aptly put it: "[H]is intuition persuades, not so much because it corresponds to our own intuition of reality, but because we are very susceptible to persuasive language. To the extent that we are persuaded, and modify our behaviour, there is a new reality" (1992, 415).

Notes

1. Quoted in Skidelsky 2000, 407. Richard Leffingwell, an American lawyer, was at the time director of J. P. Morgan.
2. For instance, Keynes wrote to Robertson: "I certainly date all my emancipation from the discussion between us which preceded your *Banking Policy and the Price Level*" (JMK to DHR, December 13, 1936, *CWK* 14, 94). And he wrote of Kahn that "he is a marvellous critic and suggester and improver—there never was anyone in the history of the world to whom it was so helpful to submit one's stuff" (JMK to Joan Robinson, March 29, 1934, *CWK* 13, 422). On the collaboration with Kahn, see Marcuzzo 2002; on the collaboration with Robertson, see Sanfilippo 2005.
3. Keynes's own arguments were set out in a memorandum of October 27, 1940, drawn to assist British Treasury official Frederick Philipps in preparation for his visit to Washington (*CWK* 23, 13–26).
4. Notably, Harrod 1951, Moggridge 1992, Skidelsky 2000, DeLong 2002, and Pressnell 2003.
5. "[Keynes] held fast to the illusion that what Britain deserved could be made to happen and . . . infected the labour government with his optimism" (Skidelsky 2000, 386).
6. "London had also made a serious tactical mistake in not including commercial specialists in the original team, although they had attached a Board of Trade official to the team at the last moment. . . . Keynes saw trade and aid as being linked but thought that they could be kept separate in the initial stages of financial talks" (Moggridge 1992, 802).
7. "Keynes's grand scheme depended on first securing a financial deal, and he was confident of being able to handle commercial policy, if it arose, in general terms; much later, perhaps a trade official or two, even a team, might join the negotiations" (Pressnell 2003, 683).
8. On the vital importance of the United States gaining access to British-controlled markets, see De Cecco 1979.
9. According to DeLong (2002, 160): "When Keynes disagreed with White, he usually lost the point because of the greater power of the United States. . . . But compared to the common view of the institutions to be built and of the goals to be accomplished, the differences between Keynes and White, while important, are orders of magnitude less important than the broad areas on which they agreed." Skidelsky (2000, 253) takes the opposite

view, going so far as to suggest that White was a Soviet spy who "wanted to cripple Britain in order to clear the ground for a post-war American-Soviet alliance." The evidence of the charges against White has been questioned by Boughton (2001).

10. Points agreed upon were the form of the ultimate statement, the size of the International Monetary Fund, the scarce currency clause, the mechanisms for altering the gold value of the units of account (Unitas), withdrawals from the fund, and selection of the currencies to be drawn from the fund. Points still to be agreed upon were the size of the initial gold subscriptions to the fund, its role in the event of exchange rate changes and in members' capital account transactions, terms of repurchase of a member's own currency, and the monetization of Unitas.
11. "It is only by a more comprehensive settlement, which attempts to offer everyone what is reasonable, and so far as we can make it, fair, that the financial consequences of the war can be liquidated. This is the aim, namely, that as between the partners to the war, its financial consequences, in so far as they affect future economic intercourse between them, should be so far as possible liquidated" (*CWK* 24, 291–92).
12. "A policy of economic isolationism and of economic rupture with the United States and Canada (and with a large part of the rest of the world also) could only be practicable if we had regained the financial reserves we have lost, and if we were prepared to live for several years after the war with rigid domestic controls and strict rationing of consumption, and with an organisation of foreign trade after the Russian model" (*CWK* 24, 256).
13. "We cannot be sure of shouldering such a burden with success, and we might find ourselves in a chronic condition of having to make humiliating and embarrassing pleas for mercy and postponement" (*CWK* 24, 278).
14. An economist at the Treasury.
15. The Permanent Secretary of the Treasury.
16. George Bolton of the Bank of England and Ernest Rowe-Dutton of the Treasury.
17. See, for instance, Harrod (1951, 496): "In the course of years he had made himself a supreme master of debate. That fine command of prose, manifested in his writings, was no less evident in oral discussion. . . . As a master of words Keynes was without peer in Washington or Bretton Woods." See also Robert Bryce (1988, 150): "In 1944 [Keynes] came twice to Ottawa as a representative of the British Treasury . . . he was a very skilled negotiator, a very persuasive and fluent expositor; indeed his exercise of fluency and charm was so powerful that the Canadian ministers preferred to take their decisions *after* they had met with him rather than while they were still under his spell." I am grateful to Robert Dimand for drawing my attention to Bryce's account.
18. *Joint Statement by Experts on the Establishment of an International Monetary Fund*, *CWK* 25, 379–92 and Appendix 4. The version signed in Washington on October 13, 1943, went though seven drafts (Editorial note, ibid., 392).

19. *Explanatory Notes by United Kingdom Experts on the Proposal for an International Monetary Fund*, *CWK* 25, 437–42. Keynes justified the need for these in a letter to the Chancellor of the Exchequer: "The experts, who are publicly stated to have *agreed* this paper as being satisfactory, are surely entitled to offer some explanation why" (J. M. Keynes to J. Anderson, April 16, 1944, in *CWK* 25, 436).
20. Overseas Financial Policy in Stage III, *CWK* 24, 256–95.
21. At the time, Treasury representative in Washington.
22. Since 1942, the Second Secretary of the British Treasury.
23. "Britain imported seventeen billion pounds' worth of goods during World War II, of which America paid in Lend-Lease and in post-World War II Marshall Plan and MSA [Mutual Security Agency] aid for seven billion. Had America paid for all seventeen billion pounds, then Britain would have had an extra ten billion pounds' worth of overseas assets at the end of World War II. At a 5 percent real return on overseas investments, this would have boosted post-World War II British GNP by 4 percent. Would Britain with 4 percent more GNP have been a truly 'great' power, the post-World War II leader of the western alliance? No. . . . It would have had no more workers and factories more productive than Britain did in reality" (DeLong 2002, 162).

References

Boughton, J. M. 2001. The case against Harry Dexter White: Still not proven. *History of Political Economy* 33:219–39.

Bryce, R. 1988. Keynes during the Great Depression and World War II. In *Keynes and public policy after fifty years*, ed. O. F. Hamouda and J. N. Smithin. Vol. 1, *Economics and policy*. Aldershot, UK: Edward Elgar.

De Cecco, M. 1979. Origins of the post-war payments system. *Cambridge Journal of Economics* 3:49.

DeLong, B. 2002. Review of Robert Skidelsky, *John Maynard Keynes: Fighting for Britain, 1937–1946*. *Journal of Economic Literature* 40:155–62.

Harrod, R. F. 1951. *The life of John Maynard Keynes*. London: Macmillan.

Kahn, R. F. 1976. Historical origins of the International Monetary Fund. In *Keynes and international monetary relations*, ed. A. P. Thirlwall. London: Macmillan.

Keynes, J. M., 1971–1989. *The collected writings of John Maynard Keynes* (*CWK*). Ed. D. Moggridge. London: Macmillan, and New York: Cambridge University Press, for the Royal Economic Society.

CWK 7, *The general theory of employment, interest and money*.
CWK 9, *Essays in persuasion*.
CWK 13, *The General Theory and after. Part I: Preparation*.
CWK 14, *The General Theory and after. Part II: Defence and development*.
CWK 17, *Activities 1920–1922: Treaty revision and reconstruction*.

CWK 23, *Activities 1940–1943: External war finance.*
CWK 24, *Activities 1944–1946: The transition to peace.*
CWK 25, *Activities 1940–1944: Shaping the post-war world: The clearing union.*
CWK 26, *Activities 1941–1946: Shaping the post-war world: Bretton Woods and reparations.*

Marcuzzo, M. C. 2002. The collaboration between J. M. Keynes and R. F. Kahn from the *Treatise* to *The General Theory*. *History of Political Economy* 34 (2): 421–47.

———. 2004. From market imperfections to market failures: Some Cambridge challenges to laissez-faire. *Annals of the Society for the History of Economic Thought* 45:1–10.

Marcuzzo, M. C., and A. Rosselli. 2005a. Introduction. In *Economists in Cambridge: A study through their correspondence, 1907–1946*, ed. M. C. Marcuzzo and A. Rosselli. London: Routledge.

———, ed. 2005b. *Economists in Cambridge: A study through their correspondence, 1907–1946*. London: Routledge.

Moggridge, D. 1992. *Maynard Keynes: An economist's biography*. London: Routledge.

Pressnell, L. S. 2003. Keynes and wartime finance: A clarification. *History of Political Economy* 35:679–84.

Robbins, L. 1932. *An essay on the nature and significance of economic science*. London: Macmillan.

Sanfilippo, E. 2005. Keynes's valuable opponent and collaborator: The correspondence between Keynes and Robertson. In *Economists in Cambridge: A study through their correspondence, 1907–1946*, ed. M. C. Marcuzzo and A. Rosselli. London: Routledge.

Skidelsky, R. 1992. *John Maynard Keynes: The economist as saviour, 1920–1937*. London: Macmillan.

———. 2000. *John Maynard Keynes: Fighting for Britain, 1937–1946*. London: Macmillan.

CHAPTER 2

LEON H. KEYSERLING, AMERICAN KEYNESIAN

THEORY, POLICY, AND PRACTICE

W. ROBERT BRAZELTON

INTRODUCTION

THE LATTER PART OF THE 1920s was a period of economic instability and speculation, especially in the stock market. This period has been analyzed by John Kenneth Galbraith in *The Great Crash* (1954), with its Keynesian and Post Keynesian implications concerning economic instabilities and uncertainties. Earlier, the works of Alvin Hansen are of interest, especially after his conversion from a neoclassicist to a Keynesian (Brazelton 1993). As a Keynesian in the 1930s, Hansen developed what became a "stagnation theory" (Hansen 1939; Brazelton 1961, 1989), a thesis that was Keynesian but had historical and institutional underpinnings. Basically, to Hansen, the American economy had stagnated in the 1930s because, in the 1920s, its three historical growth elements had declined simultaneously: The rate of population growth from a high birth rate and high immigration declined, the rate of new technology declined, and the geographic frontier in the West had ended in the 1890s. A critic might ask why, if the frontier had ended in the 1890s, investment therein would continue until the 1930s. One reply correctly pointed out that capital accumulation on the East Coast of the United States was invested in the growing cities of the American West and Midwest—Kansas City, St. Louis, Oklahoma City, Omaha, and others—which absorbed eastern capital until the late 1920s. This was an offset to the diminishing returns to capital accumulating in the already developed cities farther east. This early, basic urban investment in the western frontier lasted into the 1920s (Brazelton 1961, 1989).

Thus, Hansen realized that historic growth factors and changes therein were important in relation to continued economic growth, economic stability, and employment. Declining population growth threatened declining labor supplies and potential aggregate demand (Hansen 1939; Brazelton 1989); declining technology threatened growth, profits, and investment opportunities relating to the Keynesian "marginal efficiency of capital"; and the end of the American geographic frontier diminished the demand for new capital investments—such as resources development, railroads, and urban areas. Thus, investment reached a zenith and then declined as the growth factors declined due to economic, historical, and institutional factors. Later, of course, Hansen wrote the little book (the "Bible" of graduate students of the time), *A Guide to Keynes* (1953). In terms of his conversion to Keynesianism, Hansen became an expert in relation to countercyclical economic policy (Hansen 1941, 1949, 1953, 1957, 1964; Musgrave 1987). But Hansen also realized that the economy was not competitive in the neoclassical sense (Hansen 1939, 1957; Brazelton 1993) but was concentrated in major areas of power *à la* Berle and Means.

Berle and Means (Berle and Means 1932; Berle 1959) developed an analysis of economic concentration and power and its effect upon the economy that was non-neoclassical in fact, theory, and policy implications. Basically, an "oligopolistic" market structure allows a firm or a small group of controlling firms to set prices and limit output—steel, autos, oil, et cetera. Prices are not freely set as in the neoclassical tradition. This means, *à la* Keynes, that prices and wages are not free to adjust via the "laws of supply and demand" of neoclassical tradition but, rather, in terms of market power (Berle and Means 1932; Berle 1959). Keynes, of course, utilized "wage rigidity" in his *General Theory* but never went on to develop the implications of Berle and Means—administered pricing and price inflexibility. Others made the attempt. In micro theory, there was a recognition in the textbooks of the time of the relevance and imperfections of oligopolistic, noncompetitive market structures. Later, there was the development of the kinked demand curve by the "Marxist" Paul Sweezy (Sweezy 1939; Sweezy and Baran 1966), in which a firm's demand curve is "kinked" below certain prices, below which "competing" oligopolistic firms will not allow it to cut its prices without retaliation. Later, the wage-price analysis of Sydney Weintraub enters the picture, where prices are set as a markup over costs (especially, therein, labor costs)—a post Keynesian contribution with its roots in the market structure analysis researched by Berle and Means.

The analysis of Berle and Means was also implied by John Kenneth Galbraith. For example, in *The New Industrial State* (Galbraith 1967), he is concerned with the labor market, government, and oligopoly in terms of power—economic and political. This type of analysis introduces the reader to changes in market structure over time, uncertainties in those markets, and the economic effects and consequences of market power. Thus, Galbraith put himself into an institutionalist (evolutionist) framework and, later, expressed a recognition of the emerging Post Keynesian framework that is partly reminiscent of his earlier work, *The Great Crash* (1954). Indeed, in relation to market power, Galbraith himself, in *The New Palgrave: A Dictionary of Economics* (Galbraith 1987, 231), said that Berle (and Means) indicated that ownership of a firm "no longer conveyed power in the great enterprise. Profit maximization was now by managers, not on behalf of themselves, but for others largely unknown or, in pay and perquisites, for the managers themselves."

In relation to Means, Keyserling wrote in *The New Palgrave: A Dictionary of Economics* (Keyserling 1987a, 421) that they (Berle and Means) "revealed the monster size of existing corporations and their dominating power negated the attributes of private property as then conceived; their ability and determination to fix or 'administer' prices prevented the benign operation of supply and demand to suggest the need for government intervention at some level." Keyserling also pointed out that Berle and Means refuted the "trade-off" analysis by pointing out that "the great increases in inflation during recent decades have come mainly, not during a highly used economy near full employment, but rather during periods when the economy moved into stagnation or recession" (Keyserling 1987a, 422). As discussed below, Keyserling continually stressed the power and reality of "administered pricing" and the mistaken theory of the "trade-off" as a major cause of inflation. Thus, Keyserling is in line with Berle, Means, Galbraith (with whom he had some disagreements, despite their friendship), and Keyserling's mentor, Rexford Tugwell.

Tugwell was a major professor in the Department of Economics of Columbia University, New York. He believed in a historical analysis of economics and was a social critic of the American economy and society

(Tugwell 1924, 1974; Tugwell, Munro, and Stryker 1925, 1927). He was for planning—not of the Soviet style but democratic and transparent. He, like Berle and Means, and Keyserling himself, was important in the Roosevelt Administration; and Keyserling was important in the Truman Administration, as discussed below. Tugwell was, as Keyserling states, against the "curse of bigness and economic royalists" (Keyserling 1987b, 706). Keyserling further states that Tugwell urged "the type of . . . economic planning later used in World War II, with larger interpenetration between government and business" and said that the "patchwork" of the New Deal would not work as a further argument for more extensive planning. In retrospect, the post–World War II example of such planning envisioned by Tugwell would be close to that of "indicative planning" practiced by the French after World War II. In the years after the election of Franklin Roosevelt to the Presidency in 1932, Hansen, Berle, Means, Tugwell, and Keyserling (the latter two via Senator Robert Wagner, Democrat, NY) were called to Washington and were instrumental in the early years of the New Deal, with Keyserling continuing into the Truman Administration era of the "Fair Deal" and beyond until his death in 1987.

Keyserling: The Basics of Policy, Fiscal and Monetary

Keyserling was known primarily for fiscal policy due to his chairmanship of the Council of Economic Advisors. However, as can be seen by the titles of some of his Conference on Economic Progress pamphlets (see appendix), he definitely had monetary analysis and policy matters in mind. In fact, he was an important and constant critic of the Federal Reserve–Treasury Accord of 1951 as a significant policy mistake, as discussed below (Brazelton 1997, 2001, 2005; Keyserling 1964b, 1979, 1980).

Keyserling's anti-recessionary policy was rather orthodox in nature. He would increase expenditures or decrease taxes (or both). However, in terms of a choice, he favored an increase in expenditures as a more efficient way of getting funds into circulation where needed and to the poorer elements of society (Brazelton 2001, 2005). He realized that tax cuts were more practical politically at times, but he held that they should, if necessary, be "selective" (Brazelton 2001, 2005).

The concept of "selectivity" arises again (perhaps mainly) in his less-orthodox analysis of anti-inflationary policy. First, unlike many more-orthodox economists, Keyserling believed that inflations were primarily caused not by "excess demand" but rather by "inadequate supply." Prices rose more in slack economies than in full employment economies (Keyserling 1975, 1978, 1979, 1980; Brazelton 1997, 2001, 2005). Second, he believed, along with Berle, Means, Tugwell, and others of a more institutionalist slant, that the actual market structure was not of a competitive nature *à la* orthodox economics but "oligopolistic" in terms of bigness and power (Keyserling 2005; Brazelton 1997, 2001, 2005). Thus, the more realistic price mechanism was one of "administered pricing"—a concept later enlarged upon by the Post Keynesian Sydney Weintraub in his "markup" analysis (Weintraub 1963, 1977). Third, Keyserling believed in "economic balance": The sectors of the economy—micro and macro—must grow together. On the micro level, an increase in the output of one sector needs an increase in supplies and demand from other sectors. An increase in macro demand needs an increase in macro supply, and vice versa. Thus, if output increases, so must consumption; and wages must be kept adequate if mass production and full employment are to be maintained via mass consumption.

The orthodox anti-inflationary policy calls for cutting back on aggregate demand. This, to Keyserling, is counterproductive in that it is, in itself, inflationary. If one cuts back on aggregate demand, the firm has to cut back on its production, meaning that it may now be producing to the left of the lowest point on its average cost curve. Thus, average costs rise, which means an increase in prices, especially if there is the reality of administered pricing. Thus, inflationary pressures are increased, not decreased. Also, if the monetary authorities increase interest rates to combat inflation, this cuts back on investment, which means less output, less employment, and a divergence from "constant, full employment growth"—the latter a constant emphasis of Keyserling (Keyserling 1964a, 1975, 1978; Brazelton 2001). Thus, the lower investment decreases potential supply and is counterproductive to long-term growth; and the increased interest rates result in an increase in costs, which, via administered pricing, may be passed on to consumers. Thus, it is an incorrect policy for the short and the long run.

The correct policy would be to expand supply, as, remember, inflation, to Keyserling, was mainly caused by inadequate supply, not excess demand. Thus, expenditures, tax cuts, or both should be targeted to the areas of short supply, so as to enlarge supplies in those lagging sectors of the economy—selectivity. This can be described as a "rifle-shot" approach affecting the selected lagging sectors, not a "shotgun" approach affecting all sectors as would the overall higher interest rates of orthodox policy. If there is administered pricing in certain sectors, price controls or other tax incentives can be developed to constrain the guilty parties. Also, society must realize that certain investments (expenditures or tax incentives) are more valuable than others: An investment in education is, in the long run, more productive than a new casino or hotel. Priorities must be realized and, thus, as in Tugwell's analysis, some degree of planning is a necessity in sectors of the economy where it is needed and is of importance to the rest of the economy.

Keyserling constantly stressed full employment and output growth for the purpose of economic prosperity and social equity and justice. Thus, he developed what he referred to as the Freedom Budget, or the Nation's Economic Budget, in his Conference on Economic Progress reports (1957, 1964a, 1966, 1978; Brazelton 2003). This can be seen in his fiscal policy analysis, in the annual Economic Report to the President (and, hence, to Congress), and in his many testimonies before congressional committees. This growth emphasis can also be seen in his monetary analysis.

According to Keyserling, the money supply should grow as the economy grows, and it should "permit" the economy to grow at a full employment and full output rate. Furthermore, to permit such growth, the interest rates should be kept low enough to allow investment to do its job in stimulating growth or output and the growth of demand—micro and macro. The fact that he believed in the maintenance of low interest rates made him a critic of the Federal Reserve–Treasury Accord of 1951, which ended the post–World War II period of low interest rates achieved by the Federal Reserve's purchase of federal debt at a set interest rate, and a critic of the analysis of Milton Friedman, which would allow interest rates to fluctuate around a constant rate of increase in the money supply (Friedman 1956, 1959). Keyserling believed in a constantly increasing money supply but not a constant rate of increase *à la* Friedman. For Keyserling, the rate of increase in the money supply should be based on the needs of the economy at the time for the purpose of full employment and full output—secularly and cyclically. Thus, the Federal Reserve should not be constrained merely to control inflation but should also maintain growth, which in the long run would diminish inflation by increasing output rather than by decreasing demand and thus output.

The increase in the money supply should not be constant. That would mean wide fluctuations in the interest rate and, thus, the level of output and employment, whereas Keyserling's goal was constant full employment and output growth. Thus, the real money supply should be increased as needed. Also, in a Keynesian or a Post Keynesian world, as the demand for money (liquidity preference) changed *à la* Keynes and Hyman Minsky, Randall Wray, and others, the money supply must also offset these factors. To increase the money supply merely on the past rate of growth overlooks too many current events and changes in the demand for money—rational or irrational—and the wide swings in economic activity that can then occur. If one then desires to introduce the concepts of "chaos," or the Davidson concepts of "hysteresis" or "non-ergodicity" (Davidson 1991, 1993), one has an even more imprecise picture of the economy emerging based on elements of Post Keynesian analysis.

The economics of Keyserling (like that of Keynes; see Tily 2007), involved both monetary and fiscal policy and the relationships between the two, as they do not stand alone. Fiscal policy and debt financing therefrom affect interest rates; interest rates are the subject of monetary policy in terms of the availability and the cost of credit (interest rates), as indicated above. However, perhaps my own simplification of Keyserling's major points may be of help.

Keyserling's premises can be summarized as follows.

1. Full employment and output growth secularly and cyclically were constant goals of Keyserling for the purpose of employment, social welfare, and social justice.
2. Growth, even during inflation, as discussed above, was the goal, because, to Keyserling, inflation was due to inadequate supply (and wars), not excess demand; and the reality of administered pricing accentuated inflationary pressures, as did orthodox, anti-inflationary policies such as increasing interest rates and cutting output, which may increase average costs on the average cost curve of firms—all inflationary.
3. Orthodox anti-inflationary policies, then, restrict growth rather than expand it, as indicated in (2) above. The best way to control inflation is to give incentives to important sectors lagging in productivity, and to exercise selective controls over wage and price increases in areas of administered pricing of crucial sectors—a point stressed by many Keynesians, institutionalists, and Post Keynesians (Keyserling 1973, 1976).
4. Low interest rates and permissive money supply growth are important for continued growth, welfare, and justice—a point of many Post Keynesians.
5. The Accord of 1951 between the Federal Reserve and the Treasury, which ended the 1946–51 pegging of U.S. interest rates at a low rate in favor of the resultant higher rates, was a crucial policy error—also a point expressed by many Keynesians and Post Keynesians (Keyserling 1964b; Brazelton 2001).

6. The fiscal budget must be a Nation's Economic Budget or a Freedom Budget for full employment output to balance the budget at full employment secularly—a policy later adopted by the Kennedy and Johnson administrations under economic advisor Walter Heller (Brazelton 2003) and included in the so-called Humphrey-Hawkins Act (Keyserling 1978; Pechman and Simler 1982, especially the chapter by Walter Heller).
7. In terms of fiscal policy to support full employment, the money supply must grow to keep interest rates low, to permit further growth as needed for full employment via the public and the private sectors, and for social justice.
8. There must be a balance between the micro and the macro sectors of the economy. In the former, firms must get supplies to feed their needs for current output and expansion. In the latter, aggregate demand must grow with aggregate supply, and vice versa. Also, the money supply must be permissive for such secular and cyclical needs of the economy.
9. Mass production depends upon mass consumption, which depends upon real wages being kept sufficient for that purpose and for social justice and equity—all three.

Keyserling's Sixteen Points: The Basic Specifics of His Policy Analysis and Wishes

In a 1975 publication of the Conference on Economic Progress, *Full Employment without Inflation*, Keyserling stressed sixteen points to accomplish the goals of full employment and output growth over time. Following are these goals and my brief comments thereon.

1. There is a need for long-term goals for full output, employment, and growth—not temporary studies for specific purposes, but goals as set forth by the Employment Act of 1946 and the Equal Opportunity and Full Employment (Humphrey-Hawkins) Act. *The latter was being discussed in 1975.*
2. In the long run, we need to enlarge our output in needed areas where shortages impede such growth; in the short run, resources should be shifted to needed priorities, but in terms of long-term growth, needs, and priorities.
3. Housing should be a priority. Housing means better living conditions for all: employment in the building trades and increases in the need for furnishings, utilities, roads, and highways—all of which increase employment and national income via the Keynesian fiscal policy multiplier effect, to achieve growth, employment, and social justice and welfare, all in one. *Keyserling continually stressed housing, in terms of permanent need and in terms of anti-recessionary fiscal policy.*

4. There should be public service employment, whereby the government provides jobs for those eligible due to unemployment or employment disabilities, for the construction and maintenance of parks, sidewalks, environmental projects, et cetera. *This is similar to the policies of many institutionalists and Post Keynesians and of the Center for Full Employment and Price Stability (CFEPS) at the Department of Economics, University of Missouri–Kansas City.*
5. There should be a "new" monetary policy that replaces high interest rates with low interest rates, to stimulate investment and lower costs. As this policy increases output, it would be anti-inflationary (as discussed above) and fuel the priority needs of the economy, the nation, and the citizenry. *Such a permissive, low–interest-rate policy was also stressed by Keynes (Tily 2007).*
6. In terms of the fiscal budget, there should be tax cuts to reduce the tax burden on the lower- and middle-income classes, to relieve those most suffering from inflation and slow economic growth, and also to help expand the economy via increased consumption and related investment.
7. Increased expenditures of the federal government should be aimed at selected shortages and priorities in such areas as food, energy, and housing. In Keyserling's view, all sectors cannot be equally stimulated by tax cuts to the public—e.g., energy, utilities, roads—and tax cuts may send funds towards less valuable investments at the loss of more valuable investments for the overall economy: New casinos and hotels are less valuable in terms of long-term growth of output, employment, and skills than are better schools and educational investments.
8. The federal budget should be balanced or even in surplus, but only after recessionary conditions are ended. *To Keyserling, this was a long-term goal, not a short-term cyclical goal, and it assumed the closing of recessionary conditions and shortages. Of course, he also indicates that short-term deficits increase GDP, out of which future public tax revenues and private savings may be gleaned. This was, of course, the argument for the "full employment budget concept" of Keyserling and, later, Walter Heller (Brazelton 2003, 2005).*
9. National defense expenditures are necessary, and they should be based upon a "most responsible appraisal of the international situation, difficult though that appraisal always is" (Keyserling 1975, 39). *Keyserling had indicated, in a previous memo to President Truman, that, by militarily outspending the less productive Soviet system, the United States could defeat it (Brazelton 2001). This, of course, was finally done in 1989–91, during the Reagan Administration, more than forty years later.*
10. There should be income supports for social justice, income maintenance, and social security; and these supports would involve a more progressive tax system.
11. The societal income supports discussed above (item 10) should be aimed at replacing the "ragbag of costly and grossly inadequate 'welfare' programs" and would be both economical and humane.

12. National farm policies should be aimed at providing farm output sufficient to give an adequate diet to all Americans, eliminate the income disparities between rural (poorer) and urban (more affluent) Americans, and reduce the spread between what the farmers receive for their produce at the local markets and the higher prices at the retail stores. This would reduce the price of agricultural goods and would thus be anti-inflationary. There should also be an income support system for farm families (the Brannan Plan) rather than the price support system for agricultural produce; this would allow farm prices to fall to market levels (anti-inflationary) and, at the same time, give direct income supports to farmers who needed them.
13. There should be stronger, coordinated manpower training programs for available jobs, both for today and tomorrow. This would decrease unemployment and keep the workforce trained for the jobs of tomorrow in an ever-changing, globalized world.
14. Anti-trust laws should restrain price increases and illegal acts, especially in relation to administered pricing. *Keyserling, like Berle, Means, and others, understood that big business was necessary in the modern, high-technology world, but not the illegal acts and not the administered pricing permitted by bigness and the control of markets assumed by bigness itself. These policies of preventing illegal acts and administered pricing would be anti-inflationary and pro-growth. He was also willing to talk to business leaders, and frequently did, concerning the needs and the policies of the Truman Administration (Brazelton 1997, 2001, 2005).*
15. There should be direct controls over wages and prices where they are excessive. *Keyserling was aware of the dangers of such controls, but he thought that "effective price control, by preventing recurrent imbalances between investment and profits on the one hand and wages and other consumer incomes on the other, would be conducive to a healthy economy. Under such conditions, real wage rates would not be excessive, even without wage controls. However, it may be impractical to institute a system of price controls, understood and supported by the public, without including wages also" (Keyserling 1975, 42–43). This, of course, related to his emphasis on macro balance—the balance between aggregate supply and aggregate demand for long-term growth and its sustainability.*
16. Lastly, there must be both "energy expansion and conservation." *Keyserling mentioned, in 1975, the costs and dangers of depending upon foreign sources of oil, and he desired public and private cooperatives to develop new energy sources to decrease our dependence on foreign supplies and for conservation.*

In all of the sixteen points, we see an underlying interest in full employment and output growth, both cyclically and secularly. This involves price policies, tax policies, balanced budgets at full employment, the relevant Keynesian multipliers, the money supply, and money supply increases in terms of fiscal needs and growth needs (a money supply increase in real terms and in terms of the need for full employment growth—thus, at a variable, not a constant, rate) (Brazelton 1997, 2001, 2005). Constant full employment and price-constrained output growth was the goal of Keyserling. Hopefully, others will readopt such a goal in the future.

Conclusion

Keyserling was basically a Keynesian in that he used fiscal policy derived from Keynes (Brazelton 2007; Tily 2007; Turgeon 1987) and the related multipliers. He also realized that money growth was a necessary ingredient for economic growth—a reason for his constant criticism of the Federal Reserve–Treasury Accord of 1951. He did differ slightly from Keynes in that the latter was more interested in cyclical unemployment whereas Keyserling (based upon Keynesian tenets) was more interested in secular growth for full employment output; but the Keynesian fiscal, monetary, and multiplier tools were therefore applied to tax and expenditure policies. Keyserling was also influenced by the institutionalist school (via Tugwell) and by the analysis of Berle and Means, which led him to concentrate on administered pricing as an important contributor to inflation and, thus, inadequate real growth over time. Keyserling knew that, to combat administered pricing, selective controls and legal action may be necessary, but he realized the inevitability of big business in the modern industrial world. He also believed in economic balance—micro and macro—and the need for selective incentives, et cetera, to allow lagging sectors to grow according to the needs of their micro sectors and of the macro economy. Thus, within this framework, Keyserling was a constant proponent of constant full employment and output growth for reasons of economic welfare and social equity. Thus, he is a man for his time and for the future.

Appendix: The Conference on Economic Progress Pamphlets

The following pamphlets by Leon H. Keyserling and his wife, economist Mary Dublin Keyserling, are deposited at the Harry S. Truman Library and Museum, Independence, Missouri, a city adjacent to Kansas City, Missouri.

Toward Full Employment and Full Production, 1954.
National Prosperity Program, 1955.

Full Prosperity for Agriculture, 1955.
The Gaps in Our Prosperity, 1956.
Consumption—The Key to Full Employment, 1957.
Wages and the Public Interest, 1958.
The "Recession"—Cause and Cure, 1958.
Toward a New Farm Program, 1958.
Inflation—Cause and Cure, 1959.
The Federal Budget and "The General Welfare," 1959.
Tight Money and Rising Interest Rates, 1960.
Food and Freedom, 1960.
Jobs and Growth, 1961.
Poverty and Deprivation in the U.S., 1962.
Key Policies for Full Employment, 1962.
Taxes and the Public Interest, 1963.
Two Top-Priority Programs to Reduce Unemployment, 1963.
The Toll of Rising Interest Rates, 1964.
Progress or Poverty, 1964.
Agriculture and the Public Interest, 1965.
The Role of Wages in a Great Society, 1966.
A "Freedom Budget" for All Americans, 1966.
Goals for Teachers' Salaries in our Public Schools, 1967.
Achieving Nationwide Educational Excellence, 1968.
Taxation of Whom and for What, 1969.
Growth with Less Inflation or More Inflation without Growth, 1970.
Wages, Prices and Profits, 1971.
The Coming Crisis in Housing, 1972.
The Scarcity School of Economics, 1973.
Full Employment without Inflation, 1975.
Toward Full Employment within Three Years, 1976.
The Humphrey-Hawkins Bill: "Full Employment and Balanced Growth Act of 1977," 1978.
Goals for Full Employment and How to Achieve Them under the "Full Employment and Balanced Growth Act of 1978," 1978.
"Liberal" and "Conservative" National Economic Policies and Their Consequences, 1919–79, 1979.
Money, Credit and Interest Rates: Their Gross Mismanagement by the Federal Reserve System, 1980.
How to Cut Unemployment to Four Percent and End Inflation and Deficits by 1987, 1983.

References

Berle, Adolf, Jr. 1959. *Power without prosperity: A new development in American political economy*. New York: Harcourt, Brace, World.

Berle, Adolf, Jr., and Gardiner Means. 1932. *The modern corporation and private property*. New York: Commerce Clearing House.

Brazelton, W. Robert. 1961. A critical analysis of the growth theories of Alvin H. Hansen and William J. Fellner. PhD diss., University of Oklahoma, Norman, OK.

———. 1989. Alvin Harvey Hansen: Economic growth and a more perfect society. *The American Journal of Economics and Sociology* 48 (October): 427–40.

———. 1993. Alvin Harvey Hansen: A note on his analysis of Keynes, Hayek and Commons. *Journal of Economic Issues* 28 (9): 1–9.

———. 1997. Retrospectives: The economics of Leon H. Keyserling. *Journal of Economic Perspectives* 11 (4): 187–97.

———. 2001. *Designing U.S. economic policy: An analytical biography of Leon H. Keyserling*. London: Palgrave Macmillan.

———. 2003. The Council of Economic Advisors and the full employment budget concept: Keyserling before Heller. *Journal of Economics* 29:87–102.

———. 2005. Research papers report and oral interview, Leon H. Keyserling, University of Missouri–Kansas City. Archives of the Harry S. Truman Library and Museum, Independence, MO; and Library/Archives, University of Missouri–Kansas City, 377–455.

———. 2007. On the "orthodoxy" of Leon H. Keyserling: Selected major analytical and policy concepts and advice to presidents. *The American Economist* 51 (Spring): 15–28.

Davidson, Louise, ed. 1991. *The collected works of Paul Davidson*, 2 vols. New York: University of New York Press.

Davidson, Paul. 1993. The elephant and the butterfly: On hysteresis and Post Keynesian economics. *Journal of Post Keynesian Economics* 15 (3): 309–22.

Friedman, Milton. 1956. The quantity theory of money: A restatement. In *Studies in the quantity theory of money*, ed. Milton Friedman. Chicago: University of Chicago Press.

———. 1959. The demand for money: Some theoretical and empirical results. *Journal of Political Economy* 67 (4): 327–51.

Galbraith, John Kenneth. 1954. *The great crash, 1929*. New York: Houghton-Mifflin.

———. 1967. *The new industrial state*. New York: Houghton-Mifflin.

———. 1987. Berle, Adolf, Jr. In *The new Palgrave: A dictionary of economics*, ed. John Eatwell, Murray Milgate, and Peter Newman. New York: Macmillan.

Hansen, Alvin H. 1939. Economic progress and declining population growth. *American Economic Review* 29 (March): 1–17.

———. 1941. *Fiscal policy and business cycles*. New York: Norton Press.

———. 1949. *Monetary theory and fiscal policy*. New York: McGraw-Hill.

———. 1953. *A guide to Keynes*. New York: McGraw-Hill.

———. 1957. *The American economy*. New York: McGraw-Hill.

———. 1964. *Business cycles and national income*, expanded ed. New York: Norton Press.

Keyserling, Leon H. 1957. *Consumption—The key to full employment.* Washington, DC: Conference on Economic Progress.

———. 1964a. *Progress or poverty.* Washington, DC: Conference on Economic Progress.

———. 1964b. *The toll of rising interest rates: The one great waste of the federal budget.* Washington, DC: Conference on Economic Progress.

———. 1966. *A "freedom budget" for all Americans.* Washington, DC: Conference on Economic Progress.

———. 1973. *The scarcity school of economics and the shortages it has wrought.* Washington, DC: Conference on Economic Progress.

———. 1975. *Full employment without inflation.* Washington, DC: Conference on Economic Progress.

———. 1976. *Toward full employment within three years.* Washington, DC: Conference on Economic Progress.

———. 1978. *Goals for full employment and how to achieve them under the "Full Employment and Balanced Growth Act of 1978."* Washington, DC: Conference on Economic Progress.

———. 1979. *"Liberal" and "conservative" national economic policies and their consequences, 1919–79.* Washington, DC: Conference on Economic Progress.

———. 1980. *Money, credit and interest rates: Their gross mismanagement by the Federal Reserve System.* Washington, DC: Conference on Economic Progress.

———. 1987a. Means, Gardiner Coit. In *The new Palgrave: A dictionary of economics,* ed. John Eatwell, Murray Milgate, and Peter Newman. New York: Macmillan.

———. 1987b. Tugwell, Rexford Guy. In *The new Palgrave: A dictionary of economics,* ed. John Eatwell, Murray Milgate, and Peter Newman. New York: Macmillan.

———. 2005. Two oral interviews. Harry S. Truman Library and Museum, Independence, MO (includes Brazelton 2005).

Minsky, Hyman. 1977. The financial instability hypothesis and an alternative to standard theory. *Nebraska Journal of Economics and Business* 169 (1): 5–16.

Musgrave, Richard A. 1987. Hansen, Alvin H. In *The new Palgrave: A dictionary of economics,* ed. John Eatwell, Murray Milgate, and Peter Newman. New York: Macmillan.

Pechman, Joseph, and N. J. Simler. 1982. *Economics in the public service: Papers in honor of Walter W. Heller.* New York: Norton.

Sweezy, Paul. 1939. Demand under conditions of oligopoly. *Journal of Political Economy* 47:568–73.

Sweezy, Paul, and Paul Baran. 1966. *Monopoly capital: An essay on the American economic and social order.* New York: Monthly Review Press.

Tily, Geoff. 2007. *Keynes's general theory, the rate of interest and "Keynesian" economics: Keynes betrayed.* New York: Palgrave Macmillan.

Tugwell, Rexford Guy, ed. 1924. *The trend of economics.* New York: Knopf.

———. 1974. *The emerging constitution.* New York: Harper's Magazine Press.

Tugwell, Rexford Guy, Thomas Munro, and Roy Stryker, ed. 1925. *American economic life and the means of its improvement.* New York: Harcourt.

———. 1927. *Industry's coming of age.* New York: Harcourt.

Turgeon, Lynn. 1987. Keyserling, Leon Hirsch. In *The new Palgrave: A dictionary of economics*, ed. John Eatwell, Murray Milgate, and Peter Newman. New York: Macmillan.

Weintraub, Sydney. 1963. *Some aspects of wage theory and policy.* Philadelphia: Chilton Books.

———, ed. 1977. *Modern economic thought.* Philadelphia: University of Pennsylvania Press.

Wray, L. Randall. 1992. Commercial banks, the central bank, and endogenous money. *Journal of Post Keynesian Economics* 14 (3): 272–310.

———. 1988. *Understanding modern money.* Cheltenham, UK: Edward Elgar.

CHAPTER 3

HOW KEYNES CAME TO CANADA
MABEL TIMLIN AND KEYNESIAN ECONOMICS

ROBERT W. DIMAND*

CANADIAN ECONOMICS AND THE KEYNESIAN REVOLUTION

CANADA HAS ATTRACTED LITTLE ATTENTION from historians of economic thought studying the international spread of economic ideas. It was omitted, for instance, from a conference volume on the international diffusion of Keynesianism (Hall 1991) and from a *History of Political Economy* supplement on the post-1945 internationalization of economics. John Kenneth Galbraith (1965), writing on "How Keynes Came to America," included a passing mention of Robert Bryce taking Keynesian ideas from Cambridge to Ottawa, because Bryce conducted a study group on Keynes while a graduate student at Harvard before returning to Canada. However, Bryce's career is by no means the whole story of "How Keynes Came to Canada," nor is that story a mere repetition of the experience of other countries.

Keynesian economics came to Canada through two channels. One channel was a group of senior federal civil servants with academic backgrounds who formed a symbiotic relationship with the ruling Liberal Party. Two members of the group had studied with Keynes at Cambridge:

---

* I am grateful to Robin Neill and T. K. Rymes for helpful comments on this chapter.

Wynne Plumptre while Keynes was writing *A Treatise on Money*, and Robert Bryce, who attended Keynes's lectures from 1932 to 1934. This group, much studied in Canada (for example, Granatstein 1982 and Owram 1986), renewed direct contact with Keynes's ideas during his visits to Ottawa in 1942 and 1944 (Bryce 1988) and in negotiations with Keynes in Cambridge about the postwar Canadian loan to Britain (LePan 1979). Although the group's economic ideas were never translated neatly into economic policy, for they were filtered through a political process involving lobbying by the business community and dominion-provincial negotiations (Campbell 1987; Wolfe 1984), these civil servants shaped federal thinking about macroeconomic policy for nearly three decades after the 1945 White Paper on Employment and Income (Gordon 1965; Mackintosh 1965; Sharp 1966–1967).

The other channel, which introduced Keynesian economics into Canadian scholarly publications, conferences, and teaching, was a single remarkable career: that of Mabel Timlin of the University of Saskatchewan, author of *Keynesian Economics* (1942), which was based on a dissertation begun before the publication of Keynes's *The General Theory of Employment, Interest and Money* in 1936. This chapter examines Timlin's contribution and career to illuminate the reception of the "Keynesian revolution in Canada" and how this reception was shaped by and helped to transform the distinctive features and setting of Canadian economics.

The reception of Keynesian macroeconomics by the Canadian economics profession and by Canadian policymakers reflected, and helped to alter, distinctive Canadian circumstances and traditions in at least three ways. First, management of aggregate demand in the pursuit of macroeconomic stability, as a middle way between unfettered market forces and central planning, provided an enhanced role for the Liberal federal authorities in Canada's perpetual struggle over federal-provincial division of powers, itself a reflection of Canada's bilingual and bicultural nature. Keynesian demand management offered a middle way for the Liberals (in office federally 1935–57, 1963–79, 1980–84), between the free-market convictions of the Conservatives, who governed Ontario (1943–85), and the Second International social democracy of the Cooperative Commonwealth Federation and its successor, the New Democratic Party, which governed Saskatchewan (1944–64, 1971–82); and it was an alternative to the radical nostrums of Social Credit, which governed

Alberta (1935–71), and the provincial autonomy promoted by the Union Nationale, which ruled Quebec (1936–39, 1944–60, 1966–70).

Second, Keynesian macroeconomic theory was the vehicle for the Canadian economics profession to move beyond its focus on Canadian economic history, shaped by British historical economics and by Harold Innis and the "Toronto School of Economic History," to an interest in formal economic theory.

Third, this growing adoption of the language of formal economic models and movement beyond specifically Canadian topics led to increasing integration of Canadian economics into the international community of economics at a time when the center of gravity of economic research (including Keynesian macroeconomics) was shifting to the United States. In economics as in other areas of English Canadian thought, the United States displaced Britain as the dominant external cultural and intellectual influence in the years following the Second World War.

Mabel Timlin was prominent in all three areas: She stressed the policy relevance of economic theory and interpreted Keynesian economics to the Liberal Party as well as to a wider audience; she interpreted formal economic theory (Keynesian macroeconomics, general equilibrium analysis, and welfare economics) to a Canadian economics profession unused to formal theory; and she was active in the American Economic Association and the International Economic Association.

The first professors of political economy at English-speaking Canadian universities, the economic historian W. J. (later Sir William) Ashley at the University of Toronto in the 1890s and A. W. Flux at McGill University a decade later, were young British academics waiting for senior positions to become available at home. This was also true of the economic historian C. R. Fay at Toronto in the 1920s (and it was common in other fields, as with the physicist Ernest Rutherford at McGill). In a protectionist country where the authorities were suspicious of the free-trade leanings of economic theorists, preference in hiring was given to economic historians: Four economic historians and a sociologist were the five heads of Toronto's Department of Political Economy in its first eighty years (see Goodwin 1961and Neill 1991). Another distinctive feature of Canadian economics was that, until the 1960s, Canadian economists associated willingly with other social scientists in the Canadian Political Science Association, the *Canadian Journal of Economics and Political Science*, the University of Toronto's Department of Political

Economy (which included a notable historical sociologist, S. D. Clark), and McGill's Department of Economics and Political Science. The British connection, the emphasis on history and the lack of emphasis on theory and formal methods, and the association with other social sciences disappeared in the post–World War II internationalization (or Americanization) of Canadian economics, of which the spread of Keynesian macroeconomics in Canada was an early part.

An Extraordinary Career

Mabel Frances Timlin's *Keynesian Economics* (1942) was a significant contribution to economic theory, critically analyzing and extending J. M. Keynes's *General Theory*. It also stands as a monument to a remarkable career. It was written at a time when economic theory of any kind, let alone newfangled Keynesian macroeconomics, was very lightly represented in the Canadian economics profession, and it was the first publication—published when Timlin was fifty—of a woman who managed the rare transition from department secretary to academic eminence, including the presidency of her scholarly association.

Mabel Timlin was born in Wisconsin on December 6, 1891. She trained as a teacher for two years and taught school both in Wisconsin and in Saskatchewan, where she moved in 1917, the year after her parents died. In 1921, she was hired as a secretary in the Department of Agricultural Extension at the University of Saskatchewan in Saskatoon, and she began working towards a degree, one course at a time.

> At first she intended to take the honours degree in economics, a subject which had caught her imagination at an early age (her father, a stationmaster who took a lively interest in public issues, was given to lecturing his children on such matters as bimetallism and comparative advantage). However, the courses given by the Economics Department disappointed her; after taking a fourth course she turned to the more agreeable offerings of the English Department. She wrote of this decision some years later that "nothing was lost to my development as an economist [by it], for through systematic reading I did much better myself." (D. Spafford 1977, 279)

Timlin was director of the university's correspondence courses from 1929, when she took her BA with great distinction, until 1942. Her correspondence students in economics included the late John J. Deutsch, who became principal and vice-chancellor of Queen's University and the first chairman of the Economic Council of Canada, and Clarence Barber, later an eminent Keynesian at the University of Manitoba. In 1932, Timlin enrolled as a doctoral student in economics at the University of Washington, in Seattle, a graduate program with an unusually short residence requirement. (W. W. Swanson, her Department Head in Saskatoon, had formerly been an assistant professor at the University of Washington, which may have influenced her choice of graduate school.) By taking summer courses and one six-month leave from her job at the University of Saskatchewan, Timlin managed to complete the residence requirement for the PhD by 1935, when she was appointed instructor in economics at Saskatchewan. The dissertation that became *Keynesian Economics* was supervised by the international economist Raymond Mikesell and was accepted in 1940. (Mikesell was two decades younger than his doctoral student and lived until September 2006, when he was ninety-three.) Timlin was promoted from instructor to assistant professor in 1941, at the age of forty-nine, and to full professor in 1950, retiring as professor emeritus in 1957, with a Canada Council Senior Fellowship in 1959 (see Safarian 1976, D. Spafford 1977, Phillips 2002, Rymes 1995, and notes to Ostry 1998).

Timlin was elected a Fellow of the Royal Society of Canada in 1951, the only woman then in Section II of the society (social sciences and humanities in English). She held office in the Canadian Political Science Association (which then included economics) as a member of the executive committee from 1941 to 1943, as vice-president from 1953 to 1955, and as president from 1959 to 1960 (Gosztonyi 1995). Thirty-five years passed before another woman served as president of the successor organization, the Canadian Economics Association. Timlin also served on the executive committees of the American Economic Association (1958–1960) and the International Federation of University Women. Her honors included an LLD from her university in 1969 and the Order of Canada in 1976, the year of her death. Since 1983, the University of Saskatchewan has sponsored an annual Timlin Lecture in economics or political science.

For a woman to receive such recognition from the Canadian economics profession is unusual: Timlin was the first tenured woman economist in Canada. For an academic secretary, especially one without a college degree when she began the job, it is extraordinary. Her research did not deal with topics traditionally considered women's issues; even her survey, "The Social Sciences in Canada: Retrospect and Potential," devoted only a single parenthetical sentence to women in the social sciences (Timlin 1968, 52).[1]

Safarian notes that Timlin's summer travel to the Learned Societies meetings and to archives for research was "largely, as was common at the time, at great personal financial cost. . . . [T]he Great Depression of the thirties lasted more than a decade on the Prairies, not least in the parsimony with which university faculty were rewarded, both in salary and pensions, as prices soared after the war. . . . I note here . . . a long letter dated April 8, 1961, dealing ostensibly with pensions, but which was in fact a searing indictment of the wretched financial treatment which an entire generation of university scholars endured" (Safarian 1976, vi, x).

Mabel Timlin faced other barriers as well: "At the University of Saskatchewan reaction [to developments in economics outside Canada] took the form of the Chairman of the Department of Economics and Political Science refusing to hire or promote anyone who would not adhere to the quantity theory of money and the gold standard, that is, any Keynesian" (Neill 1991, 158; cf., S. Spafford 2000).

William Walker Swanson, Head of the Department from 1916 to 1945, expressed his hard-money commitment to the gold standard in *Depression and the Way Out* (Swanson 1931), although, as a disciple of J. Laurence Laughlin of the University of Chicago (Ferguson 1993, 25–26, 103), Swanson was not, in fact, a quantity theorist.

Timlin's research on Keynesian economics, welfare economics, and general equilibrium analysis contrasted with the less theoretical and more locally focused concerns of her leading colleagues. William W. Swanson was coauthor of *Wheat* (1930, with P. C. Armstrong of the Canadian Pacific Railway). George E. Britnell wrote *The Wheat Economy* (1939), a revision of his 1938 Toronto PhD dissertation, and, with Vernon C. Fowke, *Canadian Agriculture in War and Peace* (1962). Fowke was the author of *Canadian Agricultural Policy: The Historical Pattern* (1946), a revision of his 1942 University of Washington PhD dissertation, and of *The National Policy and the Wheat Economy* (1957). Britnell later expanded his horizons beyond prairie farming to participate in a World Bank study of Guatemala in 1951 and to write on the Guatemalan economy in the same 1953 American Economic Association *Papers and Proceedings* in which Timlin published. Britnell was a student of University of Toronto economic historian Harold Innis, and Fowke (1946, viii) credited "frequent consultation" with Innis, during a year at the University of Toronto rewriting his manuscript, with helping to give "direction and meaning to the author's researches." The work of Britnell and Fowke on wheat as a staple product complemented the work of Innis and the

"Toronto School of Economic History," which wrote Canadian economic history in terms of successive dominant staple commodities such as cod and furs.

Timlin spent the spring and summer of 1942 at the University of Toronto, revising her dissertation for publication, but her intellectual affinities there were with A. F. W. Plumptre and Keynesian macroeconomic theory, rather than with Innis and the staple approach to economic history. (See Neill 1999 and S. Spafford 2000 on economics at the University of Saskatchewan, Fowke 1962 on Britnell, and Phillips 1978 on Fowke.) Earlier economics teaching at the University of Saskatchewan emphasized the historical school rather than theory: When the university opened in 1910, all three economics courses were taught by a history professor, using books by Richard Ely and British historical economists William Ashley, Archdeacon William Cunningham, and John Kell Ingram, but not by Alfred Marshall (Goodwin 1961, 166). Brecher (1957) shows the near absence of anything resembling Keynesian macroeconomics from interwar Canada, and the limited amount of formal theorizing based on the quantity theory of money or pre-Keynesian business cycle theories (cf., Neill 1991, 124).

However, in 1935, Benjamin Higgins, a twenty-three-year-old Canadian who had just taken a master's degree at the London School of Economics, came to the University of Saskatchewan to teach for a year as an instructor in economics. Higgins (1992, 9) found, among other economists (notably Claude Isbister, who helped construct national income accounts at the Dominion Bureau of Statistics before becoming a federal Assistant Deputy Minister of Finance), "best of all, Mabel Timlin—'Timmie' as she was known to her host of friends—who hid a razor-sharp mind behind a rather matronly appearance and manner, and who wrote one of the very first and one of the very best books explaining and criticizing Keynes's *General Theory*." Higgins could claim "some modest credit for it" because, although he was a loyal disciple of Hayek when he attended the London-Cambridge economics seminar, he brought away from the seminar a mimeographed set of notes on Keynes's lectures taken by another young Canadian, Robert Bryce (later Secretary to the Treasury Board 1947–54, Clerk of the Privy Council and Secretary to the Cabinet 1954–63, and Deputy Minister of Finance 1963–70), and lent the notes to Timlin (Rymes 1987 transcribes Bryce's notes, among others). However, while Higgins refers to this paper as Bryce's lecture notes, I am persuaded by the suggestion of T. K. Rymes that the handwritten lectures notes were unlikely to have been mimeographed and that what Higgins brought to Saskatoon was actually a copy of Bryce's paper, "An Introduction to a Monetary Theory of Employment" (Bryce 1935), which was discussed at four meetings of Hayek's seminar and was strongly influenced by Keynes's lectures. Timlin, who had not been to Cambridge or met a Cambridge economist, studied Keynes's lectures in Saskatoon, while James Earley taught a course at the University of Wisconsin in 1935, based on notes on Keynes's 1933 lectures taken at Earley's request by Marvin Fallgatter, a physics student who had been Earley's undergraduate roommate (see Rymes 1989).

The General Theory was awaited by many with eager anticipation in the midst of the Depression, while others turned to other promised remedies for the Depression: Just to the west of Saskatchewan, the Social Credit Party, devoted to the unorthodox monetary theories of Major C. H. Douglas and led by William Aberhart of the Prophetic Bible Institute, won fifty-six of the sixty-three seats in Alberta's provincial legislature in 1935 and all fifteen of Alberta's seats in the federal House of Commons later that year, along with two seats from Saskatchewan (Douglas 1937; Macpherson 1953).

Canada's interwar universities did have one pocket of Keynesian influence: A. F. Wynne Plumptre of the University of Toronto (later Assistant Deputy Minister of Finance, 1954–65) had studied with Keynes from 1928 to 1930, while Keynes was writing *A Treatise on Money*, and had returned to teach the *Treatise* to Lorie Tarshis and other students. Plumptre indirectly led Timlin to Keynesian economics by recommending the young University of Toronto graduates Robert Bryce and Lorie Tarshis for admission to Keynes's lectures and the Political Economy Club in 1932. Timlin (1942, xx) thanked Plumptre and Oscar Lange, then at the University of Chicago, for reading and commenting on her dissertation, and she wrote the final draft of her book at the University of Toronto in the spring and summer of 1942. At a Canadian Political Science Association memorial session for Keynes at the Learned Societies annual meeting organized and introduced by Timlin (1947), Plumptre (1947) recalled the experience of studying with Keynes. Timlin's study of Keynesian macroeconomic theory led to this connection, rather than the other way around. As Lorie Tarshis noted in his foreword to the 1977 reissue of Timlin's *Keynesian Economics* (1942, xii): "At the time she wrote, Dr. Timlin had never been in the Cambridge which was the birthplace of *The General Theory*, and so far as I know she had had no contact with Cambridge economists. She had not even set foot in the other Cambridge which, J. K. Galbraith [1965] assures us, was the source of all that North America ever learned of The General Theory, but she made up for these deficiencies by a readiness to read Keynes' book with an open mind, and with a critical and imaginative intelligence."

Mabel Timlin contributed strongly to shaping the macroeconomic views of the Canadian economics profession in Canada's "Keynesian era," which extended from the White Paper on Employment and Income in April 1945 (accepting government responsibility for high and stable levels of employment) to the "Saskatoon Manifesto" of September 1975 (in which the governor of the Bank of Canada embraced monetarism and monetary aggregate targets to fight inflation). Her exuberant and inspiring personality gave her an influence in the profession beyond her writings: "The annual meetings of the Learned Societies were an important occasion each year both for academic reasons and for contact with her wide circle of friends" (Safarian 1976, vi). "[T]he Christmas mail brought dozens of letters from former students who addressed her, as all who knew her did (except her undergraduates, who dared not) as 'Timmie.' Her honours seminars she held in her lodgings, away from the university classroom whose atmosphere, she believed, encouraged flaccidity of thought. Her comments on seminar papers, written between the lines and up and down the margins, ran sometimes to a thousand words: one handed in one essay and got back two" (D. Spafford 1977, 280–81).

Keynesian Economics

Beyond an able and careful exposition of Keynes, Timlin (1942) was innovative in taking a general equilibrium approach to the economics of Keynes. She presented a synthesis of Keynes's *General Theory* with Oscar Lange's 1938 restatement of Keynes in Walrasian terms, noting, "With reference to Mr. Keynes' approval of Dr. Lange's 'general system' as an analysis of his own, see 'On Mr. Keynes and "Finance"'(Comment on), *Economic Journal*, XLVIII (1938), p. 321n" (Timlin 1942, 8n).

Further, after presenting her static Fundamental Model of the "Keynes-Lange system," Timlin devoted two chapters (the second of which, chapter 13, had no counterpart in her dissertation) to two Supplementary Models of shifting equilibrium in sequence economies, extensively illustrated with diagrams. (These two chapters are reprinted in Dimand 2002, vol. 4). In the first Supplementary Model, contracts for the services of factors of production were concluded on Mondays but consumption goods and services and new securities would not be sold until Tuesday, while the sequence was reversed in the second Supplementary Model (Timlin 1942, 15–16). Timlin (1942, 16–17n) noted the resemblance of this approach to the process analysis of D. H. Robertson and Bertil Ohlin, but she was original in using such process analysis to track the shifting equilibrium of a Keynesian system. Far more than most contemporary commentators, Timlin stressed the dynamic aspect of *The General Theory*, that the equilibrium of Week One would create new conditions for Week Two, altering the position of equilibrium.

Warren Young notes: "Interestingly, Timlin makes no use of the IS-LM diagram. Rather, she developed a diagrammatic representation of the 'Keynes-Lange system' which, according to her, was adequate to illustrate 'the system of shifting equilibrium which lies at the heart of Keynesian theory.' Timlin's diagrammatic interpretation of 'the character of the Keynesian system,' however, never received wide attention or, for that matter, acceptance by the economics profession, for Hicks's diagram had come to 'rule the roost'" (1987, 122).

(There were at least partial exceptions to this lack of attention: Canada, where, according to Timlin's preface to the 1948 second printing, "the publishers and I felt that, in view of continuing demand for the book, this reprint should not be postponed"; and Japan, where it was translated.)

Young argues that neglect of Timlin's "Keynes-Lange system" led to unnecessary originality in later independent rediscovery of her approach: "To be brief, they [Clower and Leijonhufvud 1975] have restated the link that Lange made between Keynes and Walras some thirty years earlier, which was subsequently developed by Timlin more than twenty years prior to Clower's 1965 paper. . . . Leijonhufvud [1983] did not pay attention to the fact that his proposed FIM [full information macroeconomic] model is similar, if not identical, to the Keynes-Lange system developed by Timlin [in her Fundamental Model] over forty years earlier" (Young 1987, 155, 156).

The diagrams in *Keynesian Economics*, including the innovative representation of shifting equilibrium, had been redrafted for Timlin by the renowned University of Toronto geometer H. S. M. (Donald) Coxeter. Coxeter later influenced the artist M. C. Escher, "who, when working on his Circle Limit III drawings, used to say, 'I'm Coxetering today'" (Roberts 2003, F11; see also Roberts 2006).

Keynesian reviewers welcomed Timlin's *Keynesian Economics*. Tom Wilson in the *Economic Journal* found "Miss Timlin's book a very thorough and well-documented commentary. . . . In spite of these criticisms [of the limited use made of the Supplementary Models] and a tendency throughout to adopt an over-elaborate method of treatment with too many diagrams, the book is an able re-statement of the fundamental ideas of the *General Theory*, and will repay preliminary study by economists trying to formulate remedies for the disastrous scourge of unemployment after the war" (1943, 225, 227).

In *Economica*, G. L. S. Shackle greeted *Keynesian Economics* as "a statement of the author's faith. She has found in the General Theory something which is both intellectually fascinating in itself, and hopeful for mankind, and she has wished to restate it in her own manner. The result is a book which makes plain on every page the high competence of the author and the very great and sustained care she has used in writing it. In its possession of clear-cut purposes and method, in its detailed thoroughness, and in consistency, good architecture, and exactness and clearness of statement, it is outstanding" (1943, 260).

Gottfried Haberler, a critic of Keynes, was much less enthusiastic in the *Canadian Journal of Economics and Political Science* (Haberler 1944, 102, 104). He allowed that *Keynesian Economics* "contains a systematic and in many places novel exposition . . . the author can be congratulated on her performance. The book will be useful as collateral reading in graduate courses." However, he warned that "it would be most undesirable to put beginners on such an unbalanced diet." Appropriately for the co-discoverer of what is now called the Haberler-Pigou real balance effect, Haberler criticized Timlin's Keynesian view that unemployment is compatible with flexible wages: "Many a Keynesian has foundered at that rock, although most of them try to glide past it" (Haberler 1944, 104; see Dimand 1991 for a contrary view). Haberler (1944, 102) noted Timlin's use of two dynamic supplementary models to go beyond the static fundamental model, but he dismissed this attempt as "a very slight one," asserting incorrectly, "Nine-tenths or more of the book is concerned with the fundamental model." In fact, the two chapters on the supplementary models of shifting equilibrium occupy 29 pages in a volume of 184 pages.

Apart from reviewers, *Keynesian Economics* was noted outside Canada by Franco Modigliani, who cited her chapters 5 and 6 on money and the interest rate (Modigliani 1944, 192n), modified her chapter 3 on the expectations of the marginal holder of a security (Modigliani 1944, 196n), and referred the reader to her chapter 3 for the conditions giving rise to a stationary state (Modigliani 1944, 234n).

Beyond the formal treatment of the economics of Keynes in her dissertation and book, Timlin offered a moving statement of her admiration of Keynes and his vision at a session she organized in his memory at the annual meeting of the Canadian Political Science Association in Quebec City on May 30, 1947. There she hailed

> the philosophy and characteristics which made Lord Keynes so great a human being, perhaps as nearly a whole person as the twentieth century can show us . . . the great economist and the invaluable public servant; . . . also as the scientific farmer and sagacious manager of his own funds and those of his College, the founder of the Cambridge Art Theatre, the bibliophile, the connoisseur of painting, the brilliant conversationalist, and even more clearly, as the lover of the ballet and the great editor and writer of incomparable prose. . . . It is plain to be seen that as a human being he was richly endowed—artistically, morally, emotionally, and intellectually. If his time had been spent in such a golden world as he himself described, he might have led a life which would have been the epitome of human excellences. It was spent instead in a troubled world and the wonder of it is that in spite of ill-health, arduous labour, and the brutality of his times, he should have contrived to live so personally, so much in harmony with what he called "the real values of life." Ladies and gentlemen, I believe we are met this evening to honour the memory of a very great man. (Timlin 1947, 363–65)

Rejecting both Marxist claims to Keynes and the stereotype that Keynes provided nothing more than a preoccupation with unemployment and a simple policy response to it, Timlin celebrated Keynes's vision of society eventually overcoming the economic problem and moving beyond the useful to the good and delightful. Timlin made clear in that introductory address that Shackle had been right to perceive *Keynesian Economics* as "a statement of the author's faith" rather than as simply an exercise in economic analysis.

Timlin included three other, carefully chosen papers in her session: Wynne Plumptre (1947) on studying with Keynes in Cambridge, G. A. Elliott (1947) of the University of Toronto on the significance of *The General Theory* (with three footnote references to Timlin's *Keynesian Economics*), and an account of "Keynes as a Public Servant" by William A. Mackintosh (1947). Mackintosh was the former Saskatchewan schoolteacher turned Queen's University economics professor (and future principal and vice-chancellor) who had drafted the 1945 White Paper. Mackintosh had effectively been vice-chair of the wartime Economic Advisory Committee (with Keynes's former student Robert Bryce as committee secretary) while serving nominally as a temporary assistant to W. Clifford Clark (a former Queen's economics professor who was Deputy Minister of Finance from 1932 until his death in 1953). Mackintosh chaired the committee when Clark was absent, even though nominally Mackintosh was not a member. From 1944 to 1946, Mackintosh was also Director-General of Economic Research for the Department of Reconstruction and Supply (whose minister, C. D. Howe, presented the White Paper to Parliament), and he filled in for an ill Clark as acting Deputy Minister of Finance for several months in 1945. Mackintosh was brought to Ottawa by Clark and by Clark's mentor Oscar D. Skelton (a former Queen's economics professor who was Undersecretary of State for External Affairs from 1925 until his death in 1941), and he was a central figure in shaping the government's economic thinking (see Ferguson 1993). Extensive wartime contact with Keynes left Mackintosh with admiration for Keynes's lucidity, charm and insight, annoyance at his occasional rudeness and arrogance, and "some interest in seeing how far some of the elements of Keynesianism could be presented as the most ordinary of common sense" (Mackintosh 1965, 14–15; cf., Mackintosh 1947, 382; Bryce 1988 for Keynes's wartime visits to Ottawa; LePan 1979, a poet's vivid recollection of Keynes's negotiation in Cambridge with a delegation led by Mackintosh; Granatstein 1982; Owram 1986; Ferguson 1993).

General Equilibrium and Welfare Economics

Timlin published seven book reviews in the *Canadian Journal of Economics and Political Science* from 1942 to 1948, as well as three major review articles on Lerner, Lange, and Myint (1945, 1946a, 1949) and another book review in 1958. The spate of review articles followed a 1945 Guggenheim Fellowship to study welfare economics. The number of invitations, especially invitations to write review articles rather than just reviews, indicates that recognition of Timlin as a key interpreter of theoretical works for the Canadian economics profession followed promptly on the publication of her revised thesis. Several other Canadian economists capable of interpreting economic theory to the Canadian economics profession—notably Jacob Viner, Lauchlin Currie, Lorie Tarshis, and Harry Johnson—had left Canada to pursue careers in

Britain or the United States. The Canadian Institute of International Affairs called on Timlin to survey the state of the British economy in the inaugural volume of the Institute's *International Journal* (1946c), and it later sponsored her monograph on immigration policy (1951a).

Timlin's study of general equilibrium and welfare economics was in keeping with her synthesis of a "Keynes-Lange system" that considered Keynes's theory in terms of Walrasian general equilibrium. Similarly, her work on monetary policy in the inflationary period of the early 1950s viewed Keynesian economics as implementing rather than overthrowing the classical wisdom of market adjustment. In addition to her review articles, Timlin (1946b) argued the case to the Canadian economics profession for the policy relevance and usefulness of general equilibrium analysis, with severe and continuous testing of formal models. Such an approach, though it would now be unremarkable, was strange and unfamiliar to Canadian economists of the time. Timlin called for such general equilibrium thinking, and she wrote review articles exposing the Canadian economics profession to what was being done elsewhere in general equilibrium analysis and welfare economics, but she did not attempt to contribute to that literature herself. Having mastered the novelties of Keynesian macroeconomics in her late forties and studying what was new in welfare economics in her fifties, she did not attempt to advance the frontier of formal general equilibrium theory and welfare economics in her sixties. While insisting on the policy relevance of formal economic theory, Timlin (1949, 559) also warned that "analysis presents us with useful frameworks within which to order our thoughts when we approach specific situations, but they give us no answers whatsoever."

Economic Policy

From her sixtieth year, Timlin, who had always been concerned with the applicability of Keynesian economics or general equilibrium analysis to policy, turned from theory to policy. Timlin (1950, 1951a) argued controversially that, given appropriate policies, increased immigration would raise physical product per person, and hence income per capita, in Canada. She discussed recent government attitudes towards immigration in her paper as a newly elected Fellow of the Royal Society of Canada in the society's prestigious but perhaps little read *Transactions* (1955b), and she discussed Canada's postwar immigration experience at an International Economic Association round-table in 1955 (Timlin 1958). The latter presentation provided then-unusual international visibility for a

Canadian economist: Only eight Canadian residents participated in any of the first twenty-six conferences of the International Economic Association (Timlin 1968, 39, where she noted that two of them subsequently moved to American universities), and no Canadian residents participated in twenty-two of the gatherings. She devoted her presidential address to the Canadian Political Science Association (then including economics and sociology as part of political economy) to a historical examination of Canada's wave of immigration before the First World War (Timlin 1960).

Although *Keynesian Economics* was a work of theoretical synthesis, Timlin was always interested in Keynesian macroeconomics for its policy relevance. She concluded her hostile review of the second volume of Arthur Marget's anti-Keynesian *Theory of Prices* by asserting, "Neither is a defence of Keynesian analysis necessary. In departments of finance at Ottawa and elsewhere this type of analysis has been found too useful in making judgements with respect to the effects of practical policies for such a defence any longer to be required" (Timlin 1944, 249).

Timlin (1955a, 61) concurred with Plumptre's "opinion that in no other English-speaking capital in the world had Keynesian thinking had more effect on policy than in Ottawa." Their shared opinion overlooks the influence of L. F. Giblin, Colin Clark, and other Keynesians in Australia (Coleman, Cornish, and Hagger 2006). Having made her contribution to macroeconomic theory, Timlin turned to macroeconomic policy as a sharp critic of postwar Canadian monetary policy, which she critiqued to international audiences (1953, 1955a). She also collaborated with her Saskatchewan colleagues on competition policy (Britnell, Fowke, Timlin, and Buckley 1956).

Addressing the American Economic Association after the September 1950 floating of the Canadian exchange rate and the December 1951 restoration of international convertibility of the Canadian dollar, Timlin was bluntly critical of both Canadian policy and the Canadian economics profession:

> It is the central position of this paper that policy would have been more rational if increases in bank reserves and bank deposits in response to rising external prices or increases in output had been deferred until the [Korean War] wartime inflation had worked itself out. This is another way of saying that monetary aims should have been given a higher place and monetary policies more generally resorted to at an earlier date. . . . It is possible, though perhaps paradoxical, that the atmosphere of continuous

> and objective criticism proper to such institutions in a democracy might free the Bank of Canada to some degree from political pressures and permit its officers to develop a theory of central banking adequate to the urgencies which may confront free societies for generations. There are only two sources for this criticism: the academic community and Parliament. But it is the misfortune of the Canadian academic community that most of those most competent to offer criticism have either disappeared permanently into the upper hierarchy of the civil service or have been so long associated with the government at the policy level during the war and the early post-war periods that their freedom of expression must be impaired. (Timlin 1953, 52–53)

Canadian economists eventually recovered their freedom of expression and became as outspoken on monetary policy as Timlin, so that a few years later a book could be titled *The Economists Versus the Bank of Canada* (Gordon 1961), when Canadian academic economists denounced the tight-money and nationalist policies of James Coyne, the second Governor of the Bank of Canada.

Timlin protested:

> In the pursuit of low interest rate policies through a series of years characterized by price inflation, what seems to have been overlooked in Canada and elsewhere have been the conditions set out in Section VI of Chapter 21 of the *General Theory* and the nature of the confirmation of that position in the last published article of Lord Keynes. It is the essence of this position that while the "classical medicine" may not "work by itself" in the fashion expected by laissez-faire theorists, nevertheless it is the proper object of policy to attempt "to use what we have learnt from modern experience and modern analysis, not to defeat, but to implement the wisdom of Adam Smith." (Timlin 1955a, 59)

Indeed, Timlin reached back four centuries before Adam Smith to cite Nicolas Oresme on debasement of the coinage. Policymakers should consider both the Keynesian problem of stabilizing output and employment at high levels and the neoclassical problem of the proper allocation of resources.

The extent to which Canada ever had a Keynesian era has been questioned, notably by Robert Campbell (1987) and David Wolfe (1984). Scott Gordon (1965) observed on the twentieth anniversary of the White Paper on Employment and Income (and the subsequent Green Book of federal proposals to the Dominion-Provincial Conference) that Keynesian ideas never penetrated deeply into Canada's journalistic and business communities. Politicians paid more immediate and conscious attention to public pressures treating budget surpluses as evidence of excessive taxation, and deficits as signs of fiscal irresponsibility, than to "some defunct economist" or "some academic scribbler of a few years back" (Keynes, *CW*, 7: 383). Still, Keynesian views permeated the group of academics and senior bureaucrats who formed a symbiotic relationship with the governing party during the long Liberal administrations of 1935–57, 1963–79, and 1980–84 (Granatstein 1982; Owram 1986). Irwin Gillespie (1991, 166, 101) held that "Keynesian fiscal stabilization policy had a minor influence on the revenue policy of federal governments . . . the 1946 and 1948 budgets articulated an appropriate fiscal stabilization policy, and then proceeded to implement a different tax policy"; even so, he conceded that a series of budgets followed in practice the Keynesian stabilization policy shaping government rhetoric: "Harris' 1955 budget presented the case, with clarity and directness, for a set of policies that would achieve a balanced budget at full employment. . . . Abbott's anti-inflation budgets of the early 1950s and Fleming's expansionary budgets of the early 1960s also contained appropriate stabilization tax policy initiatives" (Gillespie 1991, 102).

Mitchell Sharp, reviewing a book on Keynes for *The Journal of Liberal Thought* while Minister of Finance, held that

> because of Keynes, governments will never again be guilty of the follies that led to and prolonged the Great Depression. This was the revolution—this was the triumph of the ideas put forward by Keynes for which mankind has reason to be grateful. Paradoxical as it may appear, the conversion to the Keynesian approach may have been one of the chief reasons why the threat of a depression did not materialize in the post-war world. Although Keynesian principles may have been honoured as much in the breach as in the performance, there was confidence that if a serious deficiency in aggregate demand did appear, governments would not hesitate to take appropriate action. (Sharp 1966–1967, 187)

Sharp, who, as a civil servant, had worked closely with Mackintosh at the time of the 1945 White Paper, expressed the post–Second World War consensus among senior Canadian federal civil servants and Liberal policymakers in favor of aggregate demand management to prevent depression. (From 1993 to 2003, Sharp was a dollar-a-year adviser to the Prime Minister, who was his Parliamentary Secretary at the time of the book review.) The 1945 commitment to "maintenance of a high and stable level of employment and income" by use of aggregate demand management sought a middle way for federal Liberal policymakers between interventionist economic planning (advocated by the Cooperative Commonwealth Federation and its successor the New Democratic Party, social democratic parties governing Saskatchewan 1944–64, 1971–82, and since 1993 and affiliated to the Second International) and untrammelled free markets (as represented by the Conservatives, governing Ontario 1943–85 and since 1995).

Mabel Timlin contributed directly to the promotion of such Keynesian views in Liberal circles, as in her review article in *The Canadian Liberal* on Sir Roy Harrod's *Life of John Maynard Keynes* (Timlin 1951b). Her first book and scholarly papers and reviews synthesized Keynesian and general equilibrium analysis, and they helped spread Keynesian ideas in the Canadian economics profession. Robert Bryce's presentation of Keynes's ideas to Hayek's seminar at the London School of Economics and then at Harvard (Bryce 1935, published as an appendix to Patinkin and Leith 1978, 127–45, and also in Keynes 1979, *CW*, 29: 132–50) remained unpublished for four decades after Bryce returned to Canada, leaving *Keynesian Economics* to stand alone in the Canadian economics literature as an exposition and critical reformulation of *The General Theory*. Although other factors (such as federal-provincial rivalry over fiscal powers) shared in shaping policy outcomes, postwar federal Canadian economic policymaking occurred in a Keynesian atmosphere, to which Timlin's writing and teaching contributed.

Conclusion

Mabel Timlin charted her own distinctive path from secretary to a leading place among Canadian economists. Instead of studying traditional women's issues or the problems of Saskatchewan's wheat farmers, she tackled the latest developments at the heart of economics, first Keynesian macroeconomics and then welfare economics, in a department initially hostile to Keynesian ideas and a Canadian economics community uneasy with formal theory. Although the English Canadian academic community was peripheral, first to British, then to United States academic culture, and the University of Saskatchewan was peripheral to such central Canadian institutions as Queen's University or the University of Toronto, Timlin chose topics at the core of economic research, not at its margins. She helped shape the climate of economic ideas in Canada, and she anticipated some of the later neo-Walrasian reappraisal of Keynes. She blasted the Bank of Canada when she considered that the bank deserved it, and she inspired generations of students with her enthusiasm for scholarship, discarding gray academic prose to acclaim Keynes's vision. Her *Keynesian Economics*, her review articles on general equilibrium analysis and welfare economics, her teaching, and her presentations at the Learned Societies meetings contributed to making Canadian economics more theoretical (although still stressing the policy relevance of theory and models) and more international, increasingly part of North American and worldwide currents in economics in place of the earlier influence of British historical economics.

Note

1. Timlin's report included a rollicking account of a woman exercising power among Canadian economists: "Dr. Anne Bezanson, a former Maritimer . . . was at that time both a Professor of Economics at the University of Pennsylvania and allocator of funds in Canada for the Rockefeller Foundation. Dr. Bezanson, now retired and living in Massachusetts, is almost as tall for a woman as Harold Innis was for a man. One of the sights of meetings of the Canadian Political Science Association during the 1940's was that of the two tall figures proceeding through the crowds followed by a trail of hopeful scholars!" (Timlin 1968, 75).

References

Brecher, Irving. 1957. *Monetary and fiscal thought and policy in Canada, 1919–1939*. Toronto: University of Toronto Press.

Britnell, George E. 1939. *The wheat economy*. Toronto: University of Toronto Press.

———. 1953. The theory and practice of technical assistance in underdeveloped countries: Factors in the economic development of Guatemala. *American Economic Review: Papers and Proceedings* 43 (May): 104–14.

Britnell, George E., and Vernon C. Fowke. 1962. *Canadian agriculture in war and peace*. Stanford, CA: Stanford University Press.

Britnell, George E., Vernon C. Fowke, Mabel F. Timlin, and Kenneth A. H. Buckley. 1956. Workable competition and monopoly: The public interest and the control of combines in Canada. *Submission to the Royal Commission on Canada's Economic Prospects*.

Bryce, Robert B. 1935. An introduction to a monetary theory of employment. In *The collected writings of John Maynard Keynes*, ed. D. E. Moggridge. Vol. 29. London: Macmillan, for the Royal Economic Society.

———. 1988. Keynes during the Great Depression and World War II. In *Keynes and public policy after fifty years*, ed. Omar F. Hamouda and John N. Smithin. Aldershot, UK: Edward Elgar.

Campbell, Robert M. 1987. *Grand illusions: The politics of the Keynesian experience in Canada 1945–1975*. Peterborough, Ontario: Broadview.

Clower, Robert W. 1965. The Keynesian counter-revolution: A theoretical appraisal. In *The theory of interest rates*, ed. F. Hahn and F. Brechling. London: Macmillan. Repr. in Clower 1969.

———, ed. 1969. *Monetary Theory*. Harmondsworth, UK: Penguin.

Clower, Robert W., and Axel Leijonhufvud. 1975. The co-ordination of economic activities: A Keynesian perspective. *American Economic Review* 65 (May): 182–88.

Coleman, William, Selwyn Cornish, and Alf Hagger. 2006. *Giblin's platoon: The trials and triumphs of the economist in Australian public life*. Canberra: ANU E Press.

Dimand, Robert W. 1991. Keynes, Kalecki, Ricardian equivalence, and the real balance effect. *Bulletin of Economic Research* 43 (July): 289–92.

———., ed. 2002. *The origins of macroeconomics*. 10 vols. London: Routledge.

Douglas, C. H. 1937. *The Alberta experiment: An interim survey*. London: Eyre and Spottiswoode.

Elliott, G. A. 1947. The significance of the General Theory of Employment, Interest, and Money. *Canadian Journal of Economics and Political Science* 13 (August): 372–78. Repr. in Wood 1983.

Ferguson, Barry. 1993. *Remaking liberalism: The intellectual legacy of Adam Shortt, O. D. Skelton, W. C. Clark, and W. A. Mackintosh, 1890–1925*. Montreal and Kingston: McGill-Queen's University Press.

Fowke, Vernon C. 1946. *Canadian agricultural policy: The historical pattern*. Toronto: University of Toronto Press.

———. 1957. *The national policy and the wheat economy*. Toronto: University of Toronto Press.

———. 1962. George Edwin Britnell, 1903–1961. *Canadian Journal of Economics and Political Science* 28:283–91.

Galbraith, J. Kenneth. 1965. How Keynes came to America. *New York Times Book Review*, May 16. Repr. in Galbraith 1971.

———. 1971. *Economics, peace and laughter*. Boston: Houghton Mifflin.

Gillespie, W. Irwin. 1991. *Tax, borrow and spend: Financing federal spending in Canada 1867–1990*. Ottawa: Carleton University Press, Carleton Library no. 170.

Goodwin, Craufurd D. W. 1961. *Canadian economic thought: The political economy of a developing nation 1814–1914*. Durham, NC: Duke University Press, for the Duke University Commonwealth Studies Center.

Gordon, H. Scott. 1961. *The economists versus the Bank of Canada*. Toronto: Ryerson Press.

———. 1965. A twenty-year perspective: Some reflections on the Keynesian revolution in Canada. In *Canadian economic policy since the war*, ed. S. F. Kaliski. Montreal: Canadian Trade Committee.

Gosztonyi, Marianne Ainley. 1995. Mabel Frances Timlin, FRSC (1891–1976). *Canadian Women Economists Network Newsletter, A Tribute to Mabel Timlin* (November): 1–5.

Granatstein, J. L. 1982. *The Ottawa men: The civil service mandarins, 1935–1957*. Toronto: Oxford University Press.

Haberler, Gottfried. 1944. Review of *Keynesian Economics*, by Mabel F. Timlin. *Canadian Journal of Economics and Political Science* 10 (February): 102–104.

Hall, Peter, ed. 1991. *The political power of economic ideas: Keynesianism across nations*. Princeton, NJ: Princeton University Press.

Higgins, Benjamin. 1992. *All the difference: A development economist's quest*. Montreal and Kingston: McGill-Queen's University Press.

Keynes, John Maynard. 1971–1989. *The collected writings of John Maynard Keynes*. Ed. D. E. Moggridge and E. A. G. Robinson. 30 vols. London: Macmillan, for the Royal Economic Society (cited as *CW*).

Lange, Oscar. 1938. The rate of interest and the optimum propensity to consume. *Economica*, New Series, 5 (February): 12–32. Repr. in Wood 1983, vol. 2.

Leijonhufvud, Axel. 1983. What was the matter with IS-LM? In *Modern macroeconomic theory*, ed. J. Fitoussi. Oxford: Basil Blackwell.

LePan, Douglas V. 1979. Introduction to economics: Lord Keynes and the audit room meetings. In *Bright glass of memory*, D. V. LePan. Toronto: McGraw-Hill-Ryerson.

Lutz, F. A., and L. W. Mints, eds. 1951. *Readings in monetary theory*. New York: Blakiston.

Mackintosh, W. A. 1947. Keynes as a public servant. *Canadian Journal of Economics and Political Science* 13 (August): 379–83. Repr. in Wood 1983, vol. 1.

———. 1965. The white paper on employment and income in its 1945 setting. In *Canadian economic policy since the war*, ed. S. F. Kaliski. Montreal: Canadian Trade Committee.

Macpherson, C. B. 1953. *Democracy in Alberta: The theory and practice of a quasi-party system*. Toronto: University of Toronto Press.

Modigliani, Franco. 1944. Liquidity preference and the theory of interest and money. *Econometrica* 12:45–88. Reprinted in Lutz and Mints 1951.

Neill, Robin F. 1991. *A history of Canadian economic thought*. London: Routledge.

———. 1999. Economic historiography in the 1950s: The Saskatchewan School. *Journal of Canadian Studies* 34 (3): 243–60.

Ostry, Sylvia. 1998. The Timlin lecture: Globalization and the nation state: Erosion from above. Saskatoon: University of Saskatchewan.

Owram, Douglas. 1986. *The government generation: Canadian intellectuals and the state, 1900–1945*. Toronto: University of Toronto Press.

Patinkin, Don, and J. Clark Leith, eds. 1978. *Keynes, Cambridge and the General Theory*. London: Macmillan.

Phillips, Paul. 1978. The hinterland perspective: The political economy of V. C. Fowke. *Canadian Journal of Political and Social Theory* 2 (1): 73–96.

———. 2002. Mabel Timlin. In *The Canadian encyclopedia*. Toronto: The Historica Foundation of Canada, www.histori.ca.

Plumptre, A. F. W. 1947. Keynes in Cambridge. *Canadian Journal of Economics and Political Science* 13 (August): 366–71. Repr. in Wood 1983, vol. 1.

Roberts, Siobhan. 2003. Donald Coxeter 1907–2003: He kept a little flame of geometry alive. *The Globe and Mail* (Toronto), April 12.

———. 2006. *King of infinite space: Donald Coxeter, the man who saved geometry*. Toronto: Anansi.

Rymes, T. K. 1987. *Keynes's lectures, 1932–35: Notes of students*. Ottawa: Department of Economics, Carleton University.

———. 1989. *Keynes's lectures, 1932–35: Notes of a representative student*. London and Basingstoke: Macmillan.

———. 1995. Timlin and Keynesian economics. Department of Economics, Carleton University. (A shorter version is in the *Canadian Women Economists Network Newsletter, A tribute to Mabel Timlin*, November 1995, 6–9.)

Safarian, A. E. 1976. Biographical note. In *Keynesian economics*, ed. Mabel F. Timlin. University of Toronto Press. Reprinted as Carleton Library no. 107, 1977.

Shackle, G. L. S. 1943. Review of *Keynesian economics*, by Mabel F. Timlin. *Economica*, New Series, 10 (August): 260.

Sharp, Mitchell. 1966–1967. Review of *The age of Keynes*, by Robert Lekachman. *Journal of Liberal Thought* 3 (Winter): 185–88.

Spafford, Duff. 1977. In memoriam: Mabel F. Timlin. *Canadian Journal of Economics* 10 (May): 279–81.

Spafford, Shirley. 2000. *No ordinary academics: Economics and political science at the University of Saskatchewan, 1910–1960*. Toronto: University of Toronto Press.

Swanson, William W. 1931. *Depression and the way out*. Toronto: Ryerson Press.

Swanson, William W., and P. C. Armstrong. 1930. *Wheat*. Toronto: Macmillan of Canada.

Timlin, Mabel F. 1942. *Keynesian economics*. Toronto: University of Toronto Press. Repr. as Carleton Library no. 107, 1977, with biographical note by A. E. Safarian and foreword by Lorie Tarshis. Toronto: McClelland and Stewart.

———. 1944. Review of *The theory of prices*, vol. 2, by Arthur Marget. *Canadian Journal of Economics and Political Science* 10 (May): 246–49.

———. 1945. Review article on Abba Lerner, *The economics of control. Canadian Journal of Economics and Political Science* 11 (February): 285–93.

———. 1946a. Review article on Oscar Lange, *Price flexibility and employment. Canadian Journal of Economics and Political Science* 12 (May): 204–13.

———. 1946b. General equilibrium analysis and public policy. *Canadian Journal of Economics and Political Science* 12 (November): 483–95, and rejoinder 13 (May 1947): 285–87.

———. 1946c. The British economy in the world today. *International Journal* 1:324–36.

———. 1947. John Maynard Keynes. *Canadian Journal of Economics and Political Science* 13 (August): 363–65. Repr. in Wood 1983, vol. 1.

———. 1949. Review article on Hla Myint, *Theories of welfare economics. Canadian Journal of Economics and Political Science* 15 (November): 551–59.

———. 1950. Economic theory and immigration policy. *Canadian Journal of Economics and Political Science* 16 (August): 375–82.

———. 1951a. *Does Canada need more people?* Toronto: Oxford University Press, under sponsorship of the Canadian Institute of International Affairs.

———. 1951b. Review article on Roy Harrod, *The Life of John Maynard Keynes. The Canadian Liberal* 4 (Fall): 161–66.

———. 1953. Recent developments in Canadian monetary policy. *American Economic Review: Papers and Proceedings* 43 (May): 42–53, and discussion by G. Findlay Shirras, 58–60.

———. 1955a. Monetary stabilization policies and Keynesian theory. In *Post-Keynesian economics*, ed. Kenneth R. Kurihara. London: George Allen and Unwin.

———. 1955b. Recent changes in government attitudes towards migration. *Transactions of the Royal Society of Canada* 49, Series 3, Section 2, June.

———. 1958. Canadian immigration with special reference to the post-war period. In *International Migration*. International Economic Association. London: Macmillan.

———. 1960. Canada's immigration policy, 1896–1910. *Canadian Journal of Economics and Political Science* 26 (November): 517–32 (presidential address to Canadian Political Science Association).

———. 1968. The social sciences in Canada: Retrospect and potential. In *The social sciences in Canada: Two studies/Les sciences sociales au Canada: Deux etudes*, ed. Mabel F. Timlin and Albert Faucher. Ottawa: Social Science Research Council of Canada.

Wilson, Tom. 1943. Review of *Keynesian economics*, by Mabel F. Timlin. *Economic Journal* 52 (June–September): 224–26

Wolfe, David. 1984. The rise and demise of the Keynesian era in Canada: Economic policy, 1930–82. In *Readings in Canadian Social History*, ed. M. S. Cross and G. S. Kealey. Vol. 5, *Modern Canada 1930–1980*. Toronto: McClelland and Stewart.

Wood, John Cunningham. 1983. *John Maynard Keynes: Critical assessments*. 4 vols. London: Croom-Helm.

Young, Warren. 1987. *Interpreting Mr. Keynes: The IS-LM enigma*. Cambridge, UK: Polity Press.

CHAPTER 4

The Origin of Keynesian Economics and Some Applications to Restructuring and Globalization

ROBERT SKIDELSKY

IN *THE GENERAL THEORY OF EMPLOYMENT, INTEREST AND MONEY*, Keynes distinguished between "structural" and "involuntary," or "demand deficient," unemployment. What is called Keynesian unemployment is said to refer only to the latter. Thus, you hear: "Expansionary policy in Germany would lead only to inflation because its unemployment is structural."

However, until the early 1930s, Keynes's whole analytical and policy endeavor was stimulated by the problem of the heavy structural unemployment that developed in the UK after the war. Nicholas Kaldor expressed this well in his comment on the *Treatise on Money*: "[Keynes] put forward a macroeconomic 'model' of the British economy which in certain respects was superior to that put forward six years later in the *General Theory*. This is because his analysis specifically referred to Britain and examines the *modus operandi* of the British economy in the context of her peculiar institutions" (Kaldor 1982, 8).

The problem that exercised Keynes arose from the collapse of export demand for the main British staples. Before the First World War, the

British economy was "fabric and mineral-intensive." The staple industries, for both home sales and exports, were textiles, coal-mining, iron and steel, machinery, and shipbuilding. They produced 50 percent of British industrial output and employed 25 percent of the work force. Textiles made up 30 percent by value of British exports, coal almost 9 percent. Britain supplied 70 percent of the world's export of cotton goods, 80 percent of the world's coal exports, and practically the whole of the world's export of ships. It was the decline in the export demand for these goods that created the British unemployment problem of the 1920s.

Of the 9–10 percent of insured workers registered as unemployed in the 1920s, 6 percent were located in these industries. In 1928, a moderately prosperous year, unemployment averaged 22 percent in the iron and steel industry, 35 percent in shipbuilding, and16 percent in the coal industry. This was geographically specific: Lancashire, South Wales, the northeast coast, and the Clyde came to be known as the "distressed areas." The workers hung on in their industries, expecting better times to return. In textiles, job losses were minimized by short-time working. Elsewhere—in the Midlands, the London area, the South—there was moderate prosperity as new industries started up.

This situation continued in the 1930s. George Orwell's *The Road to Wigan Pier*, published in 1937, was about a town in the Lancashire coalfield where young men had traditionally gone into the pit and young women into the mill—a double disaster when both went bust.

The hard men had their own remedies, based on wage adjustments and "rationalization": Production should be concentrated in the most efficient units; displaced workers should move to new industries and force down wages there. Montagu Norman, Governor of the Bank of England, in his defense of the return to the gold standard before the Macmillan Committee in 1930, said: "I have never been able to see myself why for the last few years it should have been impossible for industry starting from within to have readjusted its own position" (quoted in Skidelsky 1992, 356). There was this much to be said for the hard men: In 1919, war-strengthened labor unions had forced up unit labor costs. It was the coincidence of the rise in unit labor costs with a deflationary monetary policy aimed at improving the sterling-dollar exchange rate that made the problems of the export industries so intractable.

Keynes developed two sets of policies in response to this situation. There was no new theory behind them, only a generous spirit. The first was to argue for a lower value of the pound. This brought him up against the policy of putting sterling back on the gold standard at its pre-war parity with the dollar. Keynes identified two bad effects of the policy of improving the exchange rate. First, it made it more difficult to export. Secondly, it required what was called "dear money." This held back the development of new industries that might absorb some of the surplus labor trapped in the old ones. A lower exchange rate would help the staples export more; lower interest rates would help restructuring.

As always, Keynes had a second-best policy. A restored gold standard mandated high interest rates and discouraged domestic borrowers, forcing savings abroad. If restoration of the gold standard could not be avoided, government should borrow the "excess savings" itself and spend them at home, in building roads, houses, telephones, schools, and public utilities, so as to "restore the balance in our economy" (Keynes 1924 [1981: 223]). Keynes started advocating this policy in 1924, and loan-financed "public works" formed the basis of the Liberal Party program of "conquering unemployment" in 1929.

Roy Harrod has recorded his impression at the time that Keynes's advocacy of domestic rather than foreign investment lacked theoretical cogency. "Orthodox theory did not appear to justify Keynes's contention that [unemployment] could be reduced by diverting investment from foreign to home channels" (Harrod 1951, 350–51). This seems to me to pinpoint the difference between the spirit of Keynes's economics and the spirit of orthodox economics. Keynes's was much more concrete. He was much less interested than most economists are in proving a case by long chains of reasoning, because uncertainty increased as one got more abstract and further away from home.

In fact, restructuring did take place in the 1930s on the rebound from the Great Depression, but very incompletely. The South and the Midlands boomed, the North stayed depressed. In 1937 there was 15 percent unemployment in the North, 5 percent in the South. In Jarrow, where the shipyard died, unemployment was 70 percent. The government was running a budget surplus.

In 1937, Keynes wrote some articles in *The Times* that have puzzled his followers. In one of them, he said, "We are in more need today of a rightly distributed demand than of a greater aggregate demand," and he warned against the dangers of inflation (Keynes 1937a [1982: 385]). The puzzle was how Keynes could advocate stabilizing demand when unemployment was still over 10 percent.

Another puzzle was his concern with a "balanced" economy. A greater measure of national self-sufficiency, he had started to argue in 1933, offered a "well-balanced" or "complete" national life, allowing a nation to display the full range of its aptitudes as well as preserve traditions. "To say the country cannot afford agriculture," he said in 1932, "is to delude oneself about the meaning of the word 'afford.' A country which cannot afford art or agriculture, invention or tradition, is a country in which one cannot afford to live" (quoted in Skidelsky 1992, 476). At a certain standard of living, Keynes claimed, the theory of comparative advantage lost much of its importance: It derived from the age of scarcity, not of plenty; as societies became wealthier, other considerations became more important. One can find in these sentiments an echo of Adam Smith's understanding that the demand for specialization would drastically narrow the skill base of a society and thus deprive it of a "full" life—something certainly worth discussing today in the context of globalization.

But, to return to the 1937 articles: The topic of debate was whether the recently announced rearmament program, to be financed by borrowing, would be inflationary. Keynes argued that it need not be. The nub of his argument was that, owing to the "unfortunate rigidity" of Britain's industrial structure, heavy surpluses of labor in the "distressed areas" coexisted with shortages in other areas. An expansion of aggregate demand would be inflationary, but inflation could be avoided if demand were directed to the areas with labor surpluses and reduced in those with labor shortages (by curtailing public-sector programs there). "Whether demand is or is not inflationary depends on whether it is directed towards trades and localities which have no surplus capacity. To organise output in the Special Areas is a means of obtaining rearmament without inflation" (Keynes 1937b [1982: 407]).

So much for Keynes; now for applications. The application to globalization is clear. Keynes would not have been an enthusiastic globalizer. I have hinted at why: It involves carrying specialization to a point at which it undermines the national quality of life. The contemporary economist who most fully captures the spirit of Keynes's argument on this matter is Dani Rodrik (1997). But, to get a full flavor of Keynes's approach, you also need to read his essay "Economic Possibilities for our Grandchildren" (Keynes 1930).

As Rodrik points out, specialization to reap the gains from trade always involves restructuring. This need is nowhere greater than in economies that were hitherto closed to international trade. Keynes is relevant because of his emphasis on the role that fiscal and monetary policy can play in restructuring. I want to give as examples two emerging markets, Russia and China, which have suffered massive demand shocks through the failure of their planned economic systems. The specifics of the two eras are different, but the general issue is the same.

Russia's main problem, like Britain's in the interwar years, is highly unbalanced growth. While the oil industry and its ancillaries have been booming, much of the rest of the economy, based on Soviet-era heavy industry and agriculture, has been seriously underheating. A 12 percent inflation rate coexists with a 10 percent unemployment rate, which is much higher in some sectors and regions and is compounded by heavy under-employment. As in Britain earlier, there are serious regional imbalances. The energy boom has increased gaps between regions, which are most marked in per capita gross regional products and life expectancy. The rise in the Gini coefficient—a measure of inequality—is an important consequence of the lack of an adequate distributional formula to redress regional inequality.

Russia's challenge is to build a broadly based economy—balanced not just in terms of what is produced but across the regions. Expert opinion believes that laissez-faire will do the job through the familiar "trickle-down" process: The government's task is to provide an appropriate climate for private investment by restraining inflation, reducing red tape, improving property rights, et cetera. In its macro policy (though not always in its micro policy), President Putin's government has basically followed this prescription by cutting taxes, amassing a huge budget surplus, liberalizing capital flows, and accumulating foreign exchange reserves. It has used the growing surpluses from the Oil Stabilization Fund (now close to $100 billion) to buy foreign securities. All of this is according to the dictates of "sound finance" and has led to a boom in the retail sector and in residential construction and property values, not only in Moscow.

However, the policy of restraining aggregate demand by hoarding a huge quantity of cash makes little economic sense when so much of the economy is depressed. As Keynes wrote in 1937, "We are in more need today of a rightly distributed demand than of a greater aggregate demand." Overall, it is the "output gap," not the "inflation gap," that is the serious drag on Russia's economic growth. A Keynesian policy would be to use the bounty from oil and gas exports to raise incomes in Russia's many depressed areas—those away from the centers of the energy economy and its retail and construction spillovers. This could best be done by investing capital from the excess surpluses of the Oil Stabilization Fund to build schools, hospitals, houses, and new transport and communications infrastructure in those areas. At the same time, special transaction taxes should be raised from the ordinary budget to cool the private housing boom, with tax breaks for small and medium-sized businesses. (Belatedly, the government has committed some revenues from the Stabilization Fund to kickstart the "knowledge" economy.) Of course, one would need to take a long hard look at the competence and integrity of government agencies before advising such a policy. But the retreat from socialism should not be carried to the lengths of eschewing all constructive attempts to "restore the balance" in the Russian economy.

China, too, has huge choices to make. China is a fabulously successful exporting economy but a highly unbalanced one. Its coastal economy booms, while its interior, home of the languishing state enterprises, stagnates. Inequality is widening rapidly. Inflation is low, while unemployment in the countryside may be of the order of 30–40 percent. Excess labor from the country flocks to the coastal provinces to be absorbed in an export drive maintained by an undervalued exchange rate and at the expense of hideous pollution and congestion. As in Russia, fiscal policy is used to fight inflation, with huge public-sector surpluses as well as central bank reserves being invested in U.S. Treasury bonds. The exchange rate is fixed to the dollar, and interest rates are very low.

Keynes would surely have been tempted to suggest for China the kind of national development loan he advocated in Britain in the 1920s. He might well have wanted to mobilize "excess Chinese savings," currently going abroad, to be invested in social and transport infrastructure, especially outside the boom areas. This would absorb much of the labor currently flooding into the coastal provinces and enlarge the domestic market at the expense of exports. Apart from getting a more balanced growth, it would also relieve the problem of China's "super-competitiveness," which will, sooner or later, provoke retaliation. The Chinese leadership seems to understand this, and its most recent five-year plan (they still have them!) calls for "harmonious" development.

Both Russia and China are reluctant to "think Keynesian," such is their recoil from state planning to free market economics. But I suggest that they do have something of value to offer, and they draw on a part of Keynes's legacy that is less well known than it should be.

Let me conclude with my opinion of what that legacy is. Keynes's critique of orthodox approaches to "restructuring" was informed by the notion of a civilized society. He was not against economic change. He did not believe that economic organization should be geared to the maintenance of obsolete plants—as happened under communism. He understood that the desire to better one's condition was universal, and that the capitalist market system was the most powerful engine yet invented for bringing this about. However, he thought that the pace of change should be adapted not to the requirements of what he called the "economic juggernaut" but to what human beings found reasonably comfortable, what they could cope with. He believed that the economic environment should be challenging, even stimulating, but not destructive of most of what made life worth living.

As I said, he had a generous spirit.

References

Harrod, R. F. 1951. *The life of John Maynard Keynes*. London: Macmillan.

Kaldor, N. 1982. Keynes as an economic adviser. In *Keynes as a policy adviser*, ed. A. P. Thirlwall. London: Macmillan.

Keynes, J. M. 1924. Does unemployment need a drastic remedy? *The Nation and Athenaeum* (May 24). Repr. in Keynes 1981.

———. 1930. Economic possibilities for our grandchildren. *The Nation and Athenaeum* (October 11 and 18). Repr. in Keynes 1972.

———. 1937a. How to avoid a slump. In *The* (London) *Times* (January 12). Repr. in Keynes 1982.

———. 1937b. Borrowing for defence: Is it inflation? In *The* (London) *Times* (March 11). Repr. in Keynes 1982.

———. 1972. *The collected writings of John Maynard Keynes*. Vol. 9. Ed. D. Moggridge. London: Macmillan, for the Royal Economic Society.

———. 1981. *The collected writings of John Maynard Keynes*. Vol. 19. Ed. D. Moggridge. London: Macmillan, for the Royal Economic Society.

———. 1982. *The collected writings of John Maynard Keynes*. Vol. 21. Ed. D. Moggridge. London: Macmillan, for the Royal Economic Society.

Rodrik, Dani. 1997. *Has globalization gone too far?* Washington, DC: Institute for International Economics.

Skidelsky, R. 1992. *John Maynard Keynes: The economist as saviour*. London: Macmillan.

CHAPTER 5

MOVING ON: WHERE TO?

AXEL LEIJONHUFVUD

THE GENERAL THEORY OF EMPLOYMENT, INTEREST AND MONEY was published seventy years ago. That is at least three or four intellectual generations ago. (I am not sure how to count in this context!) When I wrote about Keynes forty years ago, I did not expect to have much of an audience; to a graduate student in the 1960s, the origin of Keynesian economics seemed already a dated topic. It was a surprise to find that the profession was not tired of the debate. Since then, the Keynes literature has grown enormously. Today, the economics profession at large *is* tired of it. Those of us who carry on with it are talking only to each other. And that is an aging audience with not that many up-and-coming members.

I confess to feeling a bit trapped in this Keynes business. By switching attention from "Keynes and the Classics" to "Keynes and the Keynesians," I was lucky in causing some debate with my early book. Having, as I then thought, said my piece, I tried to stay out of the ensuing discussion. I did so partly because my book was meant to deal with the then-current situation in macroeconomics, and the interpretation of Keynes's contribution was subsidiary. But I was also somewhat fearful of getting stuck indefinitely in defending and elaborating my view of Keynes. Despite good intentions, however, I have found myself getting back to the topic over and over again.

Why is this? The mainstream has taken such a drastically different course that Post Keynesians—and less well-defined Keynesians like Bob Clower and I—have found themselves spending unreasonable amounts of time and effort explaining and re-explaining to an increasingly uncomprehending audience what Keynes was all about.

The term "Post Keynesian" was surely intended as a programmatic announcement from the beginning. The program was not, of course, to deny or to abandon Keynes but to move beyond him. Still, here we find ourselves once more at a conference seeking to assert "the continuing relevance" of Keynes. (Would Keynes himself have been pleased with this? Surely, he would have been impatient with us. His restless intelligence would long since have moved on to the great issues of today.) It is time we have a discussion about how we might get out of this rut. It is a matter of what in Keynes should be discarded, what should be retained and developed, and in what directions the essential themes should be developed.

I will try to outline my personal opinions on these matters. I am well aware that my opinions do not command assent. But my purpose, to repeat, is to start a discussion.

The Long Swing

I had my first encounters with economics about fifty years ago. What students were taught all over the world back then was that the market system was unstable, subject to a variety of market failures and prone to cyclical fluctuations amplified by multiplier and accelerator effects. It was also common to suppose, however, that governments in "advanced countries" were benevolent and competent and certainly solvent and able to stabilize the macroeconomy and cure most of its microproblems. Stabilization policy meant aggregate demand management.

What is taught today almost everywhere—present company not included, I guess—is that the market system will take care of all coordination problems, so that, as long as stupid macropolicies are eschewed, the economy will maintain itself on an equilibrium path. States of nature may vary stochastically but, once a state has been drawn from Nature's Urn, it is common knowledge, and all of the pre-programmed appropriate adjustments to it are immediately made. The coordinated time-path may be less than ideal if labor-market inflexibilities are tolerated, in which case the "natural rate" of unemployment may be higher than necessary. The idyllic picture is marred by the tendency of governments to run excessive deficits and engage in inflationary finance. Governments in representative democracies are, supposedly, particularly apt to be time-inconsistent and play the unstable Phillips curve for no good reason and to no good effect. Macropolicy in this doctrine becomes the political art of constraining governments so that they cannot do the harm that they are otherwise constitutionally prone to engage in.

Now, you may dismiss these as caricatures. I concede that they are hard-drawn. My point is simply that both worldviews are very inadequate and potentially dangerous guides to the reality we live in. The pessimism about markets and the optimism about governments of the earlier view were both highly exaggerated, and so are the optimism about markets and the pessimism about governments of the modern view. The problem is how to work out a coherent view of the world at some distance from both extremes. That will require a lot of work, and that work is yet to be done.

Stability: Effective Demand Failures

The juxtaposition of the two worldviews poses two issues. One concerns how governments generally function. I am not going to attempt that one. The second concerns the stability of the full employment equilibrium in a monetary economy.

Pre-Keynesian theory presumed that, if only all prices were flexible, the stability of general equilibrium was assured. The *indispensable core* of Keynes's theory is the demonstration that flexibility of prices was not a sufficient condition for stability in a monetary economy. The stability issue should be seen here in a Marshallian context. The Marshallian consumer will increase his purchases if his demand price exceeds the market price. The Marshallian producer will increase his output if the market price exceeds his supply price.[1] And the Marshallian middle man will increase the price he asks of consumers and the price he offers to producers if he experiences excess demand. Before *The General Theory*, it was generally believed that stability of the full employment equilibrium was guaranteed if *all* agents in the economy obeyed these "laws of motion." Keynes discovered that this theoretical presumption was not warranted.

Price adjustments have to be driven by *effective* excess demand in markets. But, in a money economy, the supply of labor is not, by itself, an effective demand for consumer goods. Similarly, in an economy where intertemporal trades are conducted with monetary instruments, a "fresh act of saving" is not an effective demand for future consumption. When the interest rate on the monetary instrument is too high to coordinate full-employment saving and investment, real income and employment will fall. In the resulting state of the system, there is no effective excess demand for "bonds" to correct the price that is too high for general equilibrium to be feasible; at the same time, unemployed labor constitutes an effective excess supply of labor, but the corresponding excess demand for consumer goods is ineffective. The wage rate may be the right one for general equilibrium, but it is tending away from that value. Downward flexibility of wages, however, will not restore unemployment. If they were to be very flexible, the result would be a Wicksellian deflation that would wreck the financial system.

Effective excess demands summed across all markets do not add up to zero. In this sense, Say's Law does not hold. This is essential to Keynesian policy doctrine. It is when supply does *not* create its own demand that aggregate demand management is needed. The case for stabilization policy rests on the denial of Say's Law. Theories in which the law is taken always to hold can provide no rational basis for it.

The "involuntary unemployment" state on which Keynes focused is a particular case and not as ubiquitously prevalent as it seemed to him in the midst of the Great Depression. It is not a permanent feature of capitalist economies or even a very common one. Consider some of Keynes's hypotheses: (1) The economy shows a permanent tendency to generate more saving than can be profitably invested; (2) workers live hand-to-mouth, so their consumption demand will be income-constrained; (3) the marginal efficiency of (aggregate) capital will shift abruptly and drastically. These are among a number of assumptions that do not apply today and that Keynes, surely, would not have applied to our present circumstances.

It is also true, however, that the particular case of *The General Theory* does not exhaust the effective demand failures that may get in the way of an economy homing in on something like an equilibrium path. There is at least one more type of effective demand failure: namely, when the promise of future output cannot be used as effective demand for the present inputs needed to realize that future output. This can occur when a banking system is clogged with nonperforming loans and the nonbank business sector has to concentrate on cleaning up balance sheets rather than taking on more debt. It is exemplified by Japan in the 1990s (Koo 2003). This case is not in Keynes, of course.[2] A more general version of *The General Theory* would incorporate it.

We should conclude, I believe, that effective demand failures of such magnitude as to negate the stabilizing tendencies of ordinary market adjustments are to be expected only as a result of serious financial imbalances or in the wake of financial crises. They are "out of the corridor" phenomena. We should moderate the claims made for Keynes (and for a generalized *General Theory)* accordingly.

Conversely, Keynesians should give mainstream theory its due. To dismiss neoclassical theory out of hand is an intellectually bad habit (and may be addictive!). The valid complaint is that general equilibrium theory does not help us understand the kind of disasters that originally motivated the emergence of macroeconomics as a distinct subdiscipline. This is a good enough reason to resist the total reabsorption of macroeconomics into dynamic stochastic general equilibrium theory.[3] But heterodox economists of whatever stripe should appreciate that mainstream theory does provide explanations for macroeconomic stagnation (Phelps 1994) and, in particular, for long-term unemployment (for example, Ljungqvist and Sargent 2003).

Stability: High Inflation

The theory of effective demand failures does not exhaust the possibilities of things going wrong with the stability of general equilibrium. High inflations and hyperinflations constitute another class of cases.

A high inflation economy does not converge to anything at all resembling the solution state of a monetary equilibrium model with a high inflation tax. The one thing that model gets right is the drastic decline in the demand for real balances. But, from this implication, the mainstream literature draws the wrong conclusion: namely, that the main welfare costs of inflation stem from the inefficiencies of economizing on the holding of cash balances. The more serious cost is caused by the strangulation of financial intermediation. This is missed in models where the only role of money is to determine the nominal scale of real magnitudes. This, moreover, is only one example of the myriad structural changes in the real economy that the monetary general equilibrium literature misses altogether. The set of markets is not the same as the economy would have if monetary stability had been maintained. Virtually all intertemporal markets disappear, while spot markets fragment as more and more arbitrage mechanisms fail.

Among Post Keynesians, Paul Davidson has always stressed the significance of the fact that contracts are concluded in terms of money. High inflations prove his case, in that no fully adequate substitute is found when the real value of the nominal unit becomes too volatile and uncertain to be useful. The point extends further than is often realized. Monetary accounting is used to monitor innumerable principal-agent relationships in a modern economy. This is true, for example, of the relationship between stockholders and corporate managements. When corporations cannot account for their results in a way that is meaningful to stock market participants, the market in their shares becomes almost completely inactive.

So: no stocks, no bonds, no intermediation. A high-inflation economy will not grow because growth cannot be financed. The welfare costs of a decade of inflationary stagnation are huge.

Inflation has not been a burning issue for some years now. But it is safe to say that we have not banished it forever. If dynamic stochastic general equilibrium theory is the current orthodoxy and we find it too naive and optimistic a view of the human condition, then a useful heterodoxy with which to complement it should aim for a "general theory" of what can go wrong in market systems. A serious theory of inflation processes would have to be a large component of such a heterodoxy.

Microfoundations

In the Cambridge tradition, "equilibrium" meant the point-attractor of an adaptive market *process*. With the laws of motion of quantity demanded, of output, and of price operating all at once, the market process is essentially nonlinear. The dynamics may nonetheless be well behaved—almost all of the time. But Marshall did not entirely trust his static model, even though he was dealing with only a single market. Keynes's analytical problem was *infinitely worse*. A Cantabrigian process model for a system of multiple interdependent markets with different lag-structures, further complicated by liquidity constraints, et cetera, would be a nonlinear nightmare. Keynes tried to find a Marshallian short-run equilibrium for it—but he was operating way beyond the limits of what could be accomplished with Marshall's static method. He was basically trying to *talk* his way through the dynamics of a complex system for which no adequate mathematical tools existed. It is no wonder that he needed his "Circus" as a sounding board: "It is astonishing what foolish things one can temporarily believe if one thinks too long alone, particularly in economics . . . where it is often impossible to bring one's ideas to a conclusive test either formal or empirical" (Keynes 1936, p. xxiii).[4] Nor is it any wonder that we spent decades debating what he meant and whether he was right.

No variation on IS-LM will ever put Keynesian economics on a solid foundation. It is extremely unlikely that a static model exists that, if found, will capture the essentials of Keynes's theory. IS-LM survived for so long because, in contrast to general equilibrium models, it does not obey Say's Law. As a consequence, it allows one to illustrate various Keynesian propositions, including the purposeful use of stabilization policy.

Keynesian economics was built on analytically shaky foundations. It does us no good to go on as if this were not the case. In order to move on, this situation has to be remedied. How can that be done? There has been a good deal of progress in the analysis of complex systems since the days of Marshall and Keynes. But closed-form solutions for the kind of dynamical processes that Keynes theorized about are not within reach even today.

Agent-based computational economics provides the *only* way in which the properties of complex adaptive economic systems can be explored in a reasonably disciplined way.[5] This is the road to take, I believe, to construct microfoundations for Keynesian macroeconomics.

Microfoundations: Production, Growth, and Income Distribution

Mainstream macro and distribution theory has been built on the basis of a production theory exhibiting constant returns to scale and smooth substitutability among inputs. This neoclassical production function is surely suspect. Increasing returns are all around us, everywhere you look. Where can you not get a volume discount? I do not think my marginal physical product or marginal value product can be unambiguously measured. How about yours?

The alternative to neoclassical production and distribution theory is the division-of-labor tradition running from Adam Smith through Marshall and Allyn Young to Kaldor. The division of labor is productive in that specialization generates economies of scale. It also creates complementarities.

Consider the simple example of an assembly line. The men and the machines of the line are complementary inputs. Their marginal physical products are not defined. Next, consider two assembly lines producing the same final product. One has a greater number of workstations than the other. The agents and artifacts engaged are more specialized and average total factor productivity is higher on the longer line. In all production processes, some factors are idle part of the time. If, for example, one workstation on a line is idle half of the time, output could be doubled by doubling all other inputs and fully utilizing this station. So, if twice the output could be sold, it can be produced at a lower unit cost.

Firms operating under increasing returns will be "monopolistically competitive." When the monopolistic element remains strong, such firms earn a quasi-rent. The complementarity among inputs makes this a joint rent. In general, capital has control and labor is hired, while labor in control and capital equipment rented is a rare exception. In this asymmetric situation, capital tends to appropriate the entire rent. Labor has to unionize to get any part of it. Labor-management conflict arises naturally out of the technology under which the factors cooperate. When, sooner or later, competition erodes the firm's monopolistic advantage, the producer's rent turns into a consumer's surplus, and neither capital nor labor can appropriate more than can be earned in the best alternative use.

However, increasing returns should not be thought of as the property of a few large, capital-intensive, and possibly monopolistic firms. When competition erodes monopoly, the technology does not change. The economy as a whole is nonconvex. It is a nonlinear (and thus non-Leontief) input-output system of interdependent production processes, most of which exhibit increasing returns. Growth allows more of the increasing-return possibilities to be realized.[6] Measured factor productivity rises in the process (the Solow residual). In a system of this kind, people are productive because of the *size* of the network of cooperating producers in which they are participants. But marginal products are most often undefined, and a large part of gross domestic product (GDP) should be regarded, in effect, as a joint rent. This theory of production requires a thorough rethinking of the political economy of distribution.

Production systems of this sort are very productive at high activity levels but are incapable of scaling back output without a drop in productivity. This theory, therefore, yields a straightforward interpretation of Okun's Law and the pro-cyclical pattern of the Solow residual—but, of course, a different one from that of mainstream theory.

Now, of course, Keynes did not contribute anything whatsoever to the theory that Marshall and Young had developed from Smith. So my argument in this section cannot be considered "Post Keynesian" in any proper sense. But there is, nonetheless, a good reason why Keynesians should take an interest in amending production theory in this direction. It inheres in Smith's adage, "The division of labor is limited by the extent of the market." Productivity growth based on the increasing elaboration of the division of labor is only possible if demand is also growing. Overly restrictive aggregate demand policies can put a stop to it and produce stagnation.

Current growth theory is altogether supply-side based. The view that aggregate demand management could, at best, be irrelevant but, more likely, harmful to growth is a serious error. Effective demand failures are not the only rationale for aggregate demand policies.

Money and Finance

Thanks to Davidson, Minsky, Moore, Chick, Kregel, and, in Italy, Gallegati and Delli Gatti, Post Keynesians have made notable progress beyond Keynes in monetary theory. During the long dominance of monetarist theory, with its stress on *exogenously* controlled *outside* money, Post Keynesians kept alive and developed a theory in which *endogenous* variations in *inside* money are of central importance. Eventually, much of the profession has come around to a view that is at least closely akin to the Post Keynesian one on these issues. But this is not a time to rest on the laurels of a (qualified) victory. Instead, the way forward from these achievements, I would suggest, might start from an institutional view of money's function.[7]

Not all that long ago, students of money and banking had to learn that money had the properties of being *portable, durable, and divisible.* This piece of wisdom had been handed down through many generations of teachers concerned with explaining why other goods did not serve the same functions as metallic coin. More recently, the focus has shifted to what kinds of *book entries* in what types of institutions should be considered money. Since all macromodels contain a variable, M, knowing how it might be measured seems to be a matter of some consequence. But in recent years the technology of making payments and the forms of short-term credit have been evolving so very rapidly that the question *what things are money*? no longer seems a promising line of inquiry.

The fundamental institutional rule governing market exchange is the equal-value-in-exchange condition. In complex societies, virtually all exchange is multilateral and "money" denotes the institutional provisions for monitoring and enforcing the equal-value condition for all market participants. Various technologies exist for doing this, from handing around metallic coin to electronic clearing, and more are constantly being invented, which is why it is not very helpful to focus on what objects serve monetary functions at any particular time.

The logic of exchange is that every transaction should give rise to a debit and a credit of equal value. When credits are created without corresponding debits somewhere in the system, this arithmetical logic is violated. When one agent succeeds in violating the equal-value condition, one or more other agents have to take a loss. Individual net worth positions have to be recalculated, but it may take some time before the necessity of so doing is realized and sometimes far longer before the results become clear. When, in an inflation, the government has appropriated resources by creating outside money at a rate in excess of the growth in demand for it, the inflation tax on money balances is the necessary arithmetical correction. But, if the inflation has not been accurately predicted by all, the recalculation of the net worth of agents is further complicated by its pervasive redistributive effects.

Isolated defaults by private-sector agents will not have significant macroeconomic effects. But, if the economy has developed into a financially fragile state, major defaults will produce a cascade of failures. Such a process will sweep with it into bankruptcy many economic units that were solvent but in varying degrees illiquid. Even if such an avalanche is somehow stopped before extreme debt deflation sets in, it will take a long time for the system to sort out what promises will or will not be honored. Meanwhile, the uncertainty about what commitments agents are good for will impede economic recovery.

In modeling market behavior, we tend automatically to assume that the budget constraints always hold.[8] This may, I think, be the reason why conventional general equilibrium models do not provide sensible interpretations of the extremes of monetary instability. General equilibrium theory becomes difficult to do if you cannot assume that budget constraints hold. But the violation of budget constraints on a large scale is exactly what high inflations and deep depressions have in common.

Conclusion

Where does all of this leave us in relation to today's mainstream macroeconomics? Keynes left us a theory, never adequately formalized, that is capable of explaining long-lasting depression. This theory can be somewhat generalized to include effective demand failures of a sort he did not consider. But even so, it remains a theory, not of the normal functioning of a modern economy, but of abnormal, extreme states that will occur under certain circumstances. Much the same can be said about high inflation theory. It explains another set of malfunctions of a monetary economy, but, again, such inflations are extreme and abnormal cases.

When monetary instability is not a dominant concern, we are back with one or another variety of conventional theory. The issues then become: How strong are the operative tendencies towards (temporary) equilibrium, and how much attention has to be paid to "frictions" of one sort or another? The point is, however, that, when an economy performs more or less as a dynamic stochastic general equilibrium system, the social value added by macroeconomists is at best trivial (Lucas 2003). When coordination can be taken for granted, economic theory reverts to the traditional issues of incentives and efficient allocation. The primary social responsibility of macroeconomists is to try as best they can to understand the extremes of monetary instability. Great depressions and high inflations wreak utter havoc on the lives of millions of people. It is by focusing on these phenomena that macroeconomists can hope to be useful.

There is one note to add. Mainstream theory is probably justified in presuming that, under normal conditions, market mechanisms work well enough—albeit with "frictions"—that one need not worry about instabilities of equilibrium of the Keynesian sort. But all is not well within the corpus of standard theory. One cannot invest much faith in neoclassical production and distribution theory or in the growth theory developed from it. Moreover, if this core component of mainstream theory is as ill-founded as I suspect it is, this will turn out to have important implications for macroeconomic policy theory.

Notes

1. Note that, while the Walrasian *tâtonnement* gives us rules for the adjustment only of prices, the Marshallian process gives us "laws of motion" also for the quantities on both sides of the market.
2. Note that, since the problem is not to alleviate income constraints on households, public works programs, for example, are not the right policy strategy in this case. Unthinking use of old Keynesian folk remedies will be of little use—as the Japanese experience gradually proved.
3. This is a good enough reason but not, of course, the only reason. While I tend to the belief that, "within the corridor," existing markets tend towards clearing, intertemporal coordination is still confounded by missing markets and strategic complementarities (Cooper and John 1988, Bryant 1983).
4. Can you imagine any self-respecting economic theorist making this statement today? But then, not many theorists today try to deal with dynamical systems of a complexity beyond the analytical tools at their disposal.
5. For promising beginnings on this enterprise, cf. Howitt and Clower 2000, Howitt 2006, van der Hoog 2005, and Gintis 2007.

6. The McKinsey Global Institute has conducted a number of studies comparing productivity developments, by industry, in a number of countries. The findings are summarized in Lewis 2004. In case after case, the keys to good productivity performance are found to be two: (1) exploiting new economies of scale and (2) allowing competition to drive out the old, less productive activities.
7. Here I should acknowledge, as did Charles Goodhart in his paper at the conference, the influence of Martin Shubik's "mathematical institutionalism." His work on monetary theory over many years culminated in Shubik 1999.
8. Or we assume at least that all default risks are, in principle, insurable.

References

Bryant, John. 1983. A simple rational expectations Keynes-type model. *Quarterly Journal of Economics* 98 (3): 525–28.

Cooper, Russell W., and Andrew John. 1988. Coordinating coordination failures in Keynesian models. *Quarterly Journal of Economics* 103 (3): 441–63.

Gintis, Herb. 2007. The dynamics of general equilibrium. *Economic Journal* 117 (523): 1280–1309.

Howitt, Peter. 2006. The microfoundations of the Keynesian multiplier process. *Journal of Economic Interaction and Coordination* 1 (1): 33–44.

Howitt, Peter, and Robert Clower. 2000. The emergence of economic organization. *Journal of Economic Behavior and Organization* 41 (1): 55–84.

Keynes, J. M. 1936. *The General Theory of Employment, Interest and Money*. London: Macmillan.

Koo, Richard C. 2003. *Balance sheet recession: Japan's struggle with uncharted economics and its global implications.* Singapore: John Wiley & Sons (Asia).

Lewis, William W. 2004. *The power of productivity: Wealth, poverty, and the threat to global stability*. Chicago: University of Chicago Press.

Ljungqvist, Lars, and Thomas J. Sargent. 2003. European unemployment: From a worker's perspective. In *Knowledge, information and expectations in modern macroeconomics: In honor of Edmund S. Phelps*, ed. Phillippe Aghion et al. Princeton, NJ: Princeton University Press.

Lucas, Robert E., Jr. 2003. Macroeconomic priorities. *American Economic Review* 93 (1): 1–14.

Phelps, Edmund S. 1994. *Structural slumps: The modern equilibrium theory of unemployment, interest and assets.* Cambridge, MA: Harvard University Press.

Shubik, Martin. 1999. *The theory of money and financial institutions.* Vols. 1 and 2. Cambridge, MA: MIT Press.

van der Hoog, Sander. 2005. *Microeconomic disequilibrium dynamics*. Amsterdam: Thela Thesis. Available online at http://dare.uva.nl/record/150442.

Note: My own attempts to pursue the lines of inquiry sketched in this chapter can be found at www.ceel.economia.unitn.it/staff/leijonhufvud.

Part II

Keynes's Continuing Impact on Policy

CHAPTER 6

Keynes in Latin America and Latin American Keynesianism

Julio López G.*

> The Keynesian revolution was one of the great modern accomplishments in social design . . . [However] the history of the revolution is, perhaps, the worst told story of our era. It is time that we knew better this part of our story and those who made it.
>
> —John K. Galbraith, 2001

MANY READERS ARE FAMILIAR with the name Raúl Prebisch and know of his central role at the Economic Commission for Latin America and the Caribbean (ECLAC) and the United Nations Conference for Trade and Development (UNCTAD). But probably few know that Prebisch also wrote the widely read *Introduction to Keynes*. And probably even fewer know that he played a decisive role in framing two Keynesian economic recovery plans for his native Argentina.

Similarly, it may surprise many readers to hear that several Latin American countries had important Keynesian demand management episodes. Some of these took place during the crisis of the 1930s, and

* I want to thank Patricia Audino, Carlos Mallorquín, and Arturo O'Connell for their help; but, most of all, I thank Ignacy Sachs, with whom I have discussed many of the ideas developed in this paper. I also acknowledge the financial support received from Universidad Nacional Autónoma de México, through DGAPA/PAPIIT-Proyecto IN301606.

some of them occurred during the Second World War. All of these left a big imprint on Keynesian-inspired economic thought in our region.

In telling the story of Prebisch and the historical episodes, I will adhere to the approach followed by Galbraith (2001) in his authoritative account of Keynes's arrival in the other America. But I will also give some factual antecedents that will, I hope, allow for a better understanding of the impact of Keynes's thought in our region. Besides that, I will give an account of how Latin American economists further developed Keynes's ideas.

Historical Episodes

Before the crisis of the 1930s, all Latin American economies had strong links with the world economy as suppliers of raw materials and foodstuffs. Therefore, the crisis hit them hard, causing a severe decline in prices and volume of exports. The export multiplier worsened the impact of the decline of exports on domestic demand. Besides, since export taxes represented most of the public revenues, the normal, orthodox reaction was a tightening of government spending, which provoked another round of demand contraction.

Sometimes, however, the government policy stance deviated from this pattern. The first episode involving what we would call Keynesian economic policy measures took place in Brazil. Celso Furtado, one of the greatest Latin American economists, masterfully analyzed this episode, and probably the best I can do is follow closely his description of the events (Furtado 1954, 1962).

When the crisis hit Brazil, the country was the largest coffee producer in the world. (It had significantly raised its production capacity as a result of huge investments made in the preceding period.) Excess supply appeared, and coffee prices declined to one-third of their previous level.

Brazil had an important previous experience with government intervention to protect coffee prices when confronted with adverse external shocks. The procedure was known as "valorization" of production—meaning that the government used external credit to purchase surplus production and thus stabilize prices.

When the 1930s world crisis arrived, Brazil had to face the ineluctable decline of its import capacity, by about 50 percent, coupled with the need to finance huge stocks of coffee that did not find a market abroad. This involved a great government effort. Consider that, in some years, the value of coffee production the government bought reached about 10 percent of gross domestic product (GDP), and that external credit for this action was not now available. The authorities had to destroy a large part of these stocks to avoid the costs of stocking the product.

Government purchase of the coffee surplus implied an expansion of loan-financed expenditure, which preserved monetary incomes of landlords and peasants despite the decline in the value of exports. Therefore, it conserved domestic and aggregate demand and employment. Brazil had a small industrial base, but it was nevertheless capable of responding to the demand forthcoming for domestic output with increased supply. As Furtado put it, "The value of the [coffee] product destroyed was much below the value of the income created. We were, in fact, building Keynes's famous pyramids" (Furtado 1962, 198).

Thanks to government policy intervention, the decline of Brazil's GDP from 1929 to the bottom of the crisis, although large—that is, about 25 percent—was not as large as it would have been otherwise. Also, already in 1933, output started to rise; that is earlier than in the United States, where the recovery began a year later.

Defense of domestic income during the world crisis entailed a balance-of-payments deficit, which provoked currency depreciation. The latter, in turn, brought about a change in relative prices in favor of manufacturing. This was of major importance. As Furtado put it:

> While defending . . . domestic money income, when import capacity had declined, the policy of favoring the coffee sector came to be, eventually, an industrialization policy. With the fast depreciation of domestic currency, the domestic prices of imports rose, even as the competitiveness of domestic producers improved. The profitability of the coffee sector and of the export sector in general, was declining, because government support only partially compensated for worsening export earnings. Manufacturing production for the domestic market became the most profitable business of the Brazilian economy. Therefore, financial resources and entrepreneurial abilities transferred from the traditional export sector, mainly coffee production and commercialization, to the novel manufacturing industries. (Furtado 1962, 94–95)

The second episode of note took place in Argentina, and its features were similar to those of the Brazilian episode. When the world crisis hit the country, the economic authorities' first reaction was an orthodox package.[1] But the crisis lasted longer than expected, and the package did not bring about good results; at the end of 1933, the government named new economic authorities, who launched the *Plan de Acción Económica Nacional.* Raúl Prebisch played an important role in devising the entire plan. In his words, "The *Plan de Acción Económica Nacional* was Keynesian, of economic expansion controlling the external sector with a selective exchange rate policy . . . and with two exchange markets: the controlled and the free one. In the first one we controlled everything. Imports were subject to selective prior authorization; exports were subject to a fixed price for the exchange. We subsidized those exports that we could not sell at international prices; namely, an internal subsidy. And financial services and nontraditional exports remained in the free market" (Magariños 1991, 94).

An important part of the plan was its proposal to set up a government institution (*Junta Reguladora de Granos*) in charge of the purchase of all cereal crops, at a price higher than the international one. The roles of the *Junta* were "i) to set minimum prices at which the State would buy all the cereal supplied; these prices stimulated farmers to plant and to harvest; ii) to control the supply of Argentine exports of cereal to the world market, to avoid a large drop in the price in times of overproduction" (González and Pollock 1991).

The plan contributed to the important economic recovery that took place in Argentina between 1933 and 1937. GDP grew by 5 percent yearly, which was a rate almost as high as the 5.7 percent achieved between 1920 and 1925, a fast-growth period. A greater use of the productive capacity allowed an economic upswing. Yet, per capita GDP in 1937 still lagged behind the level reached in 1929.

The experience gained with the world crisis left a deep imprint on all Latin American economies. Governments could see that it was possible to face the outside-induced recession with expansionary economic policy measures. Monetary and fiscal policies, in particular, were especially important to defend production and demand. Those economies that confronted the crisis with nonorthodox policies achieved positive results. Industry could respond to the greater demand with a greater use of capacity and supply, despite its small size and the low degree of development.

But the economic authorities also discovered that demand management without control of the external sector was impossible. They had to recognize the usefulness of instruments rejected by orthodox theory, such as foreign exchange control, or import tariffs. The institutions and instruments used to confront the crisis remained a part of the arsenal that Latin American countries would use in the future.

Last, but not least, the crisis forced the authorities as well as Latin American thinkers to embark on an autonomous reflection about economic policies. Recurrent crises had hit all countries of the region, but these had not been as deep and protracted as the one of the 1930s. In part because of this, Latin Americans had not had an opportunity to thoroughly reflect on the peculiarities of their economies and societies and on economic policies and strategies to confront external shocks. The experience of the crisis forced a new economic thinking in these countries.

The third episode I want to relate has more to do with ideas than with policymaking. It is again about Argentina, and again Prebisch is a central character.

Following 1937, there was a new economic downswing and, when World War Two erupted, new problems appeared, especially in the financial sector and on the external front. The European markets drastically reduced imports from Argentina, and the country had to transfer part of its demand for imports to the United States.

Under this new set-up, the Central Bank and the Ministry of Finance devised a national economic recovery plan (*Programa de Reactivación de la Economía Nacional*), which they proposed to Parliament in November 1940.[2]

The plan recognized the central role of the state in creating favorable conditions for the private sector, since the latter should be the dynamic economic agent. The plan argued that, through state intervention and especially through monetary policy, it would be possible to stimulate the economy. It thus proposed to inject a fair quantity of purchasing power and of demand into certain sectors especially affected by the crisis that, at the moment, seemed likely to respond to a greater demand with a greater output. The plan also devised a scheme to guarantee that the economic expansion would not cause insurmountable balance-of-payments problems. Following is a description of how the proponents of the plan expected to achieve economic recovery.

First, the state would purchase all wheat and corn harvests at a price higher than the world price. With this, they aimed to support producers and to avoid a drastic fall in international prices because of an excess supply. Second, the plan proposed an ambitious housing and building scheme, based on the idea that "when construction is doing well, all else will do well." The authors of the proposal stressed several important features of the construction industry. They recognized the existence of a large, unsatisfied demand; they suggested that demand expansion could rapidly mobilize idle productive capacity; and they underlined the low coefficient of imports of the industry and its important input-output connections with the rest of the economy.

Third, the plan aimed to stimulate import substitution of manufacturing goods, and it proposed financial support measures to achieve this aim. The starting point was the notion that "precisely the periods of major industrial development in Argentina had been the world crisis and the first European war. In other words, when the country was forced to industrialize to supply that which it could not import industrialization speeded up" (Prebisch 1991–1993, 4:158). Note that here we find an early rationalization of import-substitution industrialization, the view that ECLAC would later develop.

With regard to public expenditure policy, the authors of the plan took as their point of departure the following opinion: "In the prior world economic depression . . . the violent expenditures contraction . . . had worsened the problem. It created new unemployed and hit negatively industry, construction and economic activity. According to the government, [the emphasis now] is not about increasing administration expenditures, but about increasing the expenditure on the field of the private economy, without momentarily having to worry for the financial problem. As the economy recovers, the government will get greater revenues and greater opportunities to collect new tax payments. Thus we will easily solve the financial problem" (Prebisch 1991–1993, 157–58).

To finance the whole scheme, the plan proposed that the Central Bank organize an emergency medium- and long-term financing system for domestic economic activity. This should receive the necessary resources and instruments to carry out its activities. At the same time, the plan argued in favor of creating a long-term capital market, which then was almost nonexistent in Argentina.

Most importantly, the plan proposed that the emergency financing system of the Central Bank should have as essential the duty of turning short-term commercial bank deposits into fifteen-year loans for the industry and into twenty-five-year loans for construction. It also envisaged a specific procedure to increase the liquidity of the economy, which, in essence, amounted to decreasing the commercial banks' compulsory reserve coefficient. Commercial banks should transfer funds to the emergency financing system already mentioned. Banks, financial societies, and other private institutions would lend the money with resources provided by the Central Bank. Although these were private loans, the risk of the loans would be much reduced, for all of the engagements incurred by the supervising and approving organism of credit would be considered government obligations.

Last, but not least, the plan recognized that Argentina should remain an open economy. The country should make the best use of its natural comparative advantages, but it should also build new comparative advantages. Following are the measures that would achieve this objective (Llach 1984).

1. A commercial treaty with Brazil and extension of the treaty to other countries of the continent, with common commercial protectionist and preferential measures, to promote exchange with neighboring countries
2. Industrial export exchange incentives, especially for exports to the United States, since Argentina had a large commercial deficit with this country
3. Generalization of the draw-back regime
4. Special stimuli for industries processing national raw materials
5. A thorough revamping of tariffs and of the antidumping legislation

As we can see, the overall stance of the plan had clear Keynesian features. In particular, it stressed monetary and financial measures, instead of restricting itself to fiscal policy.[3]

Nevertheless, there was a feature of the plan that was novel and where it departed from Keynes's outlook. It did not pretend to close the country to foreign trade and capital flows, but it did propose a strict control of the external sector. To ensure that injection of purchasing power and of demand would not put more strain on the balance of payments, it proposed to drastically control the monetary circuit in its external connections. This would be achieved through import controls and through multiple exchange rates for different types of external payments. This idea represented, in Prebisch's words, "a clear evolution of the idea of how to make exchange control work. In its primitive conception exchange control was a mere restrictive instrument to achieve balance of payments equilibrium; we now see it as an instrument for strengthening domestic economic movements" (Prebisch 1991–1993, 159).

Unfortunately, Argentina never carried out this plan; for political reasons, the Argentine Congress denied its approval. Nevertheless, it stands out as the most remarkable Keynesian-oriented economic policy proposal in Latin America.

Raúl Prebisch's Early Thinking

It is important to discuss in more detail the remarkable career of Raúl Prebisch, the man who played the most important role in Latin American economic thought.[4]

Born in the Argentine province of Tucumán in 1901, Prebisch studied economics in Buenos Aires and became, even before completing his BA, a professor at the university. He combined teaching with an important career as a public servant, becoming Undersecretary of Finance at the age of twenty-nine and manager of the Central Bank, in whose conception he played a prominent role, at the age of thirty-four. He was one of the most influential economists with regard to Argentina's economic policy from the 1930s until 1943, when a new government terminated his employment with the bank.

There are interesting parallels between the personality of Prebisch and that of Keynes. Both were *political* economists. They had a great theoretical capacity; but, when they discussed theory, theirs was not abstract thinking but a reflection closely related to practical problems. Besides that, they were both reformists. They wanted to save capitalism, not destroy it through revolution. Therefore, they tried always to work closely with their governments and to devise policies that were susceptible for implementation in the existing social and political reality of their times. In fact, Prebisch did not have great qualms about working with a right-wing government issued from a coup d'état, probably because he felt that economic policies were politically neutral.

At the same time, Prebisch, just as much as Keynes, had been brought up in orthodox economics, and he remained committed to orthodoxy until the 1930s crisis showed him that traditional economic policy measures were useless. He was in an important economic position in his country when the crisis arrived and, from the first moment, acted to carry out a restrictive policy to confront it. It was only later, and precisely under the influence of Keynes, that he changed his approach to economic policy.[5]

Keynes's influence on Prebisch resulted from a series of papers the former wrote for *The* (London) *Times* in 1933, which he later published as *The Means to Prosperity* (Keynes 1939). Readers may recall that, in those papers, Keynes proposed that governments should stimulate or embark on large-scale loan-financed expenditure. He warned also that this required international coordination among leading capitalist countries. Keynes put forward his ideas to win over public opinion but especially to influence participants of the World Monetary Conference, organized by the League of Nations.

The League of Nations had invited Prebisch to Geneva, to take part in the preparatory work for the conference. Many years later he recollected:

> I became motivated by those five or six articles written [by Keynes] two years before his great book. . . . He turned from orthodoxy to a new heretic road. . . . I believe, after all this time, that these articles were much superior to the theorization he carried out later, in his great book. . . . It conquered me because. . . . I felt guilty of having proposed and carried out in Argentina in 1931 and half of 1932, a most orthodox economic policy, when I was Undersecretary of Finance. It was a contractionary policy, according to the orthodox theory ruling at the time, whereby the crisis could only be overcome with a series of austerity measures. . . . But afterwards, thinking on this experience and seeing the world depression continued . . . I began to have many doubts about the orthodox theory. And I started to think about an expansionary policy. This is why I was so much attracted by Keynes's articles, which converted me towards an expansionary policy. (Magariños 1991, 100)

Prebisch would also express his disappointment at the failure of the World Monetary Conference to take up Keynes's ideas. Neville Chamberlain, the Chancellor of the Exchequer at the time, gave a speech without any reference to Keynes's proposals or to expansionary policies. The U.S. delegation also remained within the confines of orthodox thinking.

As mentioned, Prebisch kept his key role in shaping and carrying out economic policy in Argentina from the Central Bank. After Prebisch left the bank and before he came to ECLAC in 1948, he devoted himself mostly to teaching and writing, and he developed his economic ideas in conferences held in several Latin American countries. The experience Prebisch had gained in government during the crisis, in teaching, and in his exchange with Latin American colleagues, stimulated him to further develop his own views and some he had taken from Keynes. Earlier I mentioned the textbook he wrote where he introduced the Latin American public to *The General Theory of Employment, Interest and Money*. It is a well-written book, still very much worth reading. However, in the book, Prebisch did not contrast his own theories with those of Keynes's. In fact, although he agreed in many areas with the author of *The General Theory*, his thinking departed from that of Keynes in some important aspects.

First, his experience led him to deduce that, in Argentina, the main autonomous determinant of effective demand, and of the overall level of economic activity, was not investment but exports (Prebisch 1991–1993, vol. 2, chaps. 89 and 113). One reason is that exports weighed heavily on demand. Also, he had noticed that exports as well as capital inflows move in sympathy, following the world cycle. He had also found that the external sector determines commercial bank lending, which amplifies the upswings and downswings of the balance of payments (Prebisch 1991–1993, vol. 2, chaps. 107 and 113). Therefore, exports and capital movements also shape private domestic demand.

There was a second reason why Prebisch thought exports are the key macroeconomic variable. Namely, if domestic demand rises, for whatever reason, that rise cannot go too far. Sooner or later, the balance-of-payments deficit brings the domestic upswing to a halt. Therefore, he proposed that, in the Argentine economy, cycles are not endogenous. Exports demand, as well as external capital inflows and outflows, shape the cycle (Prebisch 1991–1993, vol. 2, chaps. 107 and 113).

He therefore inferred that exports play a dual macroeconomic role, similar to investment in developed economies. On the one hand, they contribute to shape aggregate demand.[6] But, besides that—and this is more important in developing economies—export growth provides the foreign exchange without which output expansion cannot take place.

Prebisch later extended these ideas to the whole of Latin America. Also, they led him to frame his key concept of central and peripheral economies. He referred especially to Great Britain during its period as the center of the capitalist world. In that country, the domestic currency could fulfill its function as a store of wealth. Also, monetary authorities had a certain degree of control over the balance of payments. By raising the interest rate, they could easily attract foreign capital. This could offset any negative trade balance (Prebisch 1991–1993, vol. 2, chaps. 107 and 113). Developing economies did not have that option. Their growth was more dependent on the world economy, over whose course they had no influence.

Latin American governments and economists were aware of the overwhelming importance of the world economy for their countries. Therefore, they followed closely the discussions and proposals that finally became encapsulated in the Bretton Woods agreements.[7] Prebisch reflected a lot on these discussions. He considered that the rules agreed on there could help in the pursuit of full employment policies throughout the world. But he remarked that these rules, and the overall architecture of the International Monetary Fund, did not consider the needs of developing countries (Prebisch, 1991–1993, vol. 2, chap. 107).[8]

Besides, Prebisch thought that these rules, by themselves, could not ensure full employment. The latter needed domestic policy measures geared to that objective, and he therefore considered full employment on a world scale a precondition for multilateralism. On this, he assigned a key role to the economic policy stance within the United States. He called attention to the low import coefficient of that economy, which weakened the transmission of domestic and international impulses to the rest of the world. He also viewed of utmost importance the autonomy of individual countries to take defensive domestic and international policy measures if the world economy was stagnant, or if they were confronted with a world slump.

The last position explains why, until nearly the end of his life, he defended the so-called Roca-Runciman Pact of 1933 between Argentina and the United Kingdom (Magariños 1991, 85–87). This was a bilateral trade agreement, where each country gave preferences to the other without extending them to other countries. Keynes would surely have criticized the agreement as a typical expression of what he used to call "Schajtian" economics,[9] to which he was fervently opposed. However, Prebisch considered that, in a world slump, countries had to take whatever defensive economic measures they thought necessary, even if these went against the rules of multilateralism. Also, he believed that Argentina, the weaker country, had gained from that pact. He argued that, although Argentina may have had to grant important concessions to the UK, it nevertheless could defend a certain share of the UK market for its exports, and the latter could not have been sold, and perhaps not even produced, if the pact had not existed.

Prebisch, ECLAC, and Latin American Structuralist Economic Thought

Prebisch had shown his abilities to organize and lead a research working party while he was at the Argentine Central Bank, where he gathered an outstanding think tank. When he came to ECLAC as its executive secretary, he repeated that experience; but now he had greater material resources as well as a continental staff and field of interest. He assembled the most exceptional economics research team that has ever existed in Latin America. This team would have an enormous impact on economic thinking and policy at ECLAC and in Latin American countries.

Prebisch was not only the formal head of ECLAC but also its intellectual leader. He had the experience and the academic background.[10] Latin

Americans predominated on the team, and its members were generally young and had a more leftist leaning. Also, they came from different intellectual environments and field of interests.[11] For example, Brazilians such as Celso Furtado brought with them the debate around the need for industrialization, inspired to a certain extent by the theory of Manoilescu (1931).[12] Mexicans such as Juan F. Noyola brought with them the experience of the first social revolution that took place on the continent. Chileans such as Anibal Pinto and Jorge Ahumada had been influenced by the political experience of the government of the Frente Popular in the late 1930s and 1940s. Also, the younger members of the group had probably more of an inclination than Prebisch to combine economic with historical and sociopolitical analysis.

On the other hand, when ECLAC started its life, Keynesian economics had evolved. Several economists, most of them inspired by the work of Keynes, had carried out an important reflection on industrialization in the backward economies of Europe (Rosenstein-Rodan 1943; Mandelbaum 1945). Also, economic thinking that had developed in peripheral countries started to receive a wider audience in the rest of the world, while the independence of former colonies came to occupy a central stage in the debate on the prospects for developing economies. All of these ideas inspired economists from Latin America and from ECLAC.[13]

A rich cross-fertilization of ideas and perspectives took place at ECLAC, where economic analysis and theory blended with economic and social history and sociology. Surely this was the first group of Latin American economists with a clear Keynesian inspiration. They were able to develop a new paradigm in economics. It was mostly inspired by Prebisch's outlook and by Keynes's economic theory. But it had its own peculiarities. This paradigm came to be known as Latin American structuralism. Following are the main ideas of this paradigm.[14]

First, structuralism recognized as one of the most outstanding characteristics of underdevelopment the existence of a huge pool of structural or disguised unemployment in the countryside and in the cities, coexisting with scarce capital equipment and infrastructure.[15] Structuralism noticed that greater use of capacity could raise the demand for labor, even in the short run. But a persistent rise of aggregate demand would face important bottlenecks. Structuralism inferred that simple demand management policies would not be enough to absorb the whole labor surplus. Therefore, macroeconomic strategy in Latin American economies should stress capital accumulation and long-run, rather than pure short-run, demand-side policies (Prebisch 1951; Furtado 1953; Sunkel 1957).

Secondly, structuralists put a heavy emphasis on the asymmetrical nature of the economic world system. Prebisch is mostly known because of his criticism of the orthodox theory of international trade. We can summarize his essential ideas as follows (Prebisch 1949, 1950, and 1960–1961).

He argued that, in the world economy, central and peripheral economies interact in an asymmetrical way. Countries belonging to the center are characterized not only by higher per capita income but also by the production and export of goods and services where technical progress rises swiftly and for which world demand grows at fast rates. Further, thanks to their institutions and socioeconomic structure, they can keep for themselves the fruits of technical progress, without prices falling concurrently with cost declines. By contrast, underdeveloped countries specialize in raw materials and foodstuff, where technical progress is not very fast and for which world demand normally grows at a modest pace. This, coupled with the huge amount of surplus labor and fierce competition among producers in the world market, brings about a declining trend for their export prices and terms of trade.

Finally, structuralists saw in industrialization the best choice for Latin American countries. They argued that, if Latin American economies tried to grow by simply reproducing their pattern of specialization, the declining trend for the terms of trade would persist. They based their prediction on the experience of countries having an important share in world exports of agricultural or mineral goods, such as Argentina, Brazil, and Chile. Efforts to expand production and gain a larger share of world demand usually entailed a large decline in prices (Prebisch 1949, 1950, and 1960–1961).

Structuralists did not support import-substituting industries at whatever the cost. But they considered that what really matter are social costs and prices. They underpinned this outlook with the notion that market costs and prices are distorted, especially in underdeveloped economies. In particular, they do not give satisfactory information on macroeconomic costs and benefits (Prebisch 1951). Therefore, underdeveloped economies need barriers to protect the domestic market. But these should be purely temporary measures, needed only to give breathing space to new industries until they became efficient and competitive.

Structuralists recouped an outlook previously developed by economists such as List (1856), Manoilescu (1931), and other supporters of industrialization in backward economies. But the Latin America theory of what came to be known as import-substitution industrialization added new arguments to an old notion (Love 1996).

We can draw here an interesting contrast between Keynes and the structuralist view of unemployment. Keynes, at least in *The General Theory*, stressed the *short run* and saw the main reasons for unemployment in the *malfunctioning of the domestic economy*. Structuralists emphasized the *long run* and saw the cause of unemployment as the negative effects of the *international economy*, which stimulated a pattern of specialization unfavorable for economic growth. Therefore, Latin American structuralists built a long-run theory of growth and employment for peripheral open economies.

On the other hand, Keynes and the structuralists had similar views about the institutional setting that they envisaged for the design of macroeconomic strategy. Latin American structuralists considered that partnership between the private and the public sectors was necessary to foster economic growth. Further, this partnership required a careful planning of investment and of the whole economy. This preference for a planned "mixed economy" coincided with the previous experience of the region during the world crisis and World War Two. At that time, most countries had put into place important institutions, especially development banks, whereby the government supported private investment or carried out investment jointly with the private sector. Also, most governments agreed with the idea of planning economic development. There was the seeming success of the communist countries; and most advanced capitalist nations were planning their economies in the period of reconstruction effort that followed World War Two. But this outlook also coincided with Keynes's overall vision, such as developed during his participation in the MacMillan Commission in the 1920s in Great Britain (Keynes 1971–1989, vol. 19), and was encapsulated in *The General Theory* in his notion of the "socialization of investments" (Crotty 1999; Carvalho, forthcoming).

Following is a brief outline of the long-run Latin American structuralist theory of growth and employment. We may start with the dynamic employment equation (in fact and identity), where ξ is the rate of growth of employment, y is the actual rate of growth of output, and α is the average rate of growth of labor productivity. Namely:

(1) $\xi = y - \alpha$

In the structuralists' theory, the long-term growth of the economy results from the interaction of demand and supply and of internal and external factors. Also, they understood the long run as the outcome of a succession of short-run periods, where each short-run period affects the long run, mostly through its influence on investment. They viewed, at least by implication, the long-run period's output growth rate as the upshot of the interplay between three rates of growth: of effective demand, y^D; of productive capacity, y^K; and of output compatible with external equilibrium, y^X. In symbols:

(2) $y = \min(y^D, y^K, y^X)$

Structuralists accepted that the state could shape effective demand through state expenditure and through monetary policy. On the other hand, they stressed the negative influence that the income inequality that was widespread in Latin American had on aggregate demand and growth. In their view, income inequality has multifarious effects on long-run growth (more on this later).

Structuralists also used Domar's well-known formula to specify the rate of growth of the productive capacity (Prebisch 1951; Furtado 1953). Namely:

(3) $$y^K = \frac{i}{k} - \delta$$

where y^K is the growth rate of the productive capacity, k is the capital-output ratio, i is the relative share of gross investment in GDP, and δ is the (effective) depreciation rate, that is, the output loss caused by elimination of the old capital equipment (as a relative share of GDP).

Finally, to express the growth rate of output compatible with external equilibrium (y^X), Prebisch, in fact, anticipated the so-called Thirlwall's Law. That is:

(4) $$y^X = \frac{x}{\pi}$$

where x is the rate of growth of exports and π is the income-elasticity of imports. We also assume that no foreign credits are available.

Structuralists further argued that a high rate of growth of output faces three important barriers.

The first barrier has to do with the difficulty of raising the share of investment (i in equation 3). High income concentration, pervasive in the region, seemingly should be beneficial for investment. But it is not, in fact, because of the high consumption propensity of the rich and the well-to-do.[16] Also, the pattern of technical progress and the price system favor capital-intensive investment and premature scrapping of capital equipment, thus raising parameters k and δ. Structuralists argued also that changes in the pattern of demand and of production tend to raise the capital-output ratio. On the one hand, income concentration and the "international demonstration effect" bias demand in favor of "modern" goods, characterized by high-capital intensity. Besides, when import-substitution industrialization advances from light to heavy industries, capital requirements per unit of output grow because of the technical necessities of production. The rises in k and in δ have a harmful effect on the growth rate of the productive capacity.

The second barrier to raising the growth rate of output is inflation. Here I think it necessary to say a few words about the structuralist theory of inflation, which, to my mind, was and remains an important contribution to economic theory. In the structuralist view, disequilibria between demand and supply of particular sectors provoke inflation. Thus, growth acceleration in underdeveloped economies will easily bring about inflation, because of bottlenecks omnipresent in these economies. Note that the term "structural" refers not only to the long-lasting nature of the disequilibrium but also implies that it will not be overcome by simply changing relative prices. In other words, the rise in the relative price and profitability of the laggard sector does not bring about a sufficient increase in the rate of expansion of its supply; it lags behind the rate of growth of demand.

Structuralist authors identified two such typical disequilibria. One is between the rapid rate of growth of demand and the sluggish growth of supply of agricultural goods.[17] The second one arises because a slow rate of growth of the import capacity confronts a high rate of growth of the demand for foreign exchange. As Noyola put it in his seminal paper, "The basic inflationary pressure in Mexico has . . . arisen out of the incapability of exports to grow at the same rate as the domestic economy. Thus balance of payment disequilibria have appeared, which have brought about repeated currency depreciations. Exchange rate subsidies have not been able to mitigate the impact of depreciation on the domestic price level" (1956 [1987: 74]).

Noyola also proposed that monetary expansion was not the original cause of inflation but rather a "propagation" mechanism that allowed the price rise to persist. Finally, he argued that the needs of trade endogenously brought about money expansion. In his words, "Credit expansion . . . has been the most passive of the propagation mechanisms. Its role has been to provide the economy with enough liquidity in real terms. Liquidity follows the rate of growth of prices" (Noyola 1956 [1987: 73]).[18]

In the structuralist view, inflation does not directly harm the rate of growth of output. However, it does contribute to a shift of income from low- to high-income groups, with a negative impact on effective demand. Besides that, the government policy stance normally becomes contractionary under conditions of high inflation, which also depresses demand.

The third obstacle to raising the growth rate of output is the foreign trade barrier encapsulated in equation 4. Structuralists considered that any economy should preserve an external trade equilibrium in the long run. Therefore, the growth rate compatible with the external equilibrium rate will normally be the one that finally plays the role of a binding constraint on long-run growth. So, the sustainable rate of growth cannot exceed the difference between the growth rate of exports and the coefficient growth rate of imports.

I mentioned the close connection between the notion of the foreign-exchange limit to growth specified by structuralists and the so-called Thirlwall's Law (1979). However, structuralists stressed mostly the supply side of their theory. They claimed that import substitution needed the build-up of new productive capacities, which called for capital accumulation, especially in the import-substitution industries.

Structuralists gave prominence to the reduction of the import coefficient through import-substitution industrialization rather than export promotion. As mentioned, they were skeptics on the long-term evolution of demand for Latin American traditional exports. Also, they considered that manufacturing exports were unviable without a well-developed industrial basis. They saw enough space for substitution, given the high import coefficient for manufacturing goods; but they also anticipated problems in the medium and the long run, because the import elasticity might start growing after an initial decline. The most significant reasons were two: First, as it advances, import substitution inevitably reaches a more difficult stage, because durable consumer goods and capital goods production need high technical knowledge and large markets, which are often beyond the reach of underdeveloped economies; second, income concentration biases consumer demand in favor of sophisticated goods with a high import content (Tavares 1964; Furtado 1966; Furtado and Maneschi 1968; Furtado and Sousa 1970).

I close this presentation of the structuralist long-run theory of growth and employment by bringing to mind a well-known image: "We must remind ourselves that there may be several slips between the cup and the lip." Paraphrasing Keynes (1971–1989, 7:173), we may say: For whilst an increase in the rate of growth of output may be expected, *ceteris paribus*, to reduce unemployment, this will not happen if the rate of growth of labor productivity accelerates. Structuralists stressed that, in Latin America, absorption of the huge labor reserve was made more difficult because the growth rate of labor productivity was unnecessarily elevated. In fact, modernization *cum* income concentration brought about this result, which hampered employment growth in Latin American economies. This was yet another reason why the structuralists placed so much emphasis on the long run.

Final Remarks

We are here today paying homage to Keynes. We all think he was a remarkable economist, for many the greatest of the last century. But each one of us could give a different reason for his or her admiration. What I wanted to do with the story I told here is to stress his influence in economic thinking. That influence went far beyond people working in the advanced societies about which Keynes reflected. The impact of his ideas on Latin American scholars was enormous; through them, he influenced policymaking in our countries. I tried here to show how much Keynes's thoughts and theory shaped the outlook of Raúl Prebisch, the greatest economist from our part of the world, and that of his associates at ECLAC.

Fortunately, Prebisch and his coworkers shared one obsession. They wanted, above all, to understand their societies in order to be able to transform them. They also had the conviction that our economies and societies have important peculiarities, which determine the economic regularities that theories should try to identify. This is why they not only received but also further developed Keynesian economics. Thanks to all of these people, we in Latin America also had our "years of high theory."

Notes

1. However, this included some nonorthodox measures, such as exchange control, progressive income taxes, and import tariffs.
2. Federico Pinedo, the Finance Minister, proposed the plan to Parliament; it therefore came to be known as the "Pinedo Plan." However, most students of the period consider Prebisch the developer of the proposal. The full text is available in Prebisch 1991–1993, vol. 2, chap. 92.
3. Kregel 1994–1995 and Carvalho 1997 rightly stress this emphasis of Keynes's overall vision.
4. For more details, see González del Solar 2006; Magariños 1991; González and Pollock 1991; Settimi, Audino, and Tohmé 2006; Mallorquín 2006.
5. Prebisch's change in economic outlook was probably also influenced by an intellectual group active in Argentina that was led by engineer-economist A. Bunge, who had for a long time been recommending protection of the domestic market and industrialization.
6. Interestingly, in some of the course books Prebisch wrote for his classes, he took a different point of departure than most textbooks when he developed the idea of the multiplier. Exports, not investment, were the autonomous part of demand shaping aggregate demand. In this sense, the Harrod (1933) foreign-trade multiplier was important in Prebisch's theory. By the way, Prebisch also argued that it is not the saving propensity, but the import coefficient, which ensures that a (positive) demand shock will not lead to an ever-increasing GDP.
7. *El Trimestre Económico*, the most prestigious Latin American journal of economics during that period, devoted a special issue (vol. 10 [3], of 1943) to the debate over the monetary proposals.
8. Keynes had written: "Twenty-one countries have been invited which clearly have nothing to contribute and merely encumber the grounds, namely Colombia, Costa Rica, Dominica, Ecuador, Salvador, Guatemala, Haiti, Honduras, Liberia, Nicaragua, Panama, Paraguay, Philippines, Venezuela, Peru, Uruguay, Ethiopia, Iceland, Iran, Iraq, Luxembourg. The most monstrous monkey-house assembled for years. To this might perhaps be added: Egypt, Chile and . . . Yugoslavia" (Keynes 1971–1989, vol. 26, p. 42).
9. The term was coined after Hjalmar Schajt (1877–1970), a German economist. He was the president of Germany's central bank and Minister of Economics between the mid-1920s and the late 1930s. He devised a series of bilateral trade agreements between Germany and less developed European countries. These were much criticized because they hampered multilateralism and because they allegedly benefited only Germany, harming its weaker associates.
10. Celso Furtado, who would become Prebisch's second-in-command, was more than fifteen years younger.
11. Love 1996 gives a beautiful account of this part of the story.
12. Manoilescu, who originally published in 1929 in his native Romania, was published in Brazil in 1931, with a special preface by the author.
13. See especially Arndt 1987 and Love 1996.

14. Please note: I do not imply that the ideas that follow were a pure Latin American invention, because economists dealing with underdeveloped economies had anticipated many of them. But Prebisch and his coworkers put them together in an original way. I will refer to this school of thought as structuralism and to the group of economists sharing this outlook as structuralists. Probably the most complete account is in Rodríguez 1980. I have also borrowed a lot of ideas from Puchet 2004.
15. At a more advanced stage of industrialization, and in close collaboration with the International Labor Office, ECLAC economists further developed their understanding of the labor market in Latin American societies. They recognized that part of the active population without employment in the "modern" or "formal" sector must work in the "informal" sector. They also stressed that the formal sector is heterogeneous, i.e., modern activities where productivity is high coexist with low-productivity "backward" activities. They added that the formal and informal sectors interact unequally, because output of the former determines output of the latter, i.e., the informal sector lacks the capacity for self-determination (Pinto 1965).
16. Structuralists did not always recognize that a rise in the saving propensity would simply reduce the rate of growth of demand. Thus, for example: "Even though it [the problem of saving in underdeveloped countries] is the key problem of economic development, it is usually misunderstood. What is missing in our economy are not investment stimuli, but saving incentives" (Furtado 1953, 120).
17. Kalecki had stressed this point in a lecture given in Mexico (Kalecki 1954). Noyola (1956) and Sunkel (1958), who wrote the original contributions to this theory, recognized the influence of Kalecki in their line of reasoning.
18. The analysis of disequilibrium between supply and demand for agricultural output is at the center of an interesting dynamical model written almost four decades ago (Olivera 1967). However, the impact of external disequilibrium on inflation has not been formalized to the same extent (but see Ros 2000 and López and Mansilla 2007).

References

Arndt, H. W. 1987. *Economic development: The history of an idea.* Chicago: University of Chicago Press.

Carvalho, F. 1997. Economic policies for monetary economies: Keynes's economic policy proposals for an unemployment-free economy. *Brazilian Journal of Political Economy* 17 (4): 31–51.

Carvalho, F. Forthcoming. Keynes and the reform of the capitalist social order. In *Keynes and macroeconomics after 70 years: Critical assessments of* The General Theory, ed. Mathew Forstater and L. Randall Wray. Cheltenham, UK: Edward Elgar.

Crotty, J. 1999. Was Keynes a corporatist? Keynes's radical views on industrial policy and macro policy in the 1920s. *Journal of Economic Issues* 33 (3): 555–78.

Furtado, C. 1953. La formación del capital y el desarrollo económico. *El Trimestre Económico* 20 (77): 88–121.

———. 1954. *A economia Brasileira.* Rio de Janeiro: Ed. A Noite.

———. 1962. *La formación económica del Brasil.* México: Fondo de Cultura Económica.

———. 1966. *Subdesenvolvimento e estagnação na América Latina.* Rio de Janeiro: Editora Civilização Brasileira.

Furtado, C., and A. Maneschi. 1968. Um modelo simulado de desenvolvimento e estagnação na América Latina. *Revista Brasileira de Economia* 12:5–32.

Furtado, C., and A. Sousa. 1970. Los perfiles de la demanda y de la inversión. *El Trimestre Económico* 37 (147): 463–87.

Galbraith, John K. 2001. How Keynes came to America. In *The essential Galbraith,* ed. Andrea D. Williams. Boston: Houghton Mifflin.

González del Solar, J. 2006. Conversaciones con Raúl Prebisch. In Textos para el estudio del pensamiento de Raúl Prebisch, C. Mallorquín. *Cinta de Moebio, Electronic Journal of Social Sciences Epistemology* 25 (March).

González, N., and D. Pollock. 1991. Del ortodoxo al conservador ilustrado: Raúl Prebisch en la Argentina. *Desarrollo Económico* 30 (120): 455–86.

Gurrieri, Adolfo, ed. 1982. *La obra de Prebisch en la CEPAL.* México: Fondo de Cultura Económica.

Harrod, R. 1933. *International economics.* Cambridge, UK: Cambridge University Press.

Kalecki, M. 1954. The problem of financing economic development. In *Collected works of Michal Kalecki,* ed. J. Osiatynsky. Vol. 5. Oxford: Oxford University Press, 1993.

Keynes, J. M. 1939. *The means to prosperity.* London: MacMillan. Repr. in Keynes 1971–1989, vol. 9.

———. 1971–1989. *The collected writings of John Maynard Keynes.* Ed. D. E. Moggridge and E. A. G. Robinson. 30 vols. London: Macmillan, for the Royal Economic Society.

Kregel, J. 1994–1995. The viability of economic policy and the priorities of economic policy. *Journal of Post Keynesian Economics* 17 (2): 261–77.

List, George Friedrich. 1856. *National system of political economy.* Philadelphia: Lippincott.

Llach, J. J. 1984. El Plan Pinedo de 1940, su significado histórico y los orígenes del la economía política del Peronismo. *Desarrollo Económico* 23 (89): 515–58.

Lopez, J., and R. Mansilla, 2007. The structuralist theory of inflation and beyond. In *Ideas, policies and economic development in the Americas,* ed. E. Perez and M. Vernengo, New York: Routledge Studies in Development Economics.

Love, J. L. 1996. *Crafting the Third World: Theorizing underdevelopment in Romania and Brazil.* Stanford, CA: Stanford University Press.

Magariños, M. 1991. *Diálogos con Raúl Prebisch.* México: Fondo de Cultura Económica.

Mallorquín, C. 2006. Raúl Prebisch antes de la era de hielo. In *Raúl Prebisch: El poder, los principios y la ética del desarrollo*, ed. E. Dosman. Buenos Aires: INTAL.

Mandelbaum, K. 1945. *The Industrialization of backward areas.* Oxford: Basil Blackwell.

Manoilescu, M. 1931. *The theory of protection and international trade.* London: P. S. King and Son.

Noyola, J. 1956. El desarrollo económico y la inflación en México y otros países Latinoamericanos. *Investigación Económica* 16 (4): 603–48. A new version appears in *Desequilibrio externo e inflación, Investigación Económica,* ed. Facultad de Economía, Universidad Nacional Autónoma de México, 1987.

Olivera, J. H. G. 1967. Aspectos dinámicos de la inflación estructural. *Desarrollo económico* 17 (7): 261–66.

Osiatynsky, J., ed. 1993. *Developing economies.* Vol. 5 of *Collected works of Michal Kalecki.* Oxford: Oxford University Press.

Pinto, A. 1965. Concentración del progreso técnico y de sus frutos en el desarrollo Latinoamericano. *El Trimestre Económico* 32 (4): 432–60.

Prebisch, R. 1949. El desarrollo económico de la América Latina y algunos de sus principales problemas. In *La obra de Prebisch en la CEPAL*, ed. Adolfo Gurrieri. México: Fondo de Cultura Económica, 1982.

———. 1950. Crecimiento, desequilibrios y disparidades: Interpretación del proceso de desarrollo económico. In *La obra de Prebisch en la CEPAL*, ed. Adolfo Gurrieri. México: Fondo de Cultura Económica, 1982.

———. 1951. Problemas teóricos y prácticos del crecimiento económico. In *La obra de Prebisch en la CEPAL*, ed. Adolfo Gurrieri. México: Fondo de Cultura Económica, 1982.

———. 1960–1961. La política comercial en los países insuficientemente desarrollados. In *La obra de Prebisch en la CEPAL*, ed. Adolfo Gurrieri. México: Fondo de Cultura Económica, 1982.

———. 1991–1993. *Obras, 1919–1948.* Buenos Aires: Fundación Raúl Prebisch.

Puchet, M. 2004. Contribuciones teóricas del pensamiento económico al desarrollo Latinoamericano. *Economía UNAM* 3 (September–December): 115–29.

Rodríguez, O. 1980. *La teoría del subdesarrollo de la CEPAL.* México: Siglo XXI Editores.

Ros, J. 2000. *Development theory and the economics of growth.* Ann Arbor, MI: University of Michigan Press.

Rosenstein-Rodan, P. 1943. Problems of industrialization of Eastern and South-Eastern Europe. *The Economic Journal* 53 (210): 202–11.

Settimi, S. M., P. Audino, and F. Tohmé. 2006. The road from orthodoxy towards structuralism: The influence of John Maynard Keynes on the economics of Raúl Prebisch. Working paper, Departamento de Economía Universidad Nacional del Sur.

Sunkel, O. 1957. Cuál es la utilidad práctica de la teoría del multiplicador? *El Trimestre Económico* 24 (3): 251–75.

———. 1958. La inflación Chilena: Un enfoque heterodoxo. *El Trimestre Económico* 25 (4): 570–99.

Tavares, M. C. 1964. The growth and decline of import substitution in Brazil. *Economic Bulletin for Latin America* 9 (1): 1–59.

Thirlwall, A. P. 1979. The balance of payments constraint as an explanation of international growth rate differences. *Banca Nazionale del Lavoro Quarterly Review* 128:45–53.

CHAPTER 7

THE CONTINUING POLICY RELEVANCE OF KEYNES'S *GENERAL THEORY*

JAN KREGEL

INTRODUCTION

TODAY, KEYNES'S *General Theory of Employment, Interest and Money* is primarily considered part of the history of economics, rather than a guide to economic policy for the new millennium. This is primarily the result of what were considered to be theoretical errors and weaknesses in the theory that Keynes put forward in the book. Most of these criticisms appeared in the immediate postwar period, which, paradoxically, was the period in which Keynesian "policy" was being applied in almost all developed countries and was taken as the foundation for the restructuring of the postwar international trade and financial system.

THREE EARLY MISINTERPRETATIONS OF *THE GENERAL THEORY*

An early criticism was that *The General Theory* was designed to combat the high levels of unemployment experienced during the Great Slump of the 1920s and 1930s. It was thus only "depression economics," without application outside rare periods of extremely depressed global economic activity. It was not useful for the reconstruction and boom that followed the war.

Another early criticism was that Keynes's analysis was undertaken in "real terms," dealing only with levels of real output, investment measured in wage units, and so forth. It thus had no explanation of the level of nominal prices and, in particular, the impact of money on prices, that is, inflation, since in the slump the problem was not considered important—rather, the opposite. The theory was thus considered incapable of dealing with the problems of inflation.

A third, related criticism was raised somewhat later: Not only was there no explanation of nominal prices, but there was no explanation of relative prices, since the theory dealt only with aggregate output, wage units, and so forth. There was no connection between its macroeconomic, aggregate relationships and the underlying individual decisions that determine those aggregate outcomes. The theory was thus considered to lack a "microeconomic" foundation for its "macroeconomic" analysis.

It is interesting that neither Keynes nor any of his immediate associates ever used the term "macroeconomics" in presenting his theory. Nonetheless, these criticisms brought forth the so-called "neoclassical synthesis," in which traditional Chicago-style price theory was proposed as the complement to Keynesian macro analysis. When the inconsistencies in this approach became too obvious, it was replaced by what was called a "new" Keynesian micro approach that placed restrictions on the adjustment of prices and/or quantities in competitive labor and product markets for institutional or other reasons, while the return of inflationary conditions produced the monetarist counterrevolution. Less than fifty years after publication of the book, it was possible to find textbook writers proposing a return to "classical" economics.

Setting the Record Straight

Anyone who has taken the trouble to attempt to understand *The General Theory*, or even read just the title of the book from beginning to end and attempted to understand that, should recognize that none of these criticisms are well-founded.

Consider the first criticism. In a short pamphlet called *How to Pay for the War* (Keynes 1940), prepared in the late 1930s as the basis for British economic policy in support of the war effort, Keynes showed how his theory applied to conditions of full employment as well as depression. Indeed, Keynes intended his theory to be general in the sense that it provided the explanation of why the economy could reach equilibrium at any level of employment and economic activity, including an overfull-employment war economy. The objective of Keynes's pamphlet was to show how the economy could produce at its maximum productive potential without producing the inflation and massive indebtedness that had characterized the First World War—and which he considered one of the major causes of the Second World War. Thus, it is quite clear that the theory can be, and was, applied outside of conditions of depression.

Further, it was the use of Keynes's theory in war planning and postwar reconstruction that provided the definition and construction of the statistics of "macroeconomic aggregates"[1] that we now see in national income and expenditure accounting. It was this experience that provided the basis for the dominance of Keynesian thinking in economic policymaking in the immediate postwar theory. Indeed, Harrod confirms that the majority of the UK Treasury economics staff working on policy problems after the war was brought up on Keynes's theory. Thus, the criticism that the theory applies only to conditions of recession is clearly false.

Second, those who believe that Keynes's analysis deals only with real macroeconomic aggregates ignore one of the most important aspects of the theory—that aggregates of real economic quantities never appear in Keynes's book. In fact, he argued that this was simply impossible and instead followed the tradition of the Scottish Enlightenment descending from John Locke and David Hume in considering the wealth of the nation to be found in its labor force. For this reason, Keynes always conducted his analysis in terms of labor units, rather than in nominal terms or in real terms. He argued that wage levels and the dispersion of wages tended to change much less rapidly than other variables and thus provided a more reliable standard.

Further, if one looks carefully at Keynes's supply and demand analysis, which in modern textbooks is presented as a relationship between aggregate prices and real quantities, one finds neither variable. Instead, Keynes uses a relationship between expected aggregate supply prices and expected aggregate demand prices and levels of employment. Very clear presentations of this point are to be found in the presentation of Keynes's aggregate supply and demand analysis provided by Sidney Weintraub (1958) and Paul Davidson and Eugene Smolensky (1964).

This provides the counter argument to the third criticism noted above, that Keynes was not concerned with price theory or inflation or monetary factors. As already noted, his aggregate supply and demand analysis represented a relationship between aggregate supply and demand prices and units of employment. Thus, nominal prices are present from the very beginning.

But, more importantly, these are money prices, because Keynes borrowed from Marx the insight that decisions to provide employment are made by entrepreneurs who are totally uninterested in real returns or real productivity. What they are interested in is the differential between their money outlays today relative to the money returns that can be expected to be earned in the future—nominal profitability. Thus, Keynes followed Marx in conducting his analysis in terms of M-C-M', the generation of a monetary surplus (see Keynes 1979, 66 and 82–83). The entrepreneur's decision was based on the relationship between money today and money tomorrow, or, more simply, the relation between the spot price of productive activity relative to its forward price. If forward prices are above spot prices, then entrepreneurs earn a profit and are willing to engage their wealth to employ workers to produce goods for future sale. Thus, Joan Robinson's suggestion that Keynes never took the five minutes necessary to understand price theory refers only to the neoclassical theory of real relative prices—real rates of exchange at a given point in time—because he thought it was inapplicable to a monetary economy in which expectations of future conditions have a direct impact on current prices and decisions. A price theory that applies to an entrepreneur capitalist economy was different from the price theory taught in microeconomic textbooks. The need to provide a neoclassical micro foundation of macroeconomics is thus also unnecessary and fails to recognize the novel approach to the formation of prices and their linkage to entrepreneurial decision-making in the level of employment that was at the heart of Keynes's book.

In this, it is clear that Keynes departed from traditional neoclassical theories of supply and demand such as those found in Marshall, where prices are determined by microeconomic decisions of consumers to buy and producers to supply. Instead, in Keynes's theory, the only microeconomic decisions are undertaken by entrepreneurs who balance present prices against future prices.

According to Keynes, in *Treatise on Money* (1930) he still considered money as something separate from the theory of prices determined by supply and demand but, in *The General Theory*, money was an integral part of the theory of prices and the theory of prices had become an integral part of the theory of the determination of output as a whole (Keynes 1936).

Thus, it should be clear from even a superficial acquaintance with the book that the theory was general in the sense that it applied to both depression and full-employment economics. It was not a theory of real variables, and it was not a theory that overlooks either the formation of prices or the role of money in determining the relation between spot and future prices; it was an attempt to forge a new approach to the analysis of a monetary economy that Keynes defined as "a method of analyzing the economic behaviour of the present under the influence of changing ideas about the future."

Understanding *The General Theory*: Reading the Title First

The question then remains: What exactly was Keynes's theory if all of the criticisms have been wide of the mark? Perhaps the easiest way to understand the theory for those unable to take the time and the effort necessary to read and understand its revolutionary approach is to read the title of the book.

The title states very clearly that the objective is the determination of the level of employment. Note that neither unemployment nor prices appear in the title (although Harrod at one stage mistakenly suggested they did). This reflects the fact that Keynes was looking at the possibility of a wide range of levels of employment, a range that went from depression economics to full employment. The title also suggests, if we read it as an equation with employment as the dependent variable, that the determinants of employment would be found in the rate of interest and money.

The rate of interest refers to Keynes's emphasis on the decision facing entrepreneurs: whether or not to employ money, their own or borrowed, to engage in productive activity that leads to an increase in employment. This is what has often been called the theory of effective demand. As noted above, this is something that Keynes believed to be behind Marx's theory of exploitation, and it clearly relates to the fact that entrepreneurs are only interested in increasing their monetary returns from employing their capital. The decision to employ labor is a decision to spend money today in order to produce goods that will produce money tomorrow. Only if the money tomorrow is greater than the amount of money today, measured as a rate of return that is higher than can be found in any other productive or nonproductive use of money, will entrepreneurs be willing to provide employment. But it is important to note that Keynes always considered that entrepreneurs had alternatives to providing employment through financing productive activity. Entrepreneurs could invest in financial assets and earn interest without any further effort on their part. If the rate of interest on financial assets was higher than the rate of return (or the rate of exploitation) from employing labor, then it would not be in the interest of entrepreneurs to take the risk of starting a production process that would increase employment.

It is for this reason that the rate of interest is the crucial variable in determining whether or not new investments for new productive activities that provide employment opportunities are undertaken. Only if the rate of interest is less attractive than the rate of return on productive activity will entrepreneurs go forward and provide employment. Thus, the title of the book tells us that the level of employment is primarily determined by relative rates of return between financial investments and returns from productive, employment-creating investments.

Finally, Keynes suggested that, under certain types of expectations about the movement of interest rates, it might be even more remunerative to not invest at all but simply hold money. The investment in a financial asset with no visible return could provide a refuge from loss, as it might for the holder of a fixed-interest obligation when interest rates are expected to rise. Such losses might be avoided simply by holding money. Thus, an asset such as money that provides a safe haven against loss would have what Keynes called a liquidity premium, and this is another reason why expectations of future conditions might impact supply and demand in such a way as to divert entrepreneurs' interest in providing employment.

A little historical context might help in understanding this argument. Keynes was in debate with a large number of economists concerning the best way to emerge from the recession that had been in existence in the United Kingdom since the early 1920s. One of these economists was Friedrich von Hayek. Hayek had argued that, if there were an increase in the demand for money that pushed the rate of interest above the rate of return on productive activity, this would bring about an increase in the employment of labor to increase the production of money. But this argument depended on the assumption that money was a real commodity, such as gold, whose supply could be increased by employing more labor to produce it. Only in this case would an increase in the demand for money increase the profitability of exploiting the gold mines and, as a byproduct, increase the employment of miners digging gold in the mines in South Africa.[2] Under these assumptions, if the rate of interest were higher than the return on other productive activity, there would be an increase in the demand for gold, which would call forth an increased demand for labor to produce it and eventually increase the supply of money sufficiently to bring down the rate of interest and bring the economy to full employment. In short, there was no difference in the response of the economy to an excess demand for the money commodity gold and an excess demand for real goods and services; there was perfect substitution between the demand for goods and the demand for money in the form of a commodity called gold.

Keynes argued against this view, first of all because he believed that, even if it were correct, it would take much too long to bring about a recovery from recession, and second because he did not believe that a modern economy worked on the basis of commodity money such as gold. Indeed, if we look at his early work on ancient monies, we see that he never believed that money was a commodity or that gold served as money because of its intrinsic value as a commodity. Instead, he argued that money was a debtor-creditor relationship and that, even in the earliest times, gold served only as a useful and enduring medium for recording those debtor-creditor contracts. In short, it was the forward contract that was written on the gold coins, rather than the intrinsic value of the gold contained in the coins, that gave them value and caused them to be money. If we look at Keynes's *Treatise on Money*, we see very clearly a delineation of the different types of money and his beliefs that a modern economy is based on what he called "representative money" and that the existence of money depended on the existence of the state. Here Keynes makes reference to the state theory of money that was first put forward by Knapp (1924).

Thus, it is to counter Hayek's argument that the last independent variable suggested in the title of the book concerns the definition of the nature of money. The ability of the relationship between the rate of return on productive activity and the rate of return on money and financial assets to determine the level of employment depends on the nature of money. It determines whether or not the economic system is a self-regulating supply and demand system, in the sense that it automatically moves to market clearing at full employment, or whether or not it can become bogged down in a state of equilibrium in which the rate of interest remains above the return on productive investment and thus produces an equilibrium at less than full employment.

Keynes dealt with these questions by formulating what he called the "essential properties" of money. In simple terms, Keynes defined a monetary economy as one in which an excess demand for money, even if it drives up the price of money, does not produce an increase in investment and employment to increase its supply and bring down its price to the level that produces full employment. These are the so-called elasticity conditions, which have caused interpreters so much difficulty. But their intent is quite clear and simple: to show that, in a modern economy, an increase in the demand for money will not bring about an increase in the employment of labor to produce money.

Indeed, if we consider money as a debtor-creditor relationship, we can see that just the opposite might be the case. If money exists because individuals have expectations of the future that have convinced them to engage in contracts to repay money at future dates (this, incidentally, is precisely how Keynes defined the rate of interest: as the amount of money today that must be paid today against receipt of an amount of money in the future), then an increase in the demand for money, whether or not it increases the rate of interest, will cause a reduction in activity that will disappoint expectations and make it more difficult for individuals to meet their future commitments to pay money. This is akin to what Keynes called an increase in liquidity preference. If this increased preference to hold money leads to an inability to meet future commitments—that is, defaults—then it will create financial instability, because the lenders of money will be unable to meet their commitments. For the lenders of money, and the banks that have liabilities to depositors who consider those deposits as assets, an increase in liquidity preference would automatically lead to a decrease in the ability of both individuals and banks to meet future commitments. These failures could then lead to an interlocking chain of defaults and would look much like what Irving Fisher (1933) would eventually characterize as a debt deflation, and which Hyman Minsky (for example, 1986) has used in his interpretation of Keynes's theory.[3]

Thus, the importance of money is crucial in explaining why the system might find a position of equilibrium at less than full employment, why the system is not self-equilibrating at full employment, and why the system might be subject to financial crises in cycles. While critics characterize Keynes's theory as one in which money plays no role, which contains no explanation of prices, and which refers only to depression economics, we can now see—from a simple reading of the title of the book—that money plays the central role in determining the level of economic activity, because it competes with productive investment via the rate of interest and determines the system of intertemporal relative prices that determine the decision of entrepreneurs to engage labor to produce future output.

But all of this deals with why the system will not automatically achieve full employment as the result of the operation of forces of supply and demand when money has particular characteristics. It says little about where the economy will actually come to rest. Here Keynes posed another condition: If a monetary economy is one that contains an asset whose return does not fall, or falls less rapidly than all other investments, when the level of activity expands, then eventually it is the return on that particular asset that will "rule the roost." It will be the return on that asset that sets the standard that has to be met by the returns on all other types of activity and will eventually divert investment from employment-creating activities to financial investments, whose supply can be expanded without an increase in employment.

Therefore, the crucial question is: What will be the nature of money that causes its return, its liquidity premium, to be independent of the level of activity or of its relative supply? In principle, it could be any non-produced commodity, but Keynes insisted that money was created through a debt-credit relationship. Or, to put the problem in the words of Hyman Minsky: How do I get others to accept my IOUs as payment for a debt? Many explanations have been proposed, including the legal tender laws and the role of high-powered central bank money in providing the ultimate means of interbank settlements. However, the simplest and most effective answer was provided by Innes (1913; see also 1914), who noted that Minsky's question can be answered by requiring those who are in your debt to extinguish their debts to you by rendering your own liabilities to others. This requires that you start out as a creditor, so that there is a net demand for your liabilities, or everyone else is a net debtor. This is the basis of Knapp's chartalist approach, to which Keynes referred.

Perhaps the easiest way to understand the approach is to recognize the adage that the only certain things in life are death and taxes. As regards the first, consider the concept of original sin. Here everyone starts out as a sinner—a net debtor—with a large liability that has to be extinguished on pain of hellfire and damnation. The debt can only be extinguished by acquiring forgiveness in the form of official indulgences issued by the church. Accumulation of a sufficient amount of these indulgences, determined by the issuer of the indulgences, extinguishes the debt. There can never be an excess supply of these, and there is always an excess demand.

The church would never think of limiting its own liabilities—otherwise, no one could aspire to redemption and salvation.

Taxes can be looked at in a similar way. They represent an original sin, a liability to the state that makes all citizens net debtors and that can only be exculpated through the acquisition of indulgences that take the form of the asset that the state will accept to extinguish the tax liability. These can be acquired only by selling assets, in the form of goods and services, to the state. Just as the church would never limit the issue of its liabilities, the state should never do so, since it would mean that the tax liabilities of its citizens taken as a whole cannot be met. In the hard times of Dickens, some or possibly all of them would thus end up in debtors' prison. Today, they would be subject to fines as well, which they could not meet.

This explanation of money as the creation of the state meets the condition that the quantity of money is independent of its physical characteristics or a physical method of production. The nature of money is found in a sociopolitical relation rather than a physical or purely economic relation.

Continued Relevance of the Policy Implications of This Interpretation

All of this is in the realm of theory, and it is relatively straightforward. It simply says that capitalist entrepreneurs will invest in those assets that give them the highest returns. Some investments produce employment; others don't. If there is a clear incentive to invest in those assets that do not create employment, the system will not achieve full employment if investing in those assets does not automatically bring about a process of substitution that transfers investment towards employment-creating expenditures. Keynes argued that, in a monetary economy, this is clearly not the case.

From the point of view of policy, it is the theory of *effective* demand that expresses entrepreneurial decisions that is crucial. There are a number of ways to view this theory, but it is important to recognize that this is not a theory of what has come to be called *aggregate* demand, that is, the summing up of the various components of demand for investment goods, of demand for consumption goods by the private sector, of demand for both by the government sector, and of net demand for both by the external sector. As noted above, the theory of effective demand is a theory of those factors that induce entrepreneurs to engage their money capital to provide employment to produce future output. Thus, policies that seek to expand the level of employment must be directed at the decisions of entrepreneurs to spend money on productive employment rather than on financial assets.

A number of very simple points of policy follow from this observation. The first is that policies that seek to increase savings in order to provide financing for investment will, in general, do precisely the opposite. This is easy to see, because decisions to save more are, in fact, decisions to consume less. Decisions to consume less mean lower demand for future output, and they therefore reduce the incentive for entrepreneurs to commit funds to hire labor to produce that output. This was also part of the famous disputes between Keynes and Hayek. Joan Robinson recounts a visit by Hayek to Cambridge University to present his theory as found in his *Prices and Production* (1931). After Hayek drew on the board a number of triangles, which no one appeared able to understand, Richard Kahn asked a question that went something like this: "Professor Hayek. You mean to say that, if I decide to spend more money to buy a new overcoat, this will reduce employment?" Hayek's response was yes, whereas Keynes's response to the same question would have been an emphatic no.

The same line of argument can be applied to the often-heard proposition that it is necessary to increase the profitability of investment by reducing wages, in order to induce entrepreneurs to commit more funds to employ labor. If wages are lower, consumption will be lower and—unless entrepreneurs have convinced themselves that consumption would rise when the purchasing power of workers is falling—there will again be no incentive to increase employment or investment; rather, the opposite. This was a point Kalecki often stressed in his aphorism: "Workers spend what they get, capitalists get what they spend." Unless capitalists were willing to increase spending autonomously, reducing wages and workers' spending would not increase profits. Indeed, in this formulation, since workers don't save, savings and profits are the same thing, so the increase in profits cannot come from workers' spending decisions.

The same logic applies when we take into account the activities of the government sector. It is often argued that the government deficit simply diverts resources from the private to the public sector, so that the appropriate government policy is to run a budget surplus, that is, to increase government savings and thus liberate resources for use by the private sector. But reducing government expenditures to produce a government surplus has exactly the same impact as reducing wage incomes. Reducing consumption overall reduces the incentive for entrepreneurs to undertake investment in capital goods that employ labor in order to produce output. Any resources liberated would run to waste.

Keynes argued that one of the basic flaws of traditional theory was its assumption of a given quantity of money irrespective of the level of activity. Therefore, if unemployment is rising and prices are falling, the real quantity of money would be increasing and would thus keep the level of aggregate demand constant. On the other hand, if money was a debt-credit relationship, the level of activity would determine the willingness to undertake debt, as well as the ability to repay debt. This is a point that Hyman Minsky, with the help of Irving Fisher's theory of debt deflation, formulated in his concept of financial fragility. But his basic point is that, since it is impossible to fix the quantity of money, it is impossible to fix the level of effective demand at full employment.

We have a very good example of the application of this principle in the modern context. In Argentina, as growth and employment continued to fall after 1998, the government was asked to run a surplus to increase savings available to meet its external debt service commitments (Kregel 2003). But, in the absence of autonomous demand arising in the private or external sector, the only results were further reductions in the level of activity and in tax yields, which more than offset the cuts in expenditures. The attempt to cut expenditures produced a larger government deficit rather than a reduced deficit or a government surplus.

The main question, then, is how to influence an entrepreneur's expectations of the profitability of producing future output. Of course, the easiest way is by getting money into the cashbox. But it is also necessary for the money that comes in to be greater than the money that goes out, and this is the result not of buying government bonds but of investing in labor and equipment. This is not an argument that the government should not borrow or run a deficit, but it is an argument that says that, when the government uses its expenditures to fill the cash boxes of private entrepreneurs, it should finance those expenditures by borrowing at a rate that is below the rate of return that entrepreneurs earn from private productive activity.

Indeed, government deficits are like snowflakes—they are all different. A deficit that simply pays interest on outstanding debt is different from a deficit that transfers income to those with a lower propensity to consume, or to those with negative incomes.

Thus, government policy should be (1) to use deficits that maximize their employment-creation impact, and (2) that the government can do so without losing its ability to determine the interest rates at which it borrows to support the deficits. That is, it is important to counter the idea that there is some relationship between the level or the share of the government deficit in national income and the rate of interest at which the government can borrow. This requires recognizing that, within the theory of effective demand, it is not the government that has to borrow in order to finance its deficit expenditures; rather, it is the existence of deficit expenditures that provides the ability to determine the rate of interest in the marketplace. As Warren Mosler (1995, 1997–98) has consistently argued, and as others here in Kansas City, such as Randall Wray (1998), Stephanie Bell Kelton (2000, 2001, 2002), and Mat Forstater (1998), have made explicit, any increase in government expenditure has its first impact in increasing the amount of unborrowed reserves in the banking system. This excess supply of reserves, in the absence of any other action, will drive the overnight Federal Funds Rate to a zero bid. In order for interest rates to remain positive, there must be a residual borrower of the excess reserves. That residual borrower is the government or its agent, the central bank. The residual borrower also decides the rate that it will bid for funds. Thus, the ability to set the rate of interest derives from the fact that the government is the residual borrower in a market with excess supplies of funds that it creates through its expenditure decisions. When demand is deficient, there is no reason for the government to have to restrict its activities in support of effective demand because the market will be unwilling to lend the money or will be unwilling to lend at a rate that is below the rate of return on private investment in productive activity.

This also shows the fallacy of the argument that governments should run either short- or long-term fiscal surpluses, even if the economy is running at full employment. This is, again, quite easy to see by recognizing the basic relationship behind the theory of effective demand. If the government is running a surplus, it is draining more demand from the economy than it is adding through its purchases of goods and services from the private sector or by employing labor in the provision of public services; that is, it is reducing the supply of its liabilities available to the private sector to meet its tax liabilities and thus the ability of private entrepreneurs to meet debt contracts and other contracts to undertake productive activity. For the government to be neutral in its impact on the economy and allow the private sector to remain solvent, the government cannot run a surplus.

If, in addition, individuals choose to hold some government liabilities in the form of money balances for transaction, precautionary, or other purposes above and beyond those necessary to meet their tax liabilities, then even a balanced budget will drain more purchasing power from the economy than is added by government expenditure. Thus, whenever there is a positive demand for money, however it is caused, a neutral government budget policy requires the government to run a deficit equivalent to the size of the public's demand for government debt in the form of money in addition to tax liabilities. This leads to the conclusion that, even at full employment, structural budgeting requires the government to run a deficit.

If the government recognizes that it has the ability to set the short-term policy rate of interest in order to support employment, it is no longer available as a tool to fight inflation. In the period of the general application of Keynesian policies, this produced a policy dilemma that did much to discredit Keynesian demand management policies. In the late 1950s and again in the late 1960s and the 1970s, policymakers were faced with falling employment and rising prices—what came to be called "stagflation." If rising prices were considered an expression of excess demand in goods markets, and rising unemployment an expression of excess supply in labor markets, Keynesian policy appeared to call for a reduction in aggregate demand through tighter fiscal policies to meet the inflation problem but an expansionary policy to meet the employment problem. An additional policy tool thus appeared to be required. Many proposed that this should be some form of incomes policy to link wages to inflation. Not only did this interfere with market forces determining wage differentials, but it did little to dampen inflationary pressures, leading the way to the monetarist counterrevolution in policymaking. This policy dilemma reflects the nature of aggregate demand management as, in Joan Robinson's words, a "blunt instrument."

Keynes had already referred to the problems of what he called "semi-inflation" as the economy approached full employment. He also noted that the analysis of the variation in the level of employment in *The General Theory* assumed expansion at constant proportions. Professor Skidelsky (2006) has drawn attention to Keynes's 1937 position, when unemployment was still over 10 percent, as, "We are in more need today of a rightly distributed demand than of a greater aggregate demand," warning against the dangers of inflation (Keynes 1937). Keynes here was clearly referring to the risks of the blunt instrument failing to provide demand in those industries that had the greatest levels of unemployment. The problem facing the UK was the collapse of export demand for Britain's major export industries: textiles, coal-mining, iron and steel, machinery, and shipbuilding. These industries accounted for some 6 percent of the 9–10 percent unemployed in the 1920s. In particular sectors, such as iron and steel, shipbuilding, and coal, unemployment rates were 22 percent, 35 percent, and 16 percent in 1928. An increased government deficit in these conditions could provide support for the overall restructuring of the economy that was necessary, but it would do little to produce the shift of labor from the declining sectors to the expanding sectors.

In these 1937 articles, the question was whether debt finance of the war rearmament would be inflationary. Keynes argued that inflation could be avoided if demand were directed to the areas with labor surpluses and reduced in those with labor shortages. "Whether demand is or is not inflationary depends on whether it is directed towards trades and localities which have no surplus capacity. To organize output in the Special Areas is a means of obtaining rearmament without inflation." Thus, Keynes is implicitly arguing that the assessment of the level of aggregate demand should be measured against the impact of the government deficit on inflation and its distribution across sectors. While the degree of government planning and directed intervention required for such sectorally differentiated demand management was possible in wartime, it has seldom been acceptable to governments in time of peace.

However, there is an answer to this problem of creating a sectorally differentiated fiscal policy in the proposal by the Center for Full Employment and Price Stability here at the University of Missouri at Kansas City. If deficits are like snowflakes, then it is imperative to choose the deficit that makes the maximum impact on the level of unemployment. As Warren Mosler has argued, the problem of unemployment can be eliminated if the government becomes the employer of last resort (ELR), offering employment to anyone who is willing and able to work. Such a policy would automatically absorb unemployment in those areas where it is greatest and provide the possibility of offering training to prepare workers for transfer to those sectors where labor is in short supply. In addition, it would have other advantages, such as preserving and improving the overall skill levels in the labor force to improve international competitiveness, and providing public social and economic infrastructure projects that might not otherwise be created because they were thought to be too expensive. In this way, it is possible to adapt the policy to support economic transformation and produce the perfect fiscal policy snowflake.

In addition, fixing the minimum employment wage paid within the ELR program would simultaneously provide an anchor for the overall level of effective demand and an anchor to prices. By offering unemployed labor the opportunity to work, fiscal policy returns to its role of being an automatic stabilizer as government expenditure increases when private-sector activity fall offs. It also acts as a buffer to prices, since there will be a supply of labor available at a wage just above the official program wage, avoiding the bidding up of wages in expanding sectors that might induce a wage-price spiral. Just as buffer stocks provide price stability by offsetting volatility in supply and demand over time, the ELR program would provide a buffer stock of labor to stabilize wages as the demand for labor rises and falls across different sectors. At the same time, it would not interfere with the operation of the market in setting relative wages. The failure to achieve growth and stability in capitalist economies may be found in their inability to combine full employment and price stability. Keynes's objective was to provide the means of making them compatible. This is also the objective of the ELR program.

Notes

1. Indeed, Keynes circulated privately a "Budget for National Resources," dealing with national income accounting principles (Harrod 1951, 491).
2. Hayek (1943), among others such as Benjamin Graham, expanded this idea to propose an international reserve currency composed of a basket of commodities. This attracted the attention of Keynes, Kaldor, and others, primarily for its ability to stabilize demand by stabilizing commodity prices.
3. However, the remedy that Fisher proposed—reflation to provide a return of prices to their original levels—is different from Keynes's proposal to provide sufficient liquidity to keep interest rates low and to use expenditure policy to support sales and expectations of future earnings.

References

Bell, Stephanie. 2000. Do taxes and bonds finance government spending? *Journal of Economic Issues* 34:603–20.

———. 2001. The role of the state and the hierarchy of money. *Cambridge Journal of Economics* 25 (2): 149–63.

Bell, Stephanie, and L. Randall Wray. 2002. Fiscal impacts on reserves and the independence of the Fed. *Journal of Post Keynesian Economics* 25 (2): 263–71.

Davidson, Paul, and Eugene Smolensky. 1964. *Aggregate supply and demand analysis*. New York: Harper and Row.

Fisher, Irving. 1933. The debt-deflation theory of great depressions. *Econometrica* 1:337–57.

Forstater, Mathew. 1998. Flexible full employment: Structural implications of discretionary public sector employment. *Journal of Economic Issues* 32 (June): 557–64.

Harrod, Roy F. 1939. *The trade cycle*. Oxford: Oxford University Press.

———. 1951. *The life of John Maynard Keynes*. London: Macmillan.

Hayek, Friedrich. 1931. *Prices and production*. 2nd ed. London: Routledge and Kegan Paul, 1935.

———. 1943. A commodity reserve currency. *Economic Journal* 53 (210/211): 176–84.

Innes, A. Mitchell. 1913. What is money? *Banking Law Journal* 30 (5): 377–408. Repr. in Wray 2004.

———. 1914. The credit theory of money. *Banking Law Journal* 31 (2): 151–68. Repr. in Wray 2004.

Keynes, J. M. 1930. *Treatise on money*, 2 vols. London: Macmillan.

———. 1936. *The general theory of employment, interest and money*. London: Macmillan.

———. 1937. How to avoid the slump. In *The* (London) *Times*, January 12–14. Repr. in Keynes 1982.

———. 1940. *How to pay for the war: A radical plan for the Chancellor of the Exchequer*. London: Macmillan.

———. 1979. *The General Theory and after: A supplement*. Vol. 29 of *The collected writings of John Maynard Keynes*. Ed. D. E. Moggridge. London: Macmillan, for the Royal Economic Society.

———. 1982. *Activities 1931–39: World crises and policies in Britain and America*. Vol. 21 of *The collected writings of John Maynard Keynes*. Ed. D. E. Moggridge. London: Macmillan, for the Royal Economic Society.

Knapp, Georg Friedrich. 1924. *The state theory of money*. Abridged edition translated by H. M. Lucas and J. Bonar. London: Macmillan.

Kregel, Jan. 2003. An alternative view of the Argentine crisis: Structural flaws in structural adjustment policy. *Investigación Económica* 243 (Enero-Marzo): 15–49.

Minsky, Hyman. 1986. *Stabilizing an unstable economy*. New Haven: Yale University Press.

Mosler, Warren. 1995. Soft currency economics. EPIC: A coalition of economic policy institutions. http://www.epicoalition.org/docs/soft0004.htm.

———. 1997–98. Full employment and price stability. *Journal of Post Keynesian Economics* 20 (2): 167–82.

Skidelsky, Robert. 2006. The origins of Keynesian economics and some applications to restructuring and globalization. Speech to the Ninth International Post Keynesian Conference, Kansas City, MO, September 18.

Weintraub, Sidney. 1958. *An approach to the theory of income distribution.* Philadelphia: Chilton.

Wray, L. Randall. 1998. *Understanding modern money: The key to full employment and price stability.* Cheltenham, UK: Edward Elgar.

———, ed. 2004. *Credit and state theories of money.* Northampton, MA: Edward Elgar.

CHAPTER 8

MACROECONOMICS OF STAGNATION AND NEW DEVELOPMENTALISM IN LATIN AMERICA

LUIZ CARLOS BRESSER-PEREIRA

AFTER THE FAILURE OF CONVENTIONAL ORTHODOXY to promote macroeconomic stability and development, Latin America has become home to a clear movement for rejecting the "macroeconomics of stagnation" that it contains. Given that, the question is whether there is an alternative to the diagnoses and policies that the North offers to Latin America. In this chapter, after examining the crisis of the national development strategy that was old developmentalism, I compare the rising new developmentalism with its earlier version, as well as with the set of diagnoses and policies that rich nations have prescribed and pushed on developing countries since the neoliberal ideological wave became prevalent worldwide: conventional orthodoxy. In the first section, I discuss old developmentalism, its initial success, its obsolescence due to a series of new facts and distortions, and its replacement with conventional orthodoxy since the late 1980s. In the second section, I discuss the importance of the concept of the nation and of the "national development strategy" institution. In the third section, I discuss new developmentalism as a "third discourse" lying between the bureaucratic left wing's populism and conventional orthodoxy's macroeconomics of stagnation. In the fourth section, I compare new and old developmentalism. In the fifth section, I compare new developmentalism with conventional orthodoxy with regard to macroeconomic policies and growth strategies.

Old Developmentalism and Its Crisis

Between the 1930s and the 1970s, Brazil and other Latin American countries grew at an extraordinary pace. They took advantage of the weakening of the center to formulate national development strategies that, in essence, implied protection of the infant national industry and the forced promotion of savings through the state. This strategy was called "developmentalism," or "national developmentalism." The purpose of such a name was to emphasize that, first, the policy's basic objective was to promote economic development, and, second, in order for this to happen, the nation—that is, businessmen, state bureaucracy, middle classes, and workers joined together in international competition—needed to define the means to reach this objective within the framework of the capitalist system, with the state as the principal collective action instrument. The notable economists who then studied development and made economic policy proposals, along with the politicians, government officials, and businessmen who were most directly involved in this process, were called "developmentalists" because they chose development as the ultimate goal for their economic analysis and political action. Latin American economists who, together with a group of international economists, took part in formulating "development economics" were affiliated with three complementary schools of thought: the classical economics of Smith and Marx, Keynesian macroeconomics, and the Latin American structuralist theory.[1]

Developmentalism was not an economic theory but a national development strategy. It employed economic theories to formulate, for each country in the capitalist periphery, a strategy capable of gradually leading to the development level attained by central countries: market-based theories, for there is no economic theory that does not spring from the markets, but also political economy theories that cast the state and its institutions in a leading role as auxiliary coordinator of the economy. Developmentalism faced opposition from neoclassical economists who practiced "conventional orthodoxy"—that is, the set of diagnoses and economic policies and institutional reforms that rich, or Northern, nations prescribed to developing, or Southern, countries. They were called "monetarists," due to the emphasis placed on the money supply as a means of controlling inflation.

Since Brazil was a peripheral, or dependent, country, whose industrial revolution was taking place 150 years after that of England and more than 100 years after that of the United States, the remarkable development between the 1930s and 1970s was only possible inasmuch as Brazil as a nation was able to use its state as an instrument to define and implement a national development strategy where the state's intervention was significant. This was not about replacing the market with the state but, rather, about strengthening the state in order to enable it to create the required conditions for firms to invest so that their businessmen could innovate. All countries, beginning with England itself, required a national development strategy to bring about their industrial revolutions and continue to develop. The use of a national development strategy was particularly evident among late-development countries such as Germany and Japan, which, therefore, were never characterized by dependence. Peripheral countries, on the other hand, like Brazil and other Latin American countries that had lived through the colonial experience, remained ideologically dependent on the center after their formal independence. Both late-development central countries and former colonies needed to formulate national development strategies, but the task was easier for the former. For peripheral countries, there was the additional hurdle of facing their own "dependence," that is, submission of the local elites to those in central countries, who were interested in nothing other than their own development. Developmentalism was the name given to the national strategy of dependent countries, those whose industrialization began no earlier than the 1930s, or during World War II. Their developmentalism was nationalist because, in order to become industrial, these countries needed to form their national state. The nationalism present in developmentalism was the ideology for forming a national state; it was the affirmation that, in order to develop, countries needed to define their own policies and institutions, their own national development strategy.[2]

Late central countries also used developmentalist strategies, although they were not given the same name. Since they were nationalistic, they always followed their own criteria rather than their competitors' to formulate policies, and they used their states deliberately to promote development.

In the 1940s, 1950s, and 1960s, developmentalists and Keynesians prevailed in Latin America; they were the mainstream. Governments used their theories first and foremost in economic policymaking. From the 1970s, however, in the context of the great neoliberal, conservative wave that began to form, Keynesian theory, development economics, and Latin American structuralism were successfully challenged by neoclassical economists, most of whom adopted a neoliberal ideology. Since the 1980s, in the context of the great foreign debt crisis that added to the rich nations' political power, these economists managed to redefine in neoliberal terms their prescriptions for developing countries. The neoliberal ideology targeting these countries became hegemonic, expressing itself through what became known as the Washington Consensus, which I prefer to call "conventional orthodoxy," not only because this is a more general expression but because, if some "consensus" existed in the 1990s, in the 2000s it broke down. During the 1980s, the national development strategy—national developmentalism—faced a major crisis and was replaced with a foreign strategy: conventional orthodoxy.

Several factors help explain this. First, during the 1960s, the national alliance that served as the political foundation for developmentalism fell apart as a direct consequence of the military coup supported by Brazilian industrialists and the American government. The national-developmentalist approach assumed the existence of a nation and, thus, of a national agreement involving industrialists, workers, and the state bureaucracy—a reasonable assumption insofar as, after a lengthy period of dependence that followed the independence movements of the early nineteenth century, these countries, since 1930, had taken advantage of the crisis up north to begin their national revolutions and form autonomous national states. Based on this fact, developmentalism proposed that each country's new industrial businessmen should become a "national bourgeoisie," as had been the case in developed countries, and associate itself with government officials and urban workers to bring about a national and industrial revolution. Therefore, in every country the sense of nation, of national society, was reinforced and the possibility dawned that this society might implement a national development strategy (developmentalism), using the state as its instrument for collective action. It was at once a proposal and an assessment of the reality represented by the accelerated industrialization process that Latin America was then experiencing. However, the Cuban revolution of 1959, by radicalizing the left wing, and the economic crisis of the early 1960s led to the dissolution of the national developmental alliance and set the stage for the establishment of military regimes in Brazil, Argentina, Uruguay, and Chile, with support from each country's businessmen and from the United States. As a consequence, the national alliance that was so essential to the constitution of a nation broke up, and Latin America's moderate left embraced the "theory of associated dependence," which rejected the possibility of a "national bourgeoisie" (Bresser-Pereira 2005). In doing so, it rejected the very idea of nation and of national development strategy on which national developmentalism was based.

Second, because old developmentalism was based on import substitution, it carried the seed of its own demise. Protection of national industry, the focus on the market, and the reduction of an economy's openness coefficient, even in a relatively large economy such as Brazil's, are greatly constrained by economies of scale. For certain industries, protection becomes absurd. As a result, when the import-substitution model was maintained through the 1970s, it was leading Latin American economies to a deep distortion. On the other hand, as Furtado remarked as early as 1966, after the initial import-substitution phase of consumer-goods industries, continued industrialization implies a substantial increase of the capital-labor ratio, with two consequences: income concentration and reduced capital productivity, or product-capital ratio (Furtado 1966). The response to income concentration was to be an expanded production of luxury consumer goods, characterizing what I have termed the "industrial underdevelopment model," which, besides being perverse, carries the seed of the dissolution of the national pro-development alliance.

Third, the great debt crisis of the 1980s, which was not directly related to the import-substitution model but already an outcome of the growth-*cum*-foreign-savings strategy, further weakened the national alliance that was behind national developmentalism. The debt crisis paved the way for the rise of high inertial inflation, which would be the scourge of the Brazilian economy for fourteen years. The military government had indexed prices since 1964, but it was only in the early 1980s that inflation topped 100 percent a year as a result of exchange-rate depreciations caused by the foreign debt crisis; from this moment up to 1994, inflation would be measured in monthly terms (5 percent, 10 percent, 20 percent a month), configuring high inertial inflation (Bresser-Pereira and Nakano 1987). After that, developmentalism was supported by only a populist left wing, which, while in office in the second half of the 1980s, proved unable to manage the Brazilian economy. This became apparent in the Cruzado Plan—the 1986 attempt to control inertial inflation—that ended in a major disastrous populist episode (Sachs 1989).

The fourth reason for the replacement of developmentalism with conventional orthodoxy lies in the strength of this ideological wave that was coming from the North. In the early 1980s, in response to the foreign debt crisis, a new and stronger conventional orthodoxy established itself bit by bit. The Baker Plan (1985), named for U.S. Secretary of the Treasury James Baker, completed the definition of the new ideas by adding market-oriented institutional reforms to orthodox macroeconomic adjustment. Developmentalism then became the target of a systematic attack. Taking advantage of the economic crisis that derived, in part, from the overcome development model and from the distortions it had suffered in the hands of populist politicians and middle classes, conventional orthodoxy gave developmentalism a negative connotation, identifying it with populism or irresponsible economic policies. In its stead, it proposed a panacea of orthodox and neoliberal institutional reforms. It further proposed that developing countries abandon the antiquated concept of "nation" that national developmentalism had adopted and accept the globalist thesis, according to which, in the age of globalization, nation-states had lost autonomy and relevance: Worldwide free markets (including financial ones) would be charged with promoting the economic development of all.

Twenty years later, what we see is conventional orthodoxy's failure to promote Latin America's economic development. While developmentalism prevailed, between 1950 and 1980, per capita income in Brazil grew almost 4 percent a year; since then, it has grown around 1 percent a year—four times less. The performance of other Latin American countries has been no different, with the exception of Chile. In the same period, however, dynamic Asian countries, including China since the 1980s and India since the 1990s, maintained or achieved extraordinary growth rates.

Why such different growth rates? At the more immediate level of economic policies, the fundamental problem relates to loss of control over the most strategic macroeconomic price in an open economy: the foreign exchange rate. Latin American countries lost control over it via open financial accounts and saw their foreign exchange rates appreciate as, from the early 1990s, they accepted the proposal of growth with foreign savings from Washington and New York. Yet, at the same time, Asian countries mostly kept current account surpluses, and they retained control over their foreign exchange rates. At the reform level, Latin American countries indiscriminately accepted all liberalizing reforms, irresponsibly privatizing monopoly utilities and opening their capital accounts, while Asians were more prudent. However, it gradually became clear to me that the main difference was to be found in a new, fundamental fact: Latin American countries interrupted their national revolutions and watched as their nations became disorganized and lost cohesiveness and autonomy; as a consequence, they were left without a national development strategy.

The national strategy that Latin American countries in general and Brazil in particular adopted between 1930 and 1980 was known as developmentalism. In this period, and mainly from 1930 to 1960, many Latin American countries were firmly nationalist, finally providing their formally independent states with a basic solidarity when it came to competing internationally. Yet, the weakening brought about by the great economic crisis of the 1980s, combined with the hegemonic force of the ideological neoliberal wave coming from the United States since the 1970s, caused the interruption of the process of national and state formation in Latin America. Local elites stopped thinking for themselves and accepted the advice and pressure from the North, while the countries, devoid of a national development strategy, saw their development stall. Conventional orthodoxy, which came to replace national developmentalism, had not been developed locally; it did not reflect national concerns and interests but, rather, the visions and objectives of rich nations. In addition, as is typical of neoliberal ideology, it was a negative proposal that assumed the markets' ability to coordinate everything automatically, proposing that the state stop playing the economic role it always had in developed countries: that of supplementing the market's coordination to promote economic development and equity.

I have been critical of conventional orthodoxy and of the macroeconomics of stagnation that it implies since it became dominant in Latin America. I was probably the first Latin American economist to criticize the Washington Consensus at my keynote lecture during the annual congress of the Brazilian National Association of Post-Graduate Economics Courses (1990 [1991]). My criticism, however, gained a new dimension since the first quarter of 1999, after having been for four and one-half years a member of the Cardoso administration, whose economic policies, after the successful and innovative Real Plan (1994), became fully orthodox. Between 1999 and 2001, I and my close associate Yoshiaki Nakano began a more systematic critique of conventional orthodoxy based on our common structuralist and Keynesian views of economics (see Bresser-Pereira 1999 [2001] and Bresser-Pereira and Nakano 2002a, 2002b). Our criticism showed that the conventional proposal, albeit inclusive of certain necessary policies and reforms, did not, in fact, promote a country's development but kept it semistagnant, incapable of competing with wealthier countries, easily falling prey to a form of economic populism: foreign exchange populism. The alternative economic strategy present in these works was innovative in that it acknowledged a series of new historical facts that implied a need to review the national development strategy. How to name this alternative? We decided that "new developmentalism" could be a good name. What does new developmentalism involve? I introduce it in this work. In the third section, I define it as a "third discourse" and a national development strategy; in the fourth section, I establish its differences from the 1950s' developmentalism; and, in the fifth section, I show how it stands as a critique and an alternative to conventional orthodoxy, that is, to the diagnoses, policies, and reforms conceived mainly in Washington for use in developing countries.

Nation and Nationalism

New developmentalism, as the national developmentalism of the 1950s, at once assumes the presence and implies the formation of a true nation, capable of formulating an informal, open, national development strategy, as is proper of democratic societies whose economies are coordinated by the market. A nation is a society of individuals or households that, sharing a common political fate, manages to organize itself as a state with sovereignty over a certain territory. A nation, therefore, like the modern state, only makes sense within the nation-state framework that arises with capitalism. For a nation to be able to share a common fate, it must have common objectives, chief among which, in historical terms, is the objective of development. Other objectives, such as freedom and social justice, are also fundamental to nations but, like the state and capitalism, arise with economic development as part of its reasoning, of its intrinsic manner of being. Nations, nation-states, capitalism, and economic development are simultaneous and intrinsically correlated historical phenomena. In its most developed form—today's globalization—capitalism's economic constituents are not only firms operating at the international level but also, if not mainly, nation-states or national states. It is not just firms that compete worldwide in the markets, as conventional economic theory proposes; nation-states, too, are fundamental competitors. The main criterion for success for the political rulers of every modern nation-state is comparative economic growth. Rulers are successful in the eyes of their people and internationally if they achieve greater growth rates than countries regarded as direct competitors. Globalization is the stage of capitalism where, for the first time, nation-states span the entire globe and compete economically through their firms.

A nation involves a basic solidarity among classes when it comes to competing internationally. Businessmen, workers, state bureaucrats, middle-class professionals, and intellectuals may come into conflict, but they know that they share a common fate and that this fate relies on their successful competitive involvement in the world of nation-states. It involves, therefore, a national agreement. A national agreement is the basic social contract that gives rise to a nation and keeps it strong or cohesive; it is the compact among social classes of a modern society that enables this society to become a true nation, that is, a society gifted with a state capable of formulating a national development strategy. The great national agreement or compact that established itself in Brazil since 1930 joined the infant national industrial bourgeoisie to the new bureaucracy or the new state technicians; add to these the urban workers and the more domestic market-oriented sectors of the old oligarchy, such as the ranchers, from which Getúlio Vargas came. Their adversaries were imperialism, represented mainly by British and American interests, and the affiliated exporting rural oligarchy. The most strategic accord in a modern nation-state is that between industrial businessmen and the state bureaucracy, which includes significant politicians but also workers and the middle classes. And there will always be domestic adversaries, somehow identified with imperialism or today's colony-less neoimperialism, as well as with local collaborationist or globalist groups. In the case of Brazil today, they are the rentiers who rely on high interest rates and the financial industry that collects commissions from the rentiers.

A nation is always nationalist, inasmuch as nationalism is the ideology of the formation of a national state and its permanent reaffirmation or consolidation. Another way to define nationalism is to say, after Ernest Gellner, that it is the ideology that pursues a correspondence between nation and state, that stands for the existence of a state for each nation.[3] This, too, is a good definition, but one typical of a thinker from Central Europe; it is a definition that becomes exhausted as soon as a nation-state is formed—when nation and state begin coinciding over a given territory, formally establishing a "sovereign state." It fails therefore, to take into account Ernest Renan's celebrated 1882 sentence: "A nation is a daily referendum."[4] It fails to explain how a nation-state may formally exist in the absence of a true nation, as in the case of Latin American countries, which, in the early nineteenth century, saw themselves endowed with a state due not only to the patriotic efforts of nationalist groups but also to the good services of England, whose aim was to oust Spain and Portugal from the region. In this way, these countries saw themselves endowed with a state in the absence of true nations, as they ceased to be colonies and became dependent on England, France, and, later, the United States. For a true nation to exist, the several social classes must, despite the conflicts that set them apart, be in solidarity when it comes to competing internationally, and they must use national criteria to make policy decisions, particularly those that involve economic policy and institutional reform. In other words, the rulers must think with their own heads instead of dedicating themselves to confidence building, and the entire society must be capable of formulating a national development strategy.

New developmentalism will become a reality when the Brazilian society becomes again a true nation. This is what happened in Brazil between 1930 and 1980, particularly from 1930 to 1960. Under the rule of Brazil's twentieth-century statesman, Getúlio Vargas, the country took national decisions into its own hands and formulated a successful national development strategy. In those thirty years (or fifty, if we include the military period, which remained nationalist, despite its political alliance with the United States against communism), Brazil changed from an agricultural to an industrial country, from a mercantilist social formation to a fully capitalist one, from semi-colonial status to national status. Developmentalism was the name given to the national development strategy and to its driving ideology. Therefore, the process of defining the new developmentalism equally involves resuming the idea of nation in Brazil and other Latin American countries. It implies, therefore, a nationalist perspective in the sense that economic policies and institutions must be formulated and implemented with the national interest as their main criterion and with each country's citizens as actors. Such a nationalism aims not to endow a nation with a state but to turn the existing state into an effective instrument for collective action by the nation, an instrument that enables modern nations, in the early twenty-first century, to consistently pursue their political objectives of economic development, social justice, and freedom within an international framework of competition, but also peace and collaboration, among nations. It implies, therefore, that such a nationalism be liberal, social, and republican, that it incorporate the values of modern industrial societies.

The "Third Discourse" and the National Development Strategy

New developmentalism is a "third discourse" between the old developmentalist discourse and conventional orthodoxy; it is a set of ideas, institutions, and economic policies through which medium-income countries attempt, in the early twenty-first century, to catch up with developed countries. Like the old developmentalism, it is not an economic theory but a strategy; it is a national development strategy, based mainly on Keynesian macroeconomics, whereby such countries may gradually catch up with rich nations. It is the set of ideas that enables developing nations to reject rich nations' proposals and pressures for reform and economic policy, like a fully open capital account and growth with foreign savings, inasmuch as such proposals are neoimperialist attempts to neutralize development—the "kicking away the ladder" practice. It is the means by which businessmen, government officials, workers, and intellectuals can stand as a true nation to promote economic development. I do not include poor countries in the new developmentalism, not because they do not require a national development strategy, but because they still need to accomplish their primitive accumulation and industrial revolutions, and the challenges they face and the strategies they require are different.

In terms of discourse or ideology, we have, on the one hand, the dominant, imperial and globalist discourse that flows from Washington and is embraced in Latin America by the neoliberal, cosmopolitan right wing, comprised mainly of the rentier class and the financial industry.[5] This is conventional orthodoxy: an ideology exported to developing countries; an anti-national strategy that, despite its generous offer to promote prosperity among medium-income countries, serves, in fact, rich nations' interest in neutralizing these countries' ability to compete. This, as it was applied in Brazil since the 1990s, has four things to say: first, that the country's major problem is the lack of microeconomic reforms capable of enabling the market to operate freely; second, that, even after the end of runaway inflation in 1994, controlling inflation remained the main purpose of economic policy; third, that, in order to achieve such control, interest rates must inevitably be high, because of the sovereign risk and of fiscal issues; fourth, that "development is a great race among countries to obtain foreign savings" and that the implicit current account deficits and foreign exchange appreciation brought about by capital inflows are no cause for concern. The disastrous effects of this discourse in terms of balance-of-payments crises and low growth for Latin American countries that adopted it since the late 1980s are well known today (see Frenkel 2003).

The opposite discourse is that of the bureaucratic-populist left wing. From this perspective, Brazil's ills are due to globalization and financial capital, which placed the country under the burden of high foreign and public indebtedness. The proposed solution was to renegotiate the country's foreign and public debt at a great discount. The second ill was insufficient demand, which could be resolved with increased public spending. And the greatest ill—unequal income distribution—could be resolved by expanding the Brazilian welfare system. This alternative was used, for example, in Peru under Alan Garcia. In Brazil, it was never fully put into practice.[6]

The first discourse served the interests of the North and reflected its deep ideological hegemony over Latin American countries. Locally, it sprang chiefly from the Brazilian rentier class, which depends essentially on interest for a living, and from economists affiliated with the financial industry; a confused, disoriented upper-middle class also shared it. The second discourse came from the lower-middle class and labor unions, reflecting the old bureaucratic left wing's perspective. Neither discourse had a chance of reaching a reasonable consensus in Brazilian society, due to their irrationality and biased nature. Neither ideology reflected national interests. Might there be a third discourse capable of achieving such a reasonable consensus? Certainly, this third discourse is possible and is being formulated, little by little. It is the discourse of new developmentalism. But is not new developmentalism also an ideology, as are conventional orthodoxy and the bureaucratic-populist discourse? Yes and no: yes, because every national strategy implies an ideology, a set of political-action–oriented ideas and values; and no, because, unlike conventional orthodoxy, which is no more than an outside proposal, new developmentalism will only make sense if it rises from internal consensus and, therefore, stands as a true national development strategy. A full consensus is impossible, but a consensus that brings together businessmen from the production sector, workers, government officials, and middle-class professionals—a national agreement, therefore—is now forming, taking advantage of the failure of conventional orthodoxy. This forming consensus regards globalization as neither a blessing nor a curse, but as a system of intense competition among national states through their firms. It realizes that, in such a competition, the state must be strengthened fiscally, administratively, and politically and must, at the same time, provide national firms with the conditions to become internationally competitive. It acknowledges, as Argentina did after its 2001 crisis, that development in Brazil is prevented, in the short term, by exceedingly high short-term interest rates determined by the Central Bank of Brazil that push long-term rates upwards and uncouple them from sovereign risk. It assumes that, for development to occur, investment rates must necessarily rise and the state must contribute by means of positive public savings that are the outcome of curbing current government expenditures and not of increasing taxes. Finally, and more generally, new developmentalism assumes that development, in addition to being prevented by the absence of democratic nationalism (an absence that favors conventional orthodoxy), is also hampered by income concentration, which, besides being unfair, is a culture medium for all forms of populism and, thus, for the bureaucratic-populist discourse.

What is a national development strategy? More than a simple ideology developed abroad like conventional orthodoxy, it is a set of economic-development–oriented institutions and policies. It is less of a national development project or plan because it is not formal; it lacks a document that accurately describes objectives to be attained and policies to be implemented in order to attain such objectives, because the inherent accord among social classes has neither text nor signatures. And it is more, because it informally comprehends all of society, or a large share thereof; it shows all a path to tread and certain very general guidelines to be observed; and, although it does not assume a conflict-free society, it does require a reasonable union of all when it comes to competing internationally. It is more flexible than a project, and it always considers the actions of opponents or competitors. It recognizes that the factor that drives individual behavior is not just personal interest but competition with other nations. A national development strategy reflects all of this. Its leadership falls on the government and the more active elements of civil society. Its fundamental instrument is the state itself: its norms, policies, and organization. Its outcome, when a major accord establishes itself, when strategy becomes truly national, when society begins sharing, loosely but effectively, methods and goals, is accelerated development—a period during which the country enjoys high per capita income and living-standard growth rates.

A national development strategy implies a set of fundamental variables for economic development. These variables are real and institutional alike.

The nation's increased savings and investment capacities; the means by which it incorporates technical advances into production; human capital development; increased national social cohesiveness, resulting in social capital or in a stronger, more democratic civil society; a macroeconomic policy capable of ensuring the state's and the nation-state's financial health, leading to conservative domestic and foreign indebtedness ratios—these are all constituents of a national development strategy. In this process, institutions, instead of mere one-size-fits-all abstractions, are seen and construed concretely, historically. A national development strategy will gain meaning and strength when its institutions—be they short-term ones I call policies or public policies, or be they relatively permanent ones (institutions proper)—respond to societal needs, when they are compatible with the economy's production-factor endowment, or, to put it more broadly, with the elements that make up society at its structural level.

Old and New Developmentalism

The developmentalism of the 1950s and the new developmentalism differ based on two variables that arose in this half-century: on the one hand, new historical facts that changed world capitalism, which moved from its "golden years" to the "globalization" phase; on the other hand, medium-income countries like Brazil that changed their own development stages and are no longer marked by infant industries.

The main change at the international level was from the capitalism of the golden years (1945–1975), when the welfare state was assembled and Keynesianism ruled, while development economics prevailed as a theory and a practice of economic development, to the neoliberal capitalism of globalization, where growth rates are smaller and competition among nation-states is far fiercer. In the golden years, medium-income countries still posed no threat to rich nations. Since the 1970s, however, with the NICs (newly industrializing countries) and, since the 1990s, with China, they became much more competitive: The threat their cheap labor poses to rich nations is clearer than ever. At that time, rich nations, and the United States in particular, in need of allies for the Cold War, were far more generous; today, only the poorest African countries can expect some generosity—but even these must be wary, because the treatment the rich nations and the World Bank afford them and the help, or alleged help, they receive are often perverse.

The main difference, at the national level, is that industry was in its infancy at that time; it is now mature. Between the 1930s and the 1960s, the import-substitution model was effective in establishing the industrial bases of Latin American countries. Since the 1960s, however, they should have begun dropping protectionist barriers and orienting themselves towards an export-led model, under which they might show themselves as competitive manufactured-goods exporters. But they did not, probably due to an export pessimism that faded out only in the 1970s. It was only in the early 1990s that trade liberalization took place, in the middle of a major economic crisis, often hurriedly and haphazardly. This twenty-year lag was one of the greatest distortions endured by the developmentalism of the 1950s.

Let us examine the difference between old and new developmentalism, as summarized in Table 8.1. New developmentalism is not protectionist: It simply emphasizes the need of a competitive exchange. It assumes that medium-income countries have already overcome the infant industry stage but still face the "Dutch disease": the tendency of countries that produce low per capita value-added goods using cheap natural resources to experience the relative appreciation of the exchange rate coupled with the current account balance, thus making unviable the key condition for growth, which is the transference of labor from low to higher per capita valued-added goods. Such transference requires not protection but management of the exchange rate to neutralize this market failure (the Dutch disease), thus supporting potentially viable industries with high knowledge that adopt state-of-the-art technology (Bresser-Pereira 2007, ch. 4). Unlike old developmentalism, which embraced the exporting pessimism of development economics, new developmentalism lays odds on developing countries' ability to export

Table 8.1 Old and New Developmentalism, Compared

Old Developmentalism	New Developmentalism
1. Industrialization is based on import substitution, and trade is export pessimistic.	1. Growth is export-led, and trade is export-realistic.
2. There is a certain complacency towards inflation.	2. There is no complacency towards inflation.
3. The state plays a leading role in terms of forced savings and investment in firms.	3. The state has a subsidiary, but important, role in both activities.

medium-value-added manufactured goods or high-value-added primary products. The experience of the past thirty years has clearly shown that this pessimism was one of the great theoretical mistakes of development economics. In the late 1960s, Latin American countries should have begun shifting decisively from the import-substitution to the export-led model, as did Korea and Taiwan. In Latin America, Chile was the first to effect such a change and, as a result, its development is often pointed out as an example of a successful neoliberal strategy. In fact, neoliberalism was fully practiced in Chile only between 1973 and 1981, coming to an end with a major balance-of-payments crisis in 1982 (see Diaz-Alejandro 1981 and Ffrench-Davis 2003). The export-led model is not specifically neoliberal because, strictly speaking, the neoclassical economic theory that underlies this ideology has no room for development strategies. Dynamic Asian countries, having adopted a developmentalist strategy in the 1950s, lent it a manufactured-goods exporting nature in the 1960s and, since the 1970s at least, can be regarded as new developmentalist countries. The export-led model has two main advantages over the import-substitution model. First, the market available to industries is not constrained to the domestic market. This is important for small countries but equally fundamental to a country with a relatively large domestic market, such as Brazil. Second, if a country adopts this strategy, economic authorities, making industrial policy to benefit their firms, get access to an efficiency criterion that will guide them: Only firms that are efficient enough to export will benefit from the industrial policy. In the case of the import-substitution model, very inefficient firms may be enjoying the benefits of protection; in the case of the export-led model, the likelihood of this happening is substantially smaller.

The fact that the strategy new developmentalism stands for is not protectionist does not mean that countries should be willing to accept indiscriminate openness. They must negotiate pragmatically at the level of the World Trade Organization and regional accords to secure mutual openness. And, above all, it does not mean that the country should give up industrial policies. Room for these has been reduced by the highly unfavorable agreements made in the WTO's Uruguay Round, but there is still room for such policies, if considered strategically, in consideration of future comparative advantages that may arise as some supported firms achieve success.

New developmentalism rejects misled notions of growth based chiefly on demand and public deficit that became popular in Latin

America in the 1960s. This was one of the most severe distortions that developmentalism endured in the hands of its latter-day populist advocates. The theoretical roots of this national development strategy lie not in Keynesian macroeconomics and in development economics, which, in turn, are based mainly on classical economics. Keynes pointed out the importance of aggregate demand and legitimized resorting to public deficits in recessive periods, but he never stood for chronic public deficits. He always assumed that a fiscally balanced national economy might, for a brief while, give up this balance to reestablish employment levels (see Bresser-Pereira and Dall'Acqua 1991). The notable economists who formulated the developmentalist strategy, such as Furtado, Prebisch, and Rangel, were Keynesian, and they regarded aggregate demand management as an important tool for promoting development. But they never defended the economic populism of chronic deficits. Those who came in their wake, however, did. When Celso Furtado, faced with the severe crisis of the early 1960s, proposed his *Plano Trienal* (1963), these second-class followers accused him of having an "orthodox rebound." In fact, what Furtado already saw, and what new developmentalism firmly defends, is fiscal balance. New developmentalism defends it not due to "orthodoxy" but because of the realization that the state is the nation's *par excellence* collective-action instrument. If the state is so strategic, its apparatus must be strong, sound, and capacious, and, for this very reason, its finances must be in balance. More than this, its debt must be small and long in maturity. The worst thing that can happen to a state as an organization (the state also stands for the rule of law) is to be in thrall to creditors, be they domestic or foreign. Foreign creditors are particularly dangerous, for they and their capital may, at any time, leave the country. However, domestic creditors, transformed into rentiers and supported by the financial system, can impose disastrous economic policies on the country, as has been the case in Brazil.

The third and final difference between the developmentalism of the 1950s and new developmentalism can be found in the state's role in promoting forced savings and investing in the economic infrastructure. Both forms of developmentalism cast the state in a leading role as regards ensuring the proper operation of the market and providing general conditions for capital accumulation, such as education, health, transportation, communications, and power infrastructures. In addition, however, under the developmentalism of the 1950s, the state also played a crucial role in promoting forced savings, thereby contributing to countries' primitive accumulation process; furthermore, the state made direct investments in infrastructure and heavy industry, where the investments required were too high for the private sector's savings.

This has changed since the 1980s. With new developmentalism, the state still can and must promote forced savings and invest in certain strategic industries, but the national private sector now has the resources and managerial ability to perform a sizable portion of the investment needed. The new developmentalism rejects the neoliberal thesis that "the state no longer has resources," because whether or not the state has resources depends on how its finances are managed. But new developmentalism understands that, in all sectors where reasonable competition exists, the state must not be an investor; instead, it must concentrate on defending and ensuring competition. Even after these investments have been excluded, there are many left to the state, financed by public savings rather than debt.

In sum, and, again, because medium-income countries are at a different stage, new developmentalism regards the market as a more efficient institution, one more capable of coordinating the economic system than did old developmentalism, although the perspective is far from conventional orthodoxy's irrational faith in the market.

New Developmentalism and Conventional Orthodoxy

Let us examine the differences between new developmentalism and conventional orthodoxy. Conventional economic orthodoxy or conventional economic knowledge is made up of the set of theories, diagnoses, and policy proposals that rich nations offer to developing countries. It is based on neoclassical economics but is not to be confused with it, because it is not theoretical but openly ideological and oriented towards proposing institutional reforms and economic policies. While neoclassical economics is based on universities, particularly in the United States, conventional orthodoxy springs mainly from Washington, home to the U.S. Treasury Department and to the two agencies that are supposedly international but are, in fact, subordinate to the Treasury: the International Monetary Fund and the World Bank. The former is charged with macroeconomic policy and the latter with development. Secondarily, conventional orthodoxy originated in New York, the seat or point of convergence of major international banks and multinationals. Therefore, we may say that conventional orthodoxy is the set of diagnoses and policies intended for developing countries and originating in Washington and

New York. Conventional orthodoxy changes over time. Since the 1980s, it has become identified with the "Washington Consensus," which cannot be understood simply as a list of ten reforms or adjustments that John Williamson wrote in the paper that gave birth to the expression (Williamson 1990). (His list included reforms and adjustments that are, indeed, necessary.) The Washington Consensus is, in fact, the effective shape that the neoliberal and globalist ideology has taken at the level of economic policies recommended to developing countries.

In some works, I distinguish between the First and the Second Washington Consensus, to highlight that the former, materialized in Williamson's list, is concerned mostly with the macroeconomic adjustment that became needed as a result of the great debt crisis of the 1980s, while the second, prevalent since the 1990s, also intends to operate as a development strategy based on an open capital account and on growth with foreign savings. Together, however, they form a single consensus—that of rich nations in relation to their competitors, the medium-income countries. Although the term Washington Consensus is useful, I prefer "conventional orthodoxy," because it is more generic and portrays a certain "orthodoxy" as merely conventional.[7]

Conventional orthodoxy is the means by which the United States, at the level of economic policies and institutions, expresses its ideological hegemony over the rest of the world and mainly over dependent developing countries that lack nations strong enough to challenge this hegemony, as has been traditionally the case of Latin American countries. This hegemony purports to be "benevolent," while, in fact, it is the arm and mouth of neoimperialism—that is, an imperialism without (formal) colonies that established itself under the aegis of the United States and other rich nations after the classic colonial system ceased to exist, after World War II.

Inasmuch as conventional orthodoxy is the practical expression of the neoliberal ideology, it is the ideology of the market versus the state. While new developmentalism wants a strong state and a strong market and sees no contradiction between them, conventional orthodoxy wishes to strengthen the market by weakening the state, as if the two institutions were party to a zero-sum game. Since the second half of the twentieth century, therefore, conventional orthodoxy has been a version of the *laissez-faire* ideology that prevailed in the previous century. Disregarding the fact that the state has grown in terms of tax load and of the level of market regulation as a result of the increased dimensions and complexity of modern societies, and disregarding the fact that a strong and relatively large state is a requirement for a strong and competitive market, conventional orthodoxy is the practical reaction against the growth of the state's apparatus. Certainly, the state has also grown out of mere clientelism, to create jobs and employ the bureaucracy, but conventional orthodoxy is not interested in distinguishing legitimate state growth from illegitimate. It is the ideology of the minimal state, of the police state, of the state that is concerned only with domestic and foreign security, leaving economic coordination, infrastructure investments, and even social services like health and education to the devices of the market. It is the individualistic ideology that assumes that all are equally capable of defending their interests. It is, therefore, a right-wing ideology, an ideology of the powerful, the rich, the better educated—the high bourgeoisie and the high technobureaucracy. Its goal is to drive down direct and indirect real wages by leaving labor unprotected and, thus, making firms more competitive in an international market of developing countries and cheap labor.

The central difference between conventional orthodoxy and new developmentalism lies in the fact that conventional orthodoxy is market fundamentalist, believing that the market is an institution that coordinates everything optimally if it is free of interference, while new developmentalism is pragmatic. It views the market as an extraordinarily efficient institution to coordinate economic systems but knows its limitations. Factor allocation is the task that the market best performs, but, even there, it faces problems. In stimulating investment and innovation, it is insufficient. It fails to ensure an exchange rate that is consistent with the transference of manpower to higher value-added per capita industries. And, in distribution of income, it's a clearly unsatisfactory mechanism, because markets privilege the stronger and the more capable. While conventional orthodoxy acknowledges market failures but asserts that state failures are worse, new developmentalism rejects such pessimism about the possibilities of collective action and asks for a strong state—not as a tradeoff of a weak market but combined with a strong market. If men are able to build institutions to regulate human actions, including the market itself, there is no reason why they are not able to strengthen the state organization or apparatus—making its administration more legitimate, its finances more solid, and its management more efficient—and to strengthen the state constitutional or law system, making its institutions increasingly adjusted to social needs. Politics and democracy exist precisely for that; and the more advanced democracies have been making major advances in this area in the last century.

Insofar as one of the foundations of new developmentalism is classical political economy, which was essentially a theory of the "wealth of nations" (Smith) or of capital accumulation (Marx), social structures and institutions are fundamental in its reasoning. Besides, as it adopts a historical approach to economic development, the teachings of the German historical school and of the American institutionalists are an essential part of its vision.[8] Thus, institutions are fundamental, and to reform them is a permanent requirement insofar as, in the complex and dynamic societies in which we live, economic activities must be constantly reregulated. In contrast, conventional orthodoxy, based on neoclassical economics, only recently acknowledged the role of institutions, in the context of "new institutionalism." In contrast to historical institutionalism, which, in relation to economic development, sees obstacles to economic growth in precapitalist institutions and in the distortions of capitalist ones and searches actively to develop a set of institutions (a national growth strategy), new institutionalism offers a simplistic answer to the problem: It is sufficient that institutions guarantee property rights and contracts, or, more broadly, the good working of markets that will automatically promote growth. According to the neoliberal jargon adopted, for instance, by *The Economist*, a good government will be a "reformist" one, involved in market-oriented reforms. According to new developmentalism, a government will be good in economic terms if it is able to promote economic growth and a more even distribution of income by the adoption of economic policies and institutional reforms that are oriented, whenever possible, to the market, but often correcting it—in other words, if it grows within the framework of a national development strategy. According to conventional orthodoxy, institutions should limit themselves almost exclusively to constitutional norms; according to new developmentalism, economic policies, and particularly monetary policies, must undergo permanent reform, permanent and gradual adjustment within the framework of a broader growth strategy. Industrial policies are also required, but, while old developmentalism gave a major role to them, new developmentalism uses a moderate industrial policy: Government should act strategically only when the business enterprise that needs support shows that it is capable of competing internationally; an industrial policy that ends up confused with protectionism is not acceptable. For new developmentalism, a moderate interest rate and a competitive exchange rate are more important than an industrial policy.

New developmentalism and conventional orthodoxy share many institutional reforms, but their objectives are often different. Take, for instance, public management reform. New developmentalism supports it because it wants a more capable and more efficient state apparatus; conventional orthodoxy supports it because it sees in such reform an opportunity to reduce the tax burden. To new developmentalism, such a consequence may be desirable, but it is a different issue. The tax burden is a political question that depends on how democratic societies assign roles to the state and on how efficient public services are. Another example: Both approaches favor more flexible labor markets, but new developmentalism looks at the experiences of Northern Europe and does not mistake flexibility for lack of protection, while conventional orthodoxy wants to make labor standards more flexible to weaken the labor force and reduce wages. In other reforms, the difference is one of degree. New developmentalism favors, for instance, an open and competitive economy because it sees commercial globalization as an opportunity for medium-income countries, but it rejects unilateral opening and requires reciprocity from trade partners. And there are cases where there is definitive disagreement, such as with regard to opening capital accounts. While conventional orthodoxy strongly favors it, new developmentalism rejects it, because the middle-income country loses control of the exchange rate. New developmentalism views commercial globalization as an opportunity but sees financial globalization as a risk that developing countries should not take.

In comparing new developmentalism and conventional orthodoxy, we can distinguish growth strategies from macroeconomic policies, although both are tightly correlated. Since growth is impossible without stability, let us begin by comparing macroeconomic policies. As we can see in Table 8.2, both views value macroeconomic stability, but, while conventional orthodoxy reduces macroeconomic stability to price stability and control of the public debt, new developmentalism requires a moderate interest rate and a competitive exchange rate that guarantee the intertemporal equilibrium of public accounts (of the state) and of foreign accounts (of the nation-state). Conventional orthodoxy's approach may be summed up as follows: In order to guarantee macroeconomic stability, a country should achieve a primary surplus that keeps the public debt/GDP relation at an acceptable level for creditors. The central bank

Table 8.2 Macroeconomic Policies Compared

Conventional Orthodoxy	New Developmentalism
1 The primary surplus is the central fiscal standard.	1. The budget deficit and public savings are the central fiscal standards.
2. The central bank has a single mandate: inflation.	2. The central bank has a triple mandate: inflation, exchange rate, and employment.
3. The central bank uses a single instrument: the exchange rate.	3. The central bank may also buy reserves or impose controls on capital inflow to control the exchange rate.
4. The short-term interest rate is endogenous and should be high.	4. The short-term interest rate is exogenous and can be moderate.
5. The exchange rate is floating and endogenous.	5. The exchange rate is floating but administered.

is supposed to have a single mandate, to control inflation, since it has at its disposal a single instrument, the short-term or basic interest rate. This rate is essentially endogenous, corresponding to the equilibrium or non–inflation-accelerating rate of interest, and, given the fiscal unbalance, it should be high. The exchange rate is also endogenous; that is, it is market defined, and its equilibrium will be automatically ensured by the market once a floating exchange rate is adopted.

New developmentalism takes a substantially different approach, a Keynesian one: Fiscal adjustment should not have as a parameter primary surplus but the budget deficit and positive public savings that allow for the required public investments. The central bank, in association with the finance ministry, should not be limited to a single mandate but should have a triple one: to control inflation, to keep the exchange rate competitive (compatible with the current account balance and the gradual transference of manpower to more knowledge-intensive or high per capita value-added industries—something that a recurrent Dutch disease prevents), and to achieve reasonably full employment. In order to perform these tasks, the central bank functions not with a single instrument (which is contradictorily viewed by conventional orthodoxy as endogenous) but with several instruments besides the interest rate: It may buy reserves and establish capital inflow controls to avoid a tendency to relative appreciation of the exchange rate that is frequent in medium-income countries. The interest rate is an instrument to control inflation, but it may be considerably lower than conventional orthodoxy supposes; the exchange rate should be kept floating, but managed—there is no such a thing as a completely free exchange rate.

Let us now compare the growth strategies that I present in Table 8.3. Conventional orthodoxy supports institutional reforms that reduce the size of the state and strengthen the market. It ascribes a minimum role to the state in investment and industrial policy, and it does not see any role for the nation (an absent concept). It proposes the opening of the capital account and a growth-*cum*-foreign-savings policy.

In contrast, new developmentalism wants institutional reforms that strengthen the state as well as the market—only a capable state organization and state normative institutions endowed of legitimacy can serve as an instrument of collective action of the nation. New developmentalism sees the nation as a national society with a sense of common destiny and of solidarity when competing internationally, as the fundamental actor defining a national growth strategy. It views the fundamental institution for this growth as the national development strategy, which creates incentives to entrepreneurs to innovate and invest. It gives priority to export industries and to industries characterized by high per capita value added, that is, industries with a high technological or knowledge content. It believes that growing domestic savings is not only possible but necessary, for all developed countries did so in the past. The Dutch disease, the growth-*cum*-foreign-savings policy recommended by conventional orthodoxy, is a major cause of exchange-rate appreciation—appreciation that must always be prevented, since a competitive exchange rate, relatively depreciated, is the central condition for growth.

Before the 1990s, conventional orthodoxy was concerned with foreign exchange rates and, during balance-of-payments crises, always demanded foreign exchange depreciations in addition to fiscal adjustments. Since the 1990s, however, the IMF has practically forgotten current account deficits (they were foreign savings, after all) and exchange-rate depreciations. The twin deficit hypothesis exempted it from worrying about current account deficits: All it had to do was concern itself with the primary surplus. For a while, it chose to talk about foreign exchange anchors and dollarization; after that strategy failed in Mexico, Brazil, and, above all, Argentina, the IMF turned to full-floating exchange to solve all external problems.

The new developmentalism is strongly critical of this perspective and wants control not only over the state's public accounts (public deficit) but also over the nation's total accounts (current account). It wants not only for the state's debt to be low but also for the state to show positive public savings. It also wants a nation-state to have foreign accounts that ensure its national security and autonomy. It wants not only interest-rate management but also foreign exchange rate management, even if it's within the framework of a floating rate regime—which it does not call "dirty," as conventional orthodoxy is wont to do, but "managed."

Each point of Table 8.3 is deserving of a lengthy analysis, but that is beyond the scope of this chapter. In both comparative tables, my objective was to show that, contrary to the hegemonic ideology that assumes that conventional orthodoxy is a "straitjacket" for all countries (Friedman 2000), there is a viable and responsible alternative. The experience of East Asian countries that never accepted conventional orthodoxy was already clear on the existence of this alternative; it became even clearer with the recent experience of Russia and Argentina. In the 1990s, these two countries adopted conventional-orthodoxy models and then fell into deep crisis; after rejecting this economic model in the 2000s, the two countries are now performing in high-growth modes. Thus, new developmentalism is not a theoretical proposal but expresses successful national experiences. And conventional orthodoxy is neither a growth strategy nor a derivation of sound development macroeconomics; it is stagnation macroeconomics.

Table 8.3 Growth Strategies Compared

Conventional Orthodoxy	New Developmentalism
1. Reforms reduce the state and strengthen the market.	1. Reforms strengthen the state and the market.
2. There is no economic role for the nation.	2. The nation defines a national growth or international competition strategy.
3. Government institutions are supposed to merely protect property rights and contracts.	3. The national growth strategy is the key development institution.
4. The state has a minimum role in investing and industrial policy.	4. The state has a moderate role in investing and industrial policy.
5. Growth is financed with foreign savings.	5. Growth is financed with domestic savings.
6. Capital accounts are open, and the exchange rate is not managed.	6. Capital inflows are controlled when necessary to manage the exchange rate.

The policies derived from sound development macroeconomics must necessarily be oriented to responsible fiscal practices, a moderate average interest rate, and a competitive exchange rate; this is the policy tripod of new developmentalism. When macroeconomists in rich countries discuss monetary and fiscal policies in their own countries, they do diverge, but they agree on the three points. The conventional orthodoxy that is applied in developing countries, however, shows a quite different practice. Although it is always asking for fiscal discipline, it is soft on this matter; Brazil, for instance, has achieved each year for the last eight years the fiscal target defined by conventional orthodoxy,[9] but fiscal problems have not been overcome. Conventional orthodoxy shows no discomfort in asserting that Brazil's real equilibrium interest rate is 9 percent a year and in defending the central bank's interest-rate policy that averaged 12 percent in real terms in the last years—a short-term interest rate that, in the special case of Brazil, directly burdens the public debt.[10] And conventional orthodoxy insists, against evidence, that it is impossible to manage the long-term exchange rate; this may be true for the United States, where the dollar is the international reserve money, but it is not true for other countries.

Out of these three policies, the crucial one is the requirement of a competitive exchange rate. I understand by "competitive" or "real equilibrium exchange rate" the exchange rate that more than equilibrates intertemporally the current account, ensuring the competitive viability of industries using state-of-the-art technologies. Developing countries face a tendency toward the relative overvaluation of their currencies for several reasons: In the case of a growth-*cum*-foreign-savings policy, the overvaluation implies a current account imbalance; in the case of the Dutch disease, a relatively overvalued currency that makes economic development just not possible is consistent with current account equilibrium. There is nothing more disagreeable to conventional orthodoxy than the exchange rate topic. For years and years, development economists did not discuss the exchange rate—that was the concern of macroeconomics. A competent development macroeconomics and, in strategic terms, new developmentalism are correcting the course and showing how central the exchange rate is to not only keeping the current account balanced but also promoting savings and investment.

Conclusion

What are the results of the two approaches? The outcome of conventional orthodoxy in Latin America is well known: quasi-stagnation. Since 1990, at least, the truth from Washington and New York became hegemonic in this region marked by dependence. Reforms and adjustments of all sorts took place, but no development ensued. The results of new developmentalism in Latin America, in turn, cannot be measured. Chile has used it, but this is a small country, and its policies are halfway between one strategy and the other. The Argentina of Kirschner and former Finance Minister Roberto Lavagna is the only concrete experiment, but this is much too recent to enable an objective appraisal. Still, new developmentalism is more than proven, because the strategy that Asia's dynamic countries have been using is none other.

Can new developmentalism become hegemonic in Latin America as developmentalism was in the past? The conventional proposal's failure assures me that, yes, it can. Argentina's 2001 crisis was a *turning point*: the requiem of conventional orthodoxy. No country was more faithful in the adoption of its prescriptions; no president was ever more dedicated to confidence building than Menen. The results are common knowledge. On the other hand, new developmentalist thinking is renewing itself. It has available a younger generation of development macroeconomists who are able to think on their own account instead of just accepting the recommendations of the international financial institutions.

There is, however, an issue of ideological hegemony to resolve. Latin American countries will only resume sustained development if their economists, businessmen, and state bureaucracies recall the successful experience that old developmentalism was and reveal themselves capable of taking a step ahead. They have already criticized the former mistakes and realized the new historical facts that affect them. They must now acknowledge that the national revolution that was under way, with the old developmentalism as the national strategy, was interrupted by the great crisis of the 1980s and by the neoliberal ideological wave from the North. They must perform an in-depth diagnosis of the quasi-stagnation that conventional orthodoxy caused. They must consider that the key policies that need change are the macroeconomic ones, particularly the ones related to the interest and the exchange rates. They must turn an attentive eye towards the national development strategy of dynamic Asian countries. They must become involved in the great collective national work of rejecting conventional orthodoxy's macroeconomics of stagnation and of formulating a new national development strategy for their countries. I believe that this resumption of awareness is fully under way. Latin America's development has always been "national-dependent," because its elites were always in conflict and ambiguous—now affirming themselves as a nation, now yielding to foreign ideological hegemony. There is a cyclical element to this process, however, and everything seems to indicate that the time of neoliberalism and conventional orthodoxy has passed and that new perspectives are opening up to the region.

Notes

1. In Brazil, the two leading economists who contributed to development economics were Celso Furtado and Ignácio Rangel. Given the former's international projection, he was also part of the founding group of development economists, which included Paul Rosentein-Rodan, Arthur Lewis, Ragnar Nurkse, Gunnar Myrdal, Raúl Prebisch, Hans Singer, and Albert Hirschman.
2. Nationalism can also be defined, as Gellner did, as the ideology that attempts to endow every nation with a state. Although this is a good definition, it is applicable to Central Europe rather than Latin America. In Latin America, nations were not yet fully formed and, still, were endowed with states. The nations, however, were incomplete, and their regime was semicolonial; with independence, the main change was that the dominant power shifted from Spain or Portugal to England and other major Central European countries.
3. Gellner 1983, 1993 (2000). Gellner, a Czech philosopher who took refuge from communism in England, was probably the most astute analyst of nationalism in the second half of the twentieth century.
4. Ernest Renan 1882 (1992: 55). In the immediately preceding part, Renan wrote: "A nation is a great solidarity made up of the sentiment of the sacrifices made and those people are still willing to make. It assumes a past; its present summation is a tangible fact: the consent, the clearly expressed desire to go on with common life."
5. By "rentier class," we no longer mean the class of large landowners but that of inactive capitalists whose livelihood relies mainly on interest income. The "financial industry," in turn, involves, besides rentiers, businessmen and managers who collect commissions from rentiers.
6. The Workers Party, PT, adopted such a discourse in Brazil, but, once in power in 2003, it adopted policies recommended by conventional orthodoxy.
7. I have no sympathy for orthodoxy, which is a way of renouncing thinking, and none for unorthodoxy, where the economist, upon identifying himself as unorthodox, renounces the implementation of his ideas and policies and reserves for himself the role of eternal minority opposition. A good

economist is neither orthodox nor unorthodox but pragmatic: He can make good economic policy based on an open, modest theory that forces him to constantly consider and decide under conditions of uncertainty.

8. The historical school is the school of Gustav Schmoller, Otto Rank, Max Weber, and, in a different line, Friedrich List; the American institutionalist school is the school of Thorstein Veblen, Wesley Mitchell, and John R. Commons.
9. Between 1999 and 2002, the primary surplus target defined by the IMF was 3.5 percent of GDP; after that, the target was increased to 4.25 percent.
10. In Brazil, there is no difference between the short- and the long-term interest rates, since it is the short-term interest rate set by the Central Bank that defines the interest paid on the Brazilian domestic treasury bonds. This is an absurd financial institution—an inheritance of the times of high inertial inflation that is carefully conserved by the representatives of conventional orthodoxy.

References

Bresser-Pereira, Luiz Carlos. 1990 (1991). Economic crisis in Latin America: Washington Consensus or fiscal crisis approach? East South Systems Transformations Project, University of Chicago, Department of Political Science, working paper no. 6, January 1991. In Portuguese: *Pesquisa e Planejamento Econômico* 21 (1): 3–23. Magna lecture at the XVIII National Meeting of Economy of ANPEC, Brasília, December 4, 1990.

———. 1999 (2001). Incompetência e confidence building por trás de 20 anos de quase-estagnação da América Latina. *Revista de Economia Política* 21 (1): 141–66. Paper presented to the Centre for Brazilian Studies of Oxford University, December 1999.

———. 2005. Do ISEB e da CEPAL à teoria da dependência. In *Intelectuais e política no Brasil: A experiência do ISEB*, org. Caio Navarro de Toledo. Rio de Janeiro: Editora Revan, 201–32.

———. 2007 *Macroeconomia da estagnação*. São Paulo: Editora 34.

Bresser-Pereira, Luiz Carlos, and Fernando Dall'Acqua. 1991. Economic populism versus Keynes: Reinterpreting budget deficit in Latin America. *Journal of Post Keynesian Economics* 14 (1): 29–38.

Bresser-Pereira, Luiz Carlos, and Yoshiaki Nakano. 1987. *The theory of inertial inflation*. Boulder: Lynne Rienner Publishers.

———. 2002a. Uma estratégia de desenvolvimento com estabilidade. *Revista de Economia Política* 21 (3): 146–77.

———. 2002b. Economic growth with foreign savings? Paper presented at the Seventh International Post Keynesian Workshop, Kansas City, MO, June 30, 2002.

Diaz-Alejandro, Carlos F. 1981. Southern Cone stabilization plans. In *Economic stabilization in developing countries*, ed. W. Cline and S. Weintraub. Washington: The Brookings Institution.

Ffrench-Davis, Ricardo. 2003. *Entre el neoliberalismo y el crescimiento com equidad*, 3rd ed. Santiago de Chile: J. C. Sáes Editor.

Frenkel, Roberto. 2003. Globalización y crisis financieras en América Latina. *Revista de Economia Política* 23 (3): 94–111.

Friedman, Thomas L. 2000. *The Lexus and the olive tree*. 2nd ed. New York: Random House.

Furtado, Celso. 1963. *Plano trienal de desenvolvimento econômico e social: 1963–1965*. Rio de Janeiro: Síntese.

Furtado, Celso. 1966. *Subdesenvolvimento e estagnação na América Latina*. Rio de Janeiro: Editora Civilização Brasileira.

Gellner, Ernest. 1983. *Nations and nationalism*. Ithaca: Cornell University Press.

———. 1993 (2000). O advento do nacionalismo e sua interpretação: Os mitos da nação e da classe. In *Um mapa da questão naciona*, 2000, org. Gopal Balakrishnan and B. Anderson. Editora Contraponto, 107–34.

Renan, Ernest. 1882 (1992). *Qu'est-ce qu'une nation*? Paris: Pocket/Agora.

Sachs, Jeffrey D. 1989. Social conflict and populist policies in Latin America. In *Labor relations and economic performance*, ed. R. Brunetta and C. Dell-Arringa. London: Macmillan.

Williamson, John. 1990. The progress of policy reform in Latin America. In *Latin American adjustment: How much has happened*?, org. John Williamson. Washington: Institute for International Economics, 353–420.

CHAPTER 9

TARGETING INFLATION *AND* FULL EMPLOYMENT IN SOUTH AFRICA

A CRITIQUE OF INFLATION TARGETING IN DEVELOPING ECONOMIES

BASIL MOORE

> If a current account deficit persists, the exchange rate is going to be weak. A weak exchange rate means that the import component is going to be higher. That means inflation will be higher and interest rates will have to go higher.
>
> —South African Reserve Bank Governor Tito Mboweni, Business Day, September 17, 2006

THE SOUTH AFRICAN RESERVE BANK (SARB) insists that keeping inflation within the 3–6 percent target range set by the government is its most important policy goal. When the expected future inflation rate rises above the target band, interest rates must be increased. Since the inflation rate breached its 6 percent target ceiling this year, SARB has raised the repo rate[1] by 250 basis points, to 11 percent, and the commercial banks' prime lending rate rose to 15 percent. The governor indicated in the 2007 annual report that he is prepared to raise the repo rate further at subsequent meetings to drive inflation within its 3–6 percent target range, irrespective of South Africa having probably the world's highest unemployment rate.

But, wearing another hat, the government frequently insists that reducing the estimated 40 percent unemployment rate is its most important underlying policy goal. It has made a commitment to reduce the official unemployment rate by one-half by 2014. Based on past policy experience, this goal clearly cannot be met under the current inflation-targeting monetary policy regime. The government knows it is whistling in the dark. However, cutting unemployment by half is a noble and vote-getting goal, and one can always get lucky.

Unlike monetary policy, fiscal policy does not have the confidence to set annual unemployment targets. No alarm bells go off when the unemployment rate rises. The South African government's past Growth, Employment and Redistribution (GEAR) policy has made no perceptible dent in unemployment, and its new Accelerated and Shared Growth Initiative for South Africa (ASGISA) appears destined for a similar fate. No annual employment targets have been introduced, and no success has been made in reducing the obstacles to growth that the government has itself identified. A UN report recently estimated that the "official" unemployment rate (which fails to count as unemployed those discouraged unemployed workers no longer actively seeking work) will increase from 26 percent to 34 percent by 2014 in the absence of any major policy shift.

Successful expansionary demand management of output and inflation requires that monetary and fiscal policy be coordinated. If the government wishes to pursue an expansionary policy, raise gross domestic product (GDP), and expand employment, the huge planned increases in government spending on capital infrastructure must be matched by reductions in interest rates. By raising asset prices and lowering borrowing costs, a reduction in the repo rate stimulates private investment spending.

The South African (SA) economy has been growing at about 4 percent. This is one-third below the 6 percent average current growth rate of all developing countries. It has been estimated that, for SA, a 6 percent growth rate of GDP and the annual creation of 500,000 new jobs are required if the growth of employment is to equal the growth of the labor force and unemployment is to be prevented from rising. Should unemployment continue to increase secularly, social disruption and despair could easily lead to the adoption of desperate populist policies, as occurred in Zimbabwe. In the face of rising unemployment, the political center may not hold. Lower interest rates are essential if investment spending is to rise sufficiently to generate the increase in employment required to prevent unemployment from rising.

The goal of expansionary deficit-spending fiscal policy is to increase total consumption and investment demand. But the effect of raising interest rates is exactly the opposite: to reduce inflation by depressing investment and consumption spending. Under all inflation-targeting regimes, the restrictive effects of rising interest rates directly offset the expansionary effects of fiscal deficits. The result is that GDP growth remains modest.

One major reason why government policies to raise output and GDP growth rates have been so disappointing is that monetary and fiscal policies are fatally uncoordinated. In SA, they typically work at cross-purposes. SARB's chief monetary policy instrument to counter inflation is to increase the level of interest rates. But higher rates directly reduce GDP by raising the cost of borrowing and the rate that future expected income streams are discounted. The prospect of higher interest rates reduces the present value of all future income streams, depresses asset prices, and lowers agents' "animal spirits." In consequence, unemployment increases secularly.

In SA, as in most other countries, inflation is not due to excess demand. Most firms are not operating at maximum capacity, most markets are highly concentrated, and most firms possess considerable market power. With the important exception of food and energy, prices of most goods are administered by firms at a stable markup over unit costs.

The core inflation rate is driven by the rate of change of unit costs. Higher interest rates raise the cost of capital to business firms, and their initial effect is to depress the rate of investment spending. The "sacrifice ratio" of restrictive monetary policy—the reduction in output and employment associated with a 1 percent reduction in the inflation rate—is extremely high in SA. Since raising interest rates is unpopular, SARB does not publicly acknowledge the existence of a sacrifice ratio in its discussion of the level at which it should set interest rates. It is solely concerned with how much rates must be raised to keep inflation within its target band.

Inflation in SA, as in most countries, is not "caused" by excess demand due to excessive growth of the money supply. Inflation is cost-determined. The "core" inflation rate is equal to the excess of average money wage growth over the growth rate of average labor productivity. Unit cost increases are passed on by firms in higher prices to realize their profit targets. Average markups are empirically quite stable over time. As a result, the domestic inflation rate is, at root, due to the conflict between business and labor over relative shares of the national pie. Both groups possess sufficient market power to set the price of the commodity they sell, and the result is cost inflation.

The inflation rate is influenced by foreign prices, as reflected in changes in the exchange rate. Depending on the openness of the economy, a rise in interest rates results in an increase in short-term capital inflows to purchase domestic bonds. An increase in interest rates leads to an increase in the demand for foreign exchange, a rise in the exchange rate, and a reduction in the domestic price of imported goods. To the delight of inflation-targeting central bankers, the inflation rate falls. This leads to a bias towards high interest rates for all inflation-targeting central bankers. But increases in interest rates may also induce a fall in equity prices. As a result, increases in interest rates may sometimes result in short-term capital outflows and a fall in exchange rates. Central bankers are also surrounded by great uncertainty concerning the consequences of their policy actions.

Nevertheless, the effectiveness of monetary policy is enormously increased in flexible-exchange-rate regimes. Increases in interest rates induce short-term capital inflows, which cause the exchange rate to appreciate. Exchange rate appreciation directly lowers the inflation rate by reducing the domestic price of imports. But, unfortunately, the opportunity cost of exchange rate appreciation—the reduction in profitability, production, and employment in the export sector, and the increase in the current account deficit—are not usually explicitly considered.

Changes in the world price of oil and in the domestic price of foodstuffs constitute external supply "shocks" that affect unit costs and the inflation rate. Such shocks are independent of changes in the interest rate. An important rule for successful targeting, which SARB has not entirely mastered, is to not target a variable over which you have little control.

SARB is mandated by the government to keep inflation within its target range. But the average inflation target the bank is delegated to hit ([3 + 6]/2 = 4.5) is too low, given the high degree of market power of both labor and business.

The ultimate goal of all trade unions is to increase union wages. In SA this is measured by the reduction in black-white salary differentials. The bargaining system by which wages are determined was designed to have a pro-labor bias. But the unintended result of greater increases in average money wages has been, primarily, higher rates of price inflation and not higher real wage levels.

In SA, wage determination in the formal sector is based on industry-wide collective bargaining, in which the unions and the leading firms in each industry participate. Once the industry wage increase is negotiated, all firms in the industry, no matter how small, must pay the negotiated increase. Due to the very high concentration of industry in SA, leading firms ordinarily can easily pass on higher unit costs in higher prices without fear of being undercut by their competitors. In consequence, the average inflation rate is higher, and the increase in real wages remains largely determined by the rate of growth of average labor productivity.

In addition to the average target (4.5 percent) being too low, the target range ([6 – 3] = 3) is much too narrow. As a result, the inflation rate is typically persistently at the top of its target range. This leads to expectations that SARB is likely to soon be forced to raise rates if it is to keep inflation within its target range. The expectation that interest rates will be raised in the future operates to depress "animal spirits," asset prices, and investment spending, whatever the current level of interest rates. Even if higher inflation targets were to lead to higher inflation rates, there is no SA (or non-SA) empirical evidence that inflation rates in the range of 6–9 percent are more closely associated with a lower rate of GDP growth than inflation rates in the range of 3–6 percent.

Resolving the dilemma of secularly rising unemployment, inflation, and slow growth requires creative policy leadership. The chief question is how to achieve full employment, price stability, and rapid growth simultaneously. In the successful Asian economies like China and the Asian "tigers," this challenge has been resolved by abandoning the Washington Consensus and developing an "incomes policy" or "social contract" for all major groups. (The "social contract" solution is analogous to the cooperative solution of the well-known "prisoner's dilemma" game, where the optimum outcome requires mutual consultation. A simple example of implicit contracts is the behavior of crowds at rugby and soccer games, where, if everyone were to stand up to see better, the result would be that everyone would have a worse view.)

To ensure that prices remain stable, the average rate of increase in money wages must remain below the average rate of increase in labor productivity in the previous period. The current situation in SA with an unemployment rate of 40 percent may be characterized as "an incomes policy of fear." This is the reason why labor unions (the Congress of South African Trade Unions), although part of the African National Congress governing alliance, are so restless and unhappy. Marx's "reserve army of unemployed" (in SA, workers in the formal and informal sectors) must be kept at about 40 percent of the labor force in order to prevent unionized workers in the formal sector from demanding higher wages.

Suppose the government were to propose the development of a "social contract" between labor, business, finance, and government. The goal of such a policy would be the simultaneous achievement of full employment, price stability, and rapid growth. Such a social contract would include the following conditions:

1. All labor unions must collectively agree to moderate their wage demands and accept an average rate of money wage increase that is equal to the average rate of growth of labor productivity of the economy in the previous year. (This would currently be in the range of 2–3 percent.) Average unit labor costs would then remain constant over the entire domestic sector. (Without the existence of a social contract, no individual union leader would dare propose such a policy of "wage moderation" for fear of losing his position at the next election, or worse.)
2. All business firms (with over, say, fifty employees) must collectively agree to not raise their markup of price over unit costs. So long as unit costs and markups remain constant, the rate of inflation in the domestic sector is zero. (Without the existence of a social contract, those individual firms faced with high increases in demand would be tempted to increase their markup.)
3. SARB must agree to lower the repo rate to, say, 2–3 percent. Since average prices remain constant, the inflation rate is zero, so the real interest rate is also 2–3 percent. In developed economies like the UK or the United States, a 40 percent unemployment rate would lead the central bank to immediately reduce the repo rate towards zero to stimulate investment demand. In developed economies, the labor force is literate and trainable by firms faced with an increased demand for their product; most unemployment is due to a deficiency of aggregate demand (AD). But an unknown proportion of unemployment in SA is "structural," due to poor work habits, illiteracy, low skills, and lack of mobility. Reducing the current huge unemployment rate requires very easy monetary policy and very low interest rates. So long as the social contract remains in place, increases in AD will lead to greater employment growth without inflation until full employment is reached.
4. The government must agree to a substantial increase in capital spending on social infrastructure, designed to stimulate AD and eliminate capital-supply constraints created by the 7–8 percent growth rate necessary to reach the government's target of halving the unemployment rate by 2014. Massive government deficit spending must be financed at low interest rates to ensure that the government's debt burden remains below the increase in tax revenue. Governments, like private firms, should borrow only when the return expected on the investment exceeds the interest cost.

5. In response to an increased demand for loans, banks must collectively agree to lower the average markup of lending rates over deposit rates, to develop a market in mortgage instruments, and to issue marketable mortgage instruments against low-cost houses. This would greatly expand AD, since lower-income households could then negotiate larger bank loans against their larger net housing equity collateral. (It would also have the desirable effect of developing a strong political constituency in favor of low interest rates.) Note that no enlarged government bureaucracy is necessary for such a social contract to succeed, since the market is still relied on to allocate private resources.

Once the discipline of such a social contract is in place, SA would be able to explore the option of joining the European Economic Community (EEC). Euroization would enable SA to free itself completely from its current account constraint vis-à-vis Euroland. The volatility of the Euro-Rand exchange rate would then be completely eliminated, and international trade would greatly expand. SA would become to Europe as the Western Cape is to SA. No one need worry about the size of the current account surplus or deficit with Euroland, with the result that it would become a nonissue.

Euroization would result in SA losing the advantage of an independent monetary policy and, with it, the ability to vary the bank rate countercyclically over the cycle. With Euroization, member economies would tend to move more in tandem. But the central point is that, without a social contract to prevent cost inflation, as unemployment falls and workers' bargaining position improves, the low interest rates that are required if full employment AD is to be achieved would be inflationary and impossible to achieve for any central bank concerned about higher inflation rates.

The Post Keynesian balance-of-payments–constrained growth model and Thirlwall's rule illustrate the manner in which economies are demand constrained, and how easily the South may be pushed into mutually reinforcing contractionary growth regimes under existing multiple currency institutional arrangements. Most Post Keynesians have still to line up on the side of dollarization and Euroization. But all Post Keynesians agree that lower average levels of world interest rates would relax the current levels of demand constraints and lead to the associated outcome of greater employment and output levels for all countries.

Due to enormously rapid technological change, the world is shrinking before our very eyes. Nevertheless, a world currency and a world central bank are unlikely to be attained in the foreseeable future, due primarily to political considerations, irrespective of their enormous potential economic benefits. Post Keynesians must hold fast to the key that joining a currency union removes all balance-of-payments constraints for all countries within the currency union. The existence of political obstacles may continue to prevent the development of a common world currency and a single world central bank within our lifetime. Nevertheless, the decision to dollarize and Euroize are within each country's political grasp. Surely it is time for Post Keynesians to get on the side of history.

Note

1. The repo rate is analogous to the Federal Funds Rate in the United States.

Part III

Extensions and New Directions

CHAPTER 10

The Structure of Post-Keynesian Economics
The Core Contributions of the Pioneers[1]

G. C. Harcourt*

I

Why post-Keynesian economics, and who were its Cambridge pioneers? Maynard Keynes, Richard Kahn, Richard Goodwin, Nicholas Kaldor, Luigi Pasinetti, Joan Robinson, and Piero Sraffa all started initially, at least in some degree, within the mainstream of their time. They all moved well and truly outside it, attempting to create either a revolutionary alternative or to rehabilitate the classical Marxian tradition, in most cases in the light of the Keynesian revolution. The one exception is Michal Kalecki, whose personal history and independent mind combined to place him virtually always outside the mainstream. This chapter, though, is not principally concerned with why and how the discontents that led them to change their minds arose. Rather, its principal object is to set out the structures of their alternative approaches in

* This was the keynote address at the July 2006 HETSA Conference at Ballarat. I am most grateful (with the usual disclaimer) to the conference participants and two anonymous referees for their comments.

This chapter was originally published in *History of Economics Review* (No. 45, winter 2007, pp. 95–105).

order to suggest modes of thinking about theoretical and policy issues in political economy.[2]

The structures presented here are based on over forty years of teaching and researching under the rubric of what is now called post-Keynesian economics. I certainly was not aware that it was so called when I started on this track in the 1950s. In fact, I have much sympathy with the stance of my old friend, the late Athanasios (Tom) Asimakopulos, who declined an invitation to be included in the first edition of the admirable *A Biographical Dictionary of Dissenting Economists* by Philip Arestis and Malcolm Sawyer (1992), because he regarded his views and contributions as belonging fully within the mainstream of economics proper, not in a dissenting stream.[3] (It was only in order to provide a suitable tribute to his influential contributions and splendid personal example as a teacher and a human being that his widow, Marika, allowed the entry on Tom to be included in the second edition of Arestis and Sawyer [2000]. See Harcourt 2000.) However, it must be admitted that my scholarly views and approaches continue to be regarded by the bulk of the profession as those of dissenters.

The most succinct definition of post-Keynesian economics comes from Joan Robinson (1978; 1979, 210): "To me, the expression *post-Keynesian* has a definite meaning; it applies to an economic theory or method of analysis which takes account of the difference between the future and the past" (emphasis in the original).

I obviously have no quarrel with this; but, as I try to be ever mindful of historical developments, I also wish to stress that the approaches to political economy which reflect post-Keynesian thought are there partly for historical reasons and partly because of logical associations. Post-Keynesianism is an extremely broad church. The overlaps at each end of a long spectrum of views are marginal (*sic*), often reflecting little more than a shared hostility towards mainstream neoclassical economics and methodology, IS-LM Keynesianism, and the "fix-price" Keynesianism of the "New Keynesians" and certain French economists. Some post-Keynesians are working actively towards a synthesis of the principal strands.[4] Others regard the search for a synthesis, for a general all-embracing structure, as a profound mistake: To quote Joan Robinson (1974; 1979, 119), a founding mother, such a search is a misguided attempt to replace "one box of tricks" by another. Post-Keynesianism should be a situation-and-issue-specific method of doing political economy, a "horses for courses" approach, itself an all-embracing structure at the methodological level (see Harcourt 2001, essay 19).

The principal object of analysis is the advanced capitalist economies of the twentieth and twenty-first centuries. It must be admitted that the tradition within which they are presented objects vigorously to the microeconomic-macroeconomic dichotomy of mainstream economics (see Joan Robinson 1977b; 1979, 4–5; for a typically forceful argument why). Basically, neither individual nor group or class behavior may be understood without making explicit the economy-wide structures and relationships that provide the backdrop to their behavior. Similarly, economy-wide structures and relationships not only influence but also are influenced by individual and group or class motivations and behavior. Thus, the microeconomic foundations of macroeconomics must always be complemented with—indeed, it could be argued, dominated by—the macroeconomic foundations of microeconomics (see Crotty 1980).[5]

The particular subsets of the mainstream literature that this happy band became increasingly dissatisfied with were: the theory of distribution, especially the marginal productivity theory in its aggregative form (but also the supply and demand approach in general; see Bharadwaj 1978); the theory of pricing at the level of the firm and the industry, principally as it came down from Marshall and Pigou; the theory of investment behavior and expenditure that is implied in Marshall and Pigou and, more explicitly, in the writings of Irving Fisher; the theory of money and finance; and the theory of growth, to which is allied the theory of the trade cycle (the business cycle, to our North American cousins), as it has been developed in the postwar period by leading neoclassical economists (some of whom—for example, James Meade, Robert Solow, and Trevor Swan—were/are also leading Keynesians). In doing so, they were inspired and stimulated—even irritated—by Roy Harrod's and Evsey Domar's seminal contributions in the late pre-war and early postwar years.

The alternative theories of the post-Keynesians under each of these heads may be combined into an overarching general framework that may then be applied in explanations of postwar happenings in the advanced capitalist world. This same framework, together with its constituent parts, may be used to rationalize various policy proposals which tackled, or should have been used to tackle, some of the major malfunctions of these economies in the same period.

In addition, it is important to take note of and record for posterity the background and the nuances to the making of the theories by people who knew these pioneers personally and who were present for at least part of the time when the ideas were developed, not only to restore them to their correct place in the narrative but also to correct the misconceptions and often neglect they suffer or experience as the third and even fourth generation of post-Keynesians increasingly come to constitute the post-Keynesian literature and canon. I do not mean to denigrate the contributions of the latter groups; but I would like to restore to their rightful place the fundamental pioneering contributions of the first contributors.[6]

II

In discussing post-Keynesian macroeconomic theories of distribution, I start with Kaldor's 1955–56 paper, using it as the backdrop to discussions of Kalecki's earlier contributions, including his review of Keynes's *General Theory of Employment, Interest and Money*, Joan Robinson's eclectic approach, and Frank Hahn's macro theory of employment and distribution, which was initially developed in his PhD dissertation at the London School of Economics in the later 1940s and early 1950s.

I start with Kaldor's paper not only because it is the best known but also because it is the most idiosyncratic. For here was Kaldor, an eminent Keynesian, arguing that a growing capitalist economy, if it is in equilibrium, must be at full employment and that the theory he developed is a long-period one. The theory is Keynesian because Kaldor insists that investment leads and saving responds. But his first two assumptions led Paul Samuelson (1964) to dub him Jean-Baptiste Kaldor. Kaldor used two empirical generalizations to complete his model: first, that prices are more flexible than money wages in the long term, and so change more rapidly than money wages in situations of excess demand or supply; second, that the marginal propensity to save of profit-receivers (profits) is greater than the marginal propensity to save of wage-earners (wages).[7] This allowed total saving (as a proportion of full-employment long-period income) to change as the distribution of income changed in response to discrepancies between planned investment (as a proportion of full-employment long-period income) and the initial value of planned saving (also as a proportion of full-employment long-period income), until planned saving and planned investment were equal to one another.

In Kalecki's earlier account of a macro theory of distribution (1936, 1971), the analysis applied to the short period, in which there is not necessarily full employment, so that both the distribution of income and the levels of activity and employment may be determined simultaneously. An explicit connection is made between the pricing practices of firms and the overall distribution of income. (In Kaldor's early models on these themes, price-setting behavior is not explicitly discussed.)

Joan Robinson's well-known exposition of Kalecki's theory (Joan Robinson 1977a, 1979) was used to instruct several generations of Cambridge undergraduates, first by Robinson and, later, by me in my lectures in the 1980s and 1990s on post-Keynesian economics.

As already noted, Joan Robinson's approach over the years to the theory of distribution was eclectic. By the time she published her magnum opus, *The Accumulation of Capital*, in 1956, she was working within Kalecki's structure, which had applications not only to an understanding of how capitalism works but also to how a democratic socialist regime could work. (Alas, the Stalinists in charge of Kalecki's native Poland never gave him a chance to put his suggestions into practice when he returned there in the 1950s.)

Robinson used Kalecki's structure by examining the real aspects of the creation and extraction of a surplus from the consumption goods sector to be used by the workers in the investment goods sector. Crucial roles are played by productivity in the consumption goods sector and the size of the real wage in the determination of the *potential* rate of accumulation; whether it is *realized* or not depends, of course, on the planned investment behavior of the capitalist class in given situations in capitalism and of planners and managers in socialism. The analysis follows David Worswick's 1959 stockade dictator version of Joan Robinson's model in *The Accumulation of Capital* (a representation with which she was not *that* pleased) and Harry Johnson's 1962 version of her model, with one technique of production available and dominant at any moment of time. (She felt that the major propositions of her theory of growth could be established without explicitly incorporating an analysis of the choice of techniques.)

Kalecki's extraordinary review article of *The General Theory* (which, unfortunately, was not published in full in English until December 1982[8]) not only shows conclusively that Kalecki independently discovered the principal propositions of *The General Theory* but also that he set the arguments in the most appropriate framework for analyzing capitalism—Marx's schemas of production and reproduction. Kalecki showed explicitly both the microeconomic foundations of macroeconomics, including a macroeconomic theory of distribution, and the reverse flow of macroeconomic foundations of microeconomics. In the process, he showed that market structures were qualitatively unimportant in establishing the main systemic results; see also Shapiro 1997 (but also Marris 1997).

With regard to post-Keynesian theories of determination of the size of the markup, I take Adrian Wood's "Golden Age" model (Wood 1975) as the benchmark, against which can be assessed the "historical time" model developed by Peter Kenyon and me (1976) and the choice of technique in the investment decision in both the orthodox and the post-Keynesian approach.[9] Wood's model is explicitly Golden Age, or steady state with expectations always realized, so that the analysis is set in logical time. Harcourt and Kenyon's model is an attempt to set the same general problem in historical time, relating pricing and the investment decision to succeeding short periods' behavior of the firm. Discussion of the latter model should be preceded by an analysis of the choice of technique in both an orthodox and a post-Keynesian setting, partly because Wood claimed that his analysis was unaffected by the choice of technique rule used, partly in order to illustrate the different results obtained, according to whether the neoclassical axiomatic approach or the post-Keynesian approach based on real world decision-making rules is employed.

Wood developed a relationship between the rate of growth of sales revenue of the firm and the size of the markup needed to provide internal finance to match the accumulation needed to sustain this rate of growth, given the supply of external finance in the existing situation. He identified an opportunity frontier and a finance frontier. The former takes in the opportunities for growth of the firm in terms of alternative pricing, investment, and sales policies. At some point, the firm encounters a tradeoff between a higher profit margin on the one hand and a higher rate of sales on the other. Rates of accumulation are the clue to how fast sales may grow, because they determine both capacity and costs of production. There is a unique opportunity frontier for the firm, which itself is usually taken to be a price leader in an oligopolistic setting, operating in situations of given overall aggregate demand.

The finance frontier relates to the tradeoff between markup levels, rates of growth of sales revenues, and the investment needed to provide the capacity to produce the output associated with the sales. Where the two frontiers intersect determines both the markup set and the rate of growth of sales (and of accumulation to back them up).

When choice of techniques is possible, the two frontiers become families, each member of which is associated with a given technique of production. Because the opportunity frontiers move out at a decreasing rate (convex to origin isoquants) while the finance frontiers fan out at a proportional rate, their intersections provide a locus which has a maximum rate of growth of sales revenue, size of markup combination. Internal finance is usually preferred to other forms of investment expenditure, and Kalecki's principle of increasing risk is the most insightful explanation (see Harcourt 2006, chapter 3).

In examining macroeconomic theories of accumulation, my starting point is a critique of the details of Keynes's theory in *The General Theory* and after. The critique stems from the writings of Abba Lerner, Kalecki, Joan Robinson, and Asimakopulos, and it argues that Keynes had the right ingredients but the wrong recipe in his chapter 11 on the marginal efficiency of capital (*mec*). Lerner (1944) provided an internal critique by pointing out that Keynes failed to distinguish between the *mec* and the marginal efficiency of investment (*mei*), even though it was the latter in which he was principally interested because it related to the short-period equilibrium flow of aggregate investment. Lerner's conclusions may be stated in two propositions:

1. In full, stock-flow equilibrium, $mec = mei = i$, where i is the exogenously given value of the rate of interest.
2. In short-period flow equilibrium, $mei = i < mec$.

Even these refinements would not suffice for Keynes's other three critics. Keynes had given two reasons why there is, in any given situation, a downward sloping relation between desired rates of accumulation and given values of *i*. The first, relating mainly to the short period, is associated with the assumption of rising marginal costs of production in the short period and marginal cost pricing being usually universal in all sectors of the economy. With given expectations about future flows of expected profits associated with possible investment projects, higher supply prices implied lower *mei*s. But, his critics argued, this may only occur in the economy as a whole *if* individual business people used, in the calculations of their *mei*s, not known current market prices of investment goods but rather their equilibrium prices, which aggregate investment, if implemented, would bring about. That is to say, Keynes had assumed rational expectations for a second time in his life. (The first was when he planned to do just enough preparation to become Twelfth Wrangler in the finals of the Mathematics Tripos at Cambridge in 1905, a respectable but not brilliant result that satisfied him but not his father.)

The second reason, a more long-period one, rested on the assumption that long-term demand curves for products were givens, while short-period supply curves in future periods would be farther and farther out to the right, the greater were the levels of investment in the current short period (because they would supply greater and greater capacities in the future). The intersections of the supply and demand curves thus implied lower and lower expected prices and therefore expected profits and so lower *mei*s, the larger the investment now.

But here Keynes was being untrue to himself, for he always argued in other contexts that the present played a large role in determining expectations about the future. As higher levels of accumulation now would imply greater sales and higher prices and profits, these should be expected in the future, and so longer-term demand curves could *not* be taken as givens. Therefore, it was not inevitable that expected prices and profits would be lower and so *mei*s less.

The solution of the critics was to take Keynes's ingredients and rewrite the recipe in terms of a two-sided relationship between profitability and accumulation. Thus, higher rates of accumulation now implied higher systemic profitability. Higher profitability now meant higher expected profitability in the future, which would induce higher rates of desired accumulation. Where the two relationships intersected gave, in effect, through Joan Robinson's famous banana diagram (Robinson 1962, 48), her version of Harrod's warranted rate of growth—for the expectations of business people in a given situation would be realized and so maintained. At least, this was so, provided the relationships themselves remained unaffected over time by what Harold Macmillan once memorably called (in a different context, of course) "events, dear boy, events." All the ingredients involved in their criticism therefore come together in Joan Robinson's well-known banana diagram.

A discussion of money and finance—whether they are exogenous or endogenous in theory and real life—might start with Keynes's 1937 articles on the finance motive, which stress the distinction between finance and saving and the ordering, at the individual and the systemic levels, of finance → investment → saving. On this base can be erected the arguments of modern scholars—for example, Kaldor 1983, Basil Moore 1988, Victoria Chick 1992, Sheila Dow 1997, and Giuseppe Fontana 2003—as to why finance, especially banking finance, is predominantly endogenous and that Keynes did *not* disagree with this. For his immediate purposes in *The General Theory*, Keynes took the supply of money as a *given* but not as an exogenous variable. His liquidity preference theory may then be restated in an endogenous money framework, as Sheila Dow

(1997) showed. I have always found money and the theory of money something of a mystery, but that does not mean I regard them as unimportant. After all, one of Keynes's greatest innovations and achievements was to analyze a monetary production economy by integrating monetary and financial considerations with real ones right from the start of the analysis.

All the previous developments can be brought together in an explanation of postwar inflationary episodes, drawing on the conflict inflation models of Steve Marglin (1984a, 1984b) and Bob Rowthorn (1977). Both authors stressed the crucial insight that lasting but not accelerating inflation serves to bring about an uneasy truce between capital and labor. Neither completely achieved his aspirations (rates of accumulation for capital, real wage levels and rates of increase for labor) but, through inflation, the nonrealization of aspirations never tended to worsen, either.

Discussions of theories of growth start with Smith's and Ricardo's theories and move on to Marx and then to Harrod's theory. (The reaction to Harrod's findings and problems by Solow and Swan, on the one hand, and Kaldor and Joan Robinson, on the other, are discussed in Harcourt 2006, chapter 7, together with Richard Goodwin's eclectic theories and Pasinetti's grand synthesis.) Later, Kaldor scrapped many of his earlier ideas in order to stress the complementarity between the production of primary products and industrial products in the world economy, and of endogenous growth theory, emphasizing how it relates to previous discussions from Smith on.

Many of the ideas presented in this chapter are discussed in detail in Harcourt 2006. The book's concluding chapter uses the approaches developed in earlier chapters to examine their application to policy issues. It discusses how "vision," approach, and method interrelate with policy recommendations; and it closes with a proposed "package deal" solution to a crucial dilemma raised by Kalecki in his classic 1943 paper on the political aspects of full employment, especially how it may be permanently sustained as opposed to attained from a deep slump.

Notes

1. The title is also the title of Harcourt 2006. In writing the book, I had in mind two sets of readers: first, undergraduate and graduate students who may be looking for alternative approaches to thinking about theoretical, applied, and policy issues in economics; second, teachers and researchers in economics, not so much perhaps for the details of the analysis, with which

many would be familiar, but for the way in which one person at least sees the interconnections and interrelationships that have emerged as our discipline has evolved and developed.

2. Some of the reasons for their discontent are given in the appendixes to Harcourt 2000. Appendix 1 contains short intellectual biographies of the main contributors, and appendix 2 contains a sketch of some of their principal arguments.

   I discuss not only the theoretical core and results of the Cambridge-Cambridge controversies in capital theory but also the implications of the Cambridge, England, findings for econometric theory and practice. In particular, I stress the dangers for econometric specification of collapsing the long period and the short period into one, even within the neoclassical framework. I confine these criticisms to an appendix because I want to emphasize in the text the positive aspects of the post-Keynesian approach and structure.
3. As with Brian Reddaway and Austin Robinson, Tom's contributions are erected firmly and securely on the base of a thorough knowledge of the writings of Marshall and Keynes and, in Tom's case, of Kalecki and Joan Robinson, as well as on a deep critical understanding of the content and method of neoclassical economics.
4. The deepest and most profound example of the attempts to provide a coherent synthesis is the splendid monograph by Heinrich Bortis, *Institutions, Behaviour and Economic Theory: A Contribution to Classical-Keynesian Political Economy* (1997). Reading successive drafts of Henry's book taught me so much. If I were ever to be persuaded that a synthesis were possible, it would be because of his arguments. A referee suggested Marc Lavoie's *Foundations of Post-Keynesian Economics* (1992) as the other significant work that should be mentioned.
5. A referee points out that, in Kalecki's approach, "certain key elements are determined at the micro level, while others are determined at the macro level, so that [the determination of] the level of total employment . . . requires both micro and macro. [Hence] it does not make sense to talk about either being a 'foundation' for the other." I do not completely agree; see my discussion of Kalecki's model in section III.
6. Paul Davidson (2003–04) has written a most idiosyncratic review article of John King's *History of Post Keynesian Economics since 1936* (King 2002). It was entitled "Setting the record straight. . . . " I was tempted to write a reply with Luigi Pasinetti entitled "*Really* setting the record straight" but desisted after I read the courteous but powerful replies to Davidson by Marc Lavoie and King himself.
7. Luigi Pasinetti's famous 1962 paper analyzes what happens when wages are not the sole source of income of wage-earners because they have saved in the past and acquired financial and other assets.
8. I asked a former Cambridge graduate student of mine, Ferdinando Targetti, and his Polish wife, Boguslawa Kinda-Hass, to translate the article

for publication in *Australian Economic Papers*, with a commentary by them (see Targetti and Kinda-Hass 1982). I regard it as the most important article published during my years as joint editor of *Australian Economic Papers*.

9. A referee has pointed out that, in the literature relating to these issues, there is a debate concerning the appropriate notion of costs as well as what determines the markup. There are also two broad approaches to the latter: One follows Kalecki in locating it in the oligopolistic conditions facing the firm; the other, which is exposited in the book, locates it in the investment plans of the firm.

REFERENCES

Arestis, P., and M. Sawyer, ed. 1992. *A biographical dictionary of dissenting economists*. Aldershot, UK: Edward Elgar.

———. 2000. *A biographical dictionary of dissenting economists*. 2nd ed. Aldershot, UK: Edward Elgar.

Bharadwaj, K. 1978. *Classical political economy and rise to dominance of supply and demand theories*. New Delhi: Longman Orient.

Chick, Victoria. 1992. *On money, method and Keynes: Selected essays*. Ed. P. Arestis and S. Dow. Houndmills, Basingstoke, Hampshire: Palgrave Macmillan.

Crotty, James R. 1980. Post-Keynesian theory: An overview and evaluation. *American Economic Review* 70:20–25.

Davidson, P. 2003–04. Setting the record straight on *A History of Post Keynesian Economics*. *Journal of Post Keynesian Economics* 26:245–72.

Dow, S. C. 1997. Endogenous money. In *A "second edition" of* The general theory, vol. 2, ed. G. C. Harcourt and P. A. Riach. London: Routledge.

Fontana, G. 2003. Post Keynesian approaches to endogenous money: A time framework explanation. *Review of Political Economy* 15:291–314.

Harcourt, G. C. 1982. *The social science imperialists: Selected essays*. Ed. Prue Kerr. London: Routledge and Kegan Paul.

———. 2000. Askimakopulos, Athanasios (Tom) (1930–1990). In *A biographical dictionary of dissenting economists*, 2nd ed., ed. P. Arestis and M. Sawyer. Aldershot, UK: Edward Elgar.

———. 2001. *50 years a Keynesian and other essays*. London: Palgrave.

———. 2006. *The structure of post-Keynesian economics: The core contributions of the pioneers*. Cambridge: Cambridge University Press.

Harcourt, G. C., and P. Kenyon. 1976. Pricing and the investment decision. *Kyklos*, 29:449–77. Repr. in Harcourt 1982.

Harcourt, G. C., and P. A. Riach, eds. 1997. *A "second edition" of* The general theory. 2 vols. London: Routledge.

Johnson, H. G. 1962. A simple Joan Robinson model of accumulation with one technique. *Osaka Economic Papers* 10:28–33.

Kaldor, N. 1955–56. Alternative theories of distribution. *Review of Economic Studies* 23:83–100.

———. 1983. Keynesian economics after fifty years. In *Keynes and the modern world: Proceedings of the Keynes Centenary Conference, Kings College, Cambridge*, ed. D. Worswick and J. Trevithick. Cambridge: Cambridge University Press.

Kalecki, M. 1936. Pare uwag o teorii Keynesa (Some remarks on Keynes's theory). *Economista* 3. Repr. in Osiatynski 1990; see also Targetti and Kinda-Hass 1982.

———. 1943. Political aspects of full employment. *Political Quarterly* 14:322–31. Repr. in Kalecki 1971 and Osiatynski 1990.

———. 1971. *Selected essays on the dynamics of the capitalist economy, 1933–1970*. Cambridge: Cambridge University Press.

Keynes, J. M. 1936. *The general theory of employment, interest and money*. London: Macmillan. Repr. in Keynes 1971–1989, vol. 7.

———. 1937a. Alternative theories of the rate of interest. *Economic Journal* 47:241–52. Repr. in Keynes 1971–1989, vol. 14.

———. 1937b. The "ex ante" theory of the rate of interest. *Economic Journal* 47:663–69. Repr. in Keynes 1971–1989, vol. 14.

———. 1971–1989. *The collected writings of John Maynard Keynes*. Ed. D. E. Moggridge and E. A. G. Robinson. 30 vols. London: Macmillan, for the Royal Economic Society.

King, J. E. 2002. *A history of post Keynesian economics since 1936*. Cheltenham, UK: Edward Elgar.

Lavoie, M. 1992. *Foundations of post-Keynesian economics*. Aldershot, UK: Edward Elgar.

Lekachman, R., ed. 1964. *Keynes' general theory: Reports of three decades*. London: Macmillan.

Lerner, A. P. 1944. *The economics of control: Principles of welfare economics*. London: Macmillan.

Marglin, S. A. 1984a. Growth, distribution and inflation: A centennial synthesis. *Cambridge Journal of Economics* 8:115–44.

———. 1984b. *Growth, distribution and prices*. Cambridge, MA: Harvard University Press.

Marris, R. L. 1997. Yes, Mrs. Robinson! *The general theory* and imperfect competition. In *A "second edition" of* The general theory, vol. 1, ed. G. C. Harcourt and P. A. Riach. London: Routledge.

Moore, B. J. 1988. *Horizontalists and verticalists: The macroeconomics of credit money*. Cambridge: Cambridge University Press.

Osiatynski, J., ed. 1990. *Capitalism: Business cycles and full employment*. Vol. 1 of *Collected works of Michal Kalecki*. Oxford: Oxford University Press.

Pasinetti, L. L. 1962. Rate of profit and income distribution in relation to the rate of economic growth. *Review of Economic Studies* 29:267–79.

Robinson, Joan. 1956. *The accumulation of capital*. London: Macmillan.

———. 1962. *Essays in the theory of growth*. London: Macmillan.

———. 1974. History versus equilibrium. London: Thames Polytechnic. Repr. in Robinson 1979.

———. 1977a. Michal Kalecki on the economics of capitalism. *Oxford Bulletin of Economics and Statistics* 39:7–17. Repr. as "Michal Kalecki" in Robinson 1979.

———. 1977b. What are the questions? *Journal of Economic Literature* 15:1318–39. Repr. in Robinson 1979.

———. 1978. Keynes and Ricardo. *Journal of Post Keynesian Economics* 1:12–18. Repr. in Robinson 1979.

———. 1979. *Collected economic papers*, vol. 5. Oxford: Basil Blackwell.

Rowthorn, B. 1977. Conflict, inflation and money. *Cambridge Journal of Economics* 1:215–39.

Samuelson, P. A. 1964. A brief survey of post-Keynesian developments [1963]. In *Keynes' general theory: Reports of three decades*, ed. R. Lekachman. London: Macmillan.

Shapiro, N. 1997. Imperfect competition and Keynes. In *A "second edition" of* The general theory, vol. 1, ed. G. C. Harcourt and P. A. Riach. London: Routledge.

Targetti, F., and B. Kinda-Hass. 1982. Kalecki's review of Keynes' *General Theory. Australian Economic Papers* 21:244–60.

Wood, A. 1975. *A theory of profits*. Cambridge: Cambridge University Press.

Worswick, G. D. N. 1959. Mrs. Robinson on simple accumulation. *Oxford Economic Papers* 11:125–41.

Worswick, D., and J. Trevithick, ed. 1983. *Keynes and the modern world: Proceedings of the Keynes Centenary Conference, Kings College, Cambridge*. Cambridge: Cambridge University Press.

CHAPTER 11

African American Reparations, Keynes, and the Transfer Problem

William Darity Jr.

The Economic Consequences of the Peace (1919) was Keynes's unsuccessful (long) essay in persuasion to convince the Allies not to impose what he perceived as an excessive reparations burden on Germany after World War I. In (long) hindsight, one can wonder if Keynes was inordinately prescient. Did he glimpse that the burden of postwar reparations would put Germany on the road to national socialism and a mission of global conquest that would lead to World War II?

Keynes's objections were largely practical and logistical. While not objecting to the notion of reparations in principle, Keynes argued that the magnitude of the payments being sought by the Allies would place an unmanageable burden on Germany. The "economic consequences of the peace" would ultimately be disastrous for both Germany and her neighbors, with the long-term effect of renewed military conflict.

In chapter 5, Keynes advances a calculation of a total bill of £2 billion sterling as a reasonable indemnity for the victors to impose upon defeated Germany for wartime hostilities. He estimated that the allocation of the total would involve a £500 million payment to Belgium, an £800 million payment to France, a £500 million payment to Britain, and £250 million to all of the other Allies, including the United States. The ambiguous and open-ended nature of the then-evolving Treaty of

Versailles led Keynes to anticipate that the magnitude of the actual reparations bill would range anywhere from £8 to 13 billion.

A bill of this size, Keynes argued, would result in Germany being compelled to make payments to the Allies into the indefinite future. Keynes (1919, 154) contended that, from 1936 onward, Germany would have to pay £650 to 780 million annually to the Allies. In his judgment, "Germany cannot pay anything approaching this sum. Until the Treaty is altered . . . Germany has in effect engaged herself to hand over to the Allies the whole of her surplus production in perpetuity." Of course, Keynes's forecast was made in the context of what he viewed as a reasonable projection concerning future increases in productive capacity in Germany. A scenario with dramatically higher growth in German productive capacity, greater inflation in the Allies' currencies than the German mark, or both, would mean that only a portion of the German surplus would have to be diverted to the Allied countries. In contrast, a scenario with stagnation in Germany productivity, greater inflation in Germany than the Allied countries, or both, would mean that the German reparations payments could become a debt infeasible to pay beyond 1936.

The Treaty of Versailles was an instance of standing victorious governments imposing payment on a standing defeated government. It can also be viewed as standing victorious national economies imposing payments on a standing defeated national economy.

There are parallels with conditions in the aftermath of the U.S. Civil War. Although the Confederate States of America no longer constituted a standing government, the South as a region could be viewed as a standing, albeit war-ravaged, economy. The states that had attempted secession were defeated and, in the view of the Radical Republicans, especially Pennsylvania Congressman Thaddeus Stevens, were conquered territories and should be treated as such. From this standpoint, the secessionists, as the defeated aggressors in the Civil War, should pay for the war. The South should be reconstituted along the terms dictated by the victors. This would have included exclusion of the supporters of secession from the voter rolls, the redrawing of state boundaries to eliminate the identity of the region as "the South" (Elliott 2006), the inclusion of the ex-slaves on the voter rolls, and the provision of a form of reparations to the ex-slaves via a land redistribution that would have provided each family of four with forty acres and a mule (McPherson 1964; Shabazz 1994).

The land redistribution scheme that was to provide African Americans with a foundation for the accumulation of wealth in the United States was embodied in General William T. Sherman's Special Field Order Number 15, the first Freedman's Bureau Act, and the Southern Homestead Act. All of these commitments to the ex-slaves were abrogated by President Andrew Johnson, who became President after Lincoln's assassination. Johnson's dislike for the Southern plantocracy was exceeded only by his dislike for blacks. The failure to provide land and mules to the ex-slaves after the Civil War—indeed, the general failure to implement the Radical Republican program for Reconstruction—leaves the unfulfilled promise of reparations for African Americans still at hand today. The case today is no longer predicated exclusively on compensation for slavery but also compensation for nearly a century of Jim Crow practices and ongoing discrimination in the United States.

The Becker-Krueger trade model of discrimination (Becker 1957; Krueger 1963) provides a framework for thinking about some of the issues associated with African American reparations, and it will circle us back to Keynes and the German reparations. In Krueger's elaboration of the model, there are two economies with segregated and immobile workforces producing the same multi-purpose good. Call one of these economies the black economy and call the other the white economy. The key difference between the two economies is that the black economy is labor intensive while the white economy is capital intensive. Even without complete mobility of labor, free mobility of capital would bring about factor-price equalization—the same wages for labor in both economies and the same rate of return on capital in both economies. But free capital mobility is hindered by a discriminatory tax placed on the flow of capital going to the black sector, where autarkical pricing would offer it a higher rate of return.

The distributive implications are interesting. With the white-imposed capital tariff maintaining a factor-price wedge between the two economies, white labor receives a higher wage than black labor and black capital receives a higher return than white capital. The political economy message suggests "strange bedfellows" in terms of alliances in support of and in opposition to the regime of economic apartheid. White laborers and black owners of capital would both support the status quo of restricted capital mobility, while black laborers and white owners of capital would be expected to oppose the status quo regime. White labor might be able to buy the support of white capital if the wage differential is large enough to compensate white capital while white labor still receives a higher net wage than black labor, the free trade wage, or the autarkical wage. Thus, the black economy virtually takes on the character of an "internal colony."

Now suppose that, at some later date, a morally enlightened white population agrees that the discriminatory tariff is reprehensible, eliminates it, and agrees to pay reparations to the black population for being subjected to racist economic practices. With a lump-sum transfer of income to blacks in this world where there is a single good being produced and whites are taxed to facilitate the transfer, there should be a deadweight loss for whites and an absolute gain in income for blacks. Although wage rates and rates of return on capital have become uniform, black income and consumption should, on average, be higher than white income and consumption, on average, in the period immediately after the transfer.

Matters become much more complicated if a variety of modifications are made to the model to make it more realistic. Suppose that the black and white economies produce different goods, so that trade involves products and not just movement of factors of production. Suppose that there are unemployed resources in either economy. Suppose, further, that each economy uses a different currency. And suppose that the environment is dynamic rather than static, so that not only are participants in each economy engaged in consumption but also saving activity and technological change take place in both economies. This pushes us back to the terrain of relevance to the German reparations payments, with attendant implications for African American reparations.

In Keynes's (1929) short essay, "The German Transfer Problem," published a decade after *The Economic Consequences of the Peace*, he proposed that there were two central issues concerning the feasibility of German payment. First, there was a budgetary problem—the sheer question of whether Germany could acquire the resources to meet the obligation, that is, actually generate the surpluses required to meet its burden of debt. (It is worth noting that, after World War II, the Allies moved in the opposite direction and made a substantial transfer to again-defeated Germany rather than extracting reparations.) Second, Keynes said, there was a transfer problem. Having solved the budgetary problem, could Germany convert the accumulated resources into the foreign currencies in which payment must be met? Considerably later, Harry Johnson (1956) was to extend the discussion into a systematic analysis of the impact of the modes of payment and allocation of the transfer as well as the effects on the exchange rate.

There is no problem of exchange stability in the context of reparations for African Americans, but there is a broader issue suggested by the discussions of the transfer problem; see Johnson (1956), Keynes (1929), and especially Bertil Ohlin's commentary (1929) on Keynes's article. Indeed, Ohlin's emphasis on aggregate demand and his hints at a multiplier type of effect suggest that, at that point in time, prior to the development of *The General Theory*, he was more Keynesian than Keynes himself. The broader issue is, who benefits from the transfer? Is it possible for the donor economy actually to benefit from making the transfer?

With respect to African American reparations, a comedy sketch on satirist Dave Chappelle's television show highlights the most substantial aspect of the transfer problem. In the Chappelle sketch, blacks receive reparations income, engage in a massive spending orgy out of their "transitory" or windfall income, and *de facto* transfer income to white-owned corporations via their consumption expenditures. If there were a well-developed black economy, and black recipients of reparations bought those goods instead, the Chappelle effect would be mitigated. But, as long as there is no black corporate structure of significance in an economy where goods are produced by private enterprises, some type of re-transfer of the reparations income must take place if funds go to a group that has little productive capacity of its own. Black-owned industry in the United States is somewhat of an oxymoron; black-owned retailers are more commonplace.

Even if there were two racially separate economies producing different goods, the marginal propensity to consume the "domestic" good versus the marginal propensity to import the "foreign" good would have to be considered to assess the full effects of the transfer. The income elasticity of the propensities to consume and import would take on central significance. There would be a recomposition of aggregate demand by the recipient of the transfer, due to the change in the intergroup distribution of income. Furthermore, the full effects of the transfer would have to take into account the way in which the transfer donors finance the payment, whether it is by taxation or by borrowing (and borrowing from whom). And where do the recipients locate their savings? Do they purchase assets that actually benefit the economic position of the donor population? Presumably, there would be some plausible combination of marginal propensities, taxation, borrowing, and portfolio decisions between blacks and whites in the United States that could produce the paradox of whites benefiting by paying reparations to blacks (Darity and Frank 2003).

Given this possibility, the scope of immediate white opposition to reparations for blacks is surprising. Perhaps it is due to the redistributive effects of the transfer potentially disproportionately benefiting white capital rather than white labor. Of course, the prospect of a Nazi backlash would be unlikely in the U.S. case, since reparations for African Americans would not be enacted by a victorious economy imposing the terms of surrender on a defeated economy. In the U.S. case, for congressional legislation to enable reparations on behalf of African Americans, white America collectively will have had to decide that it is the right thing to do. White supremacists would have had to be marginalized for such an outcome to be realized.

So what are the circumstances under which the benefits of reparations for African Americans are most likely to "stay" with African Americans? A program predicated on the widely shared buildup of black capital before the transfer is enacted and that promotes the continued extensive development of black capital might be most effective in ensuring that the benefits of reparations go to those for whom the benefits are intended. This might mean that some part of the reparations fund be devoted to human capital development and the extension of capital ownership to blacks on a scale that closes the enormous racial wealth gap in the United States. A precedent exists in Malaysia with the wealth redistribution program that has been undertaken on behalf of the native Malays. Close attention should be given to both its strengths and weaknesses in the design of a program with a similar objective on behalf of African Americans. In short, a reparations program structured to achieve a racial democraticization of the capitalist and cognitive sides of American life—a racially inclusive American capitalism and American system of educational credentials—may afford the best insurance against a reparations program resulting in a Chappelle effect.

It is critical that any program of reparations be designed with intimate awareness of the context of its application. A decontextualized indemnity payment is a dangerous indemnity payment. As Keynes (1919, 211) warned about the Treaty of Versailles, its imposition of a compensatory burden on Germany without addressing any of the other structural issues at play would lead to further crises: "The Treaty includes no provisions for the economic rehabilitation of Europe—nothing to make the defeated Central Empires into good neighbours, nothing to stabilise the new States of Europe; nothing to reclaim Russia; nor does it promote in any way a compact of solidarity amongst the allies themselves; no arrangement was reached at Paris for restoring the disordered finances of France and Italy, or to adjust the systems of the Old World and the New."

Similarly, enacting a program of reparations for African Americans without considering the transfer problem (and the Chappelle effect) would be at least as unwise.

References

Becker, Gary. 1957. *The economics of discrimination.* Chicago: University of Chicago Press.

Darity, W. A., Jr., and D. Frank. 2003. The economics of reparations. *American Economic Review* 93 (2): 326–29.

Elliott, Mark. 2006. *Color-blind justice: Albion Tourgee and the quest for racial equality from the Civil War to Plessy v. Ferguson.* New York: Oxford University Press.

Johnson, H. G. 1956. The transfer problem and exchange stability. *Journal of Political Economy* 64 (3): 212–25.

Keynes, J. M. 1919. *The economic consequences of the peace.* London: Macmillan.

———. 1929. The German transfer problem. *The Economic Journal* 39 (153): 1–7.

Krueger, Anne. 1963. The economics of discrimination. *Journal of Political Economy* 71 (5): 481–86.

McPherson, James. 1964. *The struggle for equality: Abolitionists and the Negro in the Civil War and Reconstruction.* Princeton: Princeton University Press.

Ohlin, B. G. 1929. Mr. Keynes's views on the transfer problem: A rejoinder from Professor Ohlin. *The Economic Journal* 39 (155): 388–408.

Shabazz, Amilcar, ed. 1994. *The forty acres documents: What did the United States really promise the people freed from slavery?* Baton Rouge: The Malcolm Generation.

CHAPTER 12

KEYNES AND GLOBALIZATION

JAMES K. GALBRAITH

THE TRADITIONAL WAY TO ADAPT THE BASIC CLOSED-ECONOMY Keynesian model to an open world has been to introduce the elements of external account: exports, imports, capital flow, exchange rate. Sandy Darity and I give a treatment in our textbook; it is in no way original. We also develop a series of North-South models incorporating asymmetries such as the hard-currency–soft-currency dichotomy emphasized by Pan Yotopoulos. In a paper in the *International Review of Applied Economics* long ago, I interpreted Keynesian demand fluctuations and a model of vintage capital in a transnational, North-South framework, to show the structural evolution of an advanced economy like the United States toward technological bipolarity and an unstable reliance on investment booms in technology sectors. This paper nicely anticipated the speculative and tech-driven boom and bust of 1997–2002.

All of these approaches address the global dimension from a national perspective; they are about the impact of trade and other global forces on the national scene, and they are, in that sense, merely adaptations of the national, closed-economy perspective. A step further is taken with Project LINK models, which attempt to estimate the joint impact of national economies on each other, especially through the established channels of trade. I have not been involved with this work, so I will not say much about it, save that, while "going global" in one sense, it obviously preserves the traditional focus on national economies, each now interacting with all of the others.

At a fundamental level, however, let me suggest that this way of doing business is now breaking down, and it is no longer adequate to work with national models, closed or open, independent or linked. Certain features of the global economy need to be thought of on a straightforwardly transnational or even global scale.

The clearest example of this breakdown and our incomplete response to it is in modern Europe. Europe has become a single, complete, unified economy. It has no internal borders, no trade barriers, perfect capital mobility, and no formal barriers to migration. It has a common currency, for the most part. In taking this step, it abolished international exchange rate fluctuation and also the intra-European current account. France's trade balance with Germany is today no more meaningful than that of Texas with New York.

Yet, if you wanted to know, say, the poverty rate in Europe, where would you turn? What would your concept be? Our ideas are stuck where our statistics are: at the national level. But it is obvious that, if we had European rather than national data, there would be virtually no poor in Germany and only a handful of "middle class" people in Poland or Latvia. So long as we lack correctly drawn statistics, we cannot correctly model the effects of macro policy in Europe. This permits Olivier Blanchard to go on modeling European unemployment as though all labor markets were local, when we know they are not.

In the Americas, it is equally clear that the concept of "national labor supply" has lost meaning: We have an unlimited reserve in Mexico and points south, and an even larger virtual reserve in China, India, and elsewhere. At the very least, this complicates, or should complicate, the way we think of a full employment policy. Do only "natives" count? If so, who counts as a "native"? Do we design a jobs program just for "citizens"? If so, do we then not count the ineligible among us as unemployed—even though they are every bit as present, honest, hardworking, and hungry as the eligible? And, on the other hand, if we do count everyone present on our soil as eligible, what is the right immigration policy to go with the employer-of-last-resort program?

So-called free trade agreements like NAFTA and CAFTA produce interdependencies that are not contemplated in Ricardian models, nor, I believe, effectively modeled by LINK. One of the most important connections is that between farm trade liberalization and migration. Food moves south. People move north. This should have been expected, but in all of the hullabaloo over trade costing manufacturing jobs—a minor effect, as it turns out—I do not recall that we focused on this issue. Yet, today, it is arguably the only really important actual consequence of these agreements.

The presence of a virtual reserve of labor, whether outside a country or in low-wage service activities inside it—the underemployed—should force a reconsideration of Keynesian unemployment theory. For Keynes, involuntary unemployment was due to a deficiency of effective demand: The capital and resources required to put men to work were present; capital was unemployed as well as labor. "There is work to do; there are men to do it. Why not bring them together?" That was Keynes's attitude. Unemployment could be conquered because it was a finite quantity; what was required was only the appropriate "device."

Instead, the presence of a virtual reserve places us in an Arthur Lewis world, with an infinitely elastic supply of labor at the socially determined subsistence wage, and it suggests that the appropriate model of unemployment should be derived from the Harris-Todaro model of wage inequality, migration incentives, and job search. A key implication of this model is that unemployment will vary directly with inequalities in the wage structure: The greater the inequalities, the greater the displacement, the more search for the small number of best chances, and the more unemployment.

A seeming paradox of this view is that unemployment is both voluntary and involuntary: From the individual perspective, unemployment is freely chosen; a small probability of landing a good job is better than the certainty of a poor one. Yet the rate of unemployment is entirely policy determined: Equalize the wage structure, and internal unemployment will decline; pursue real and nominal income convergence between countries, and net migration will slow, as will offshore outsourcing.

And from where comes aggregate demand sufficient to create all of the jobs? From the banks: It is a corollary of the endogeneity of money in the advanced credit economy. Conversely, if aggregate demand is constrained below full employment, inequality will necessarily be higher than it should be.

This view of the relationship between inequality and unemployment has three interesting characteristics.

1. It is directly opposed to the neoliberal idea that unemployment should be tackled by making labor markets more "flexible." In fact, that assault on the lower edges of the wage structure will make unemployment worse.
2. More broadly, it undermines the entire distinction between micro and macro, not by subsuming the latter into the former but by subsuming the former into the latter. For, if macro variables govern the structure of relative wages, the latter cannot simultaneously be determined in independent labor markets by marginal physical productivities, can they? Thus, the

entire vocabulary linking pay rates to skills needs to be discarded in favor of a simplified, unified theory that jointly determines inequality and unemployment.

3. It fits the facts extraordinarily well. Inequality and unemployment are, it turns out, intimately associated, in time series and cross-section, in North America and in Europe. More egalitarian countries have less unemployment. Inequality rises and falls with unemployment.

Once you understand this relationship, you see it everywhere. A notable case in point is China, where rapidly rising inequality between coastal cities and the rural interior has fueled an internal migration of some 150 million people, many of whom are unemployed at any given time. Yet no one would accuse China of running a slow-growth policy. Nor is it accurate to say that the Chinese economy works through repression of wages—in real terms they've risen more rapidly there than anywhere in the world.

A next step is to begin to ask questions of public policy. In particular, how might this theory of unemployment bear on the problem of mass unemployment in Europe, whose problem, we are incessantly told, is the inveterate egalitarianism of socialists and trade unions, denying that continent the inegalitarian dynamism of the United States?

We have now measured the inequality of Europe across regions, in a way precisely comparable to measuring that of the United States across states. We find that, across the EU-15, inequality is *40 percent higher* than in the United States. Across the EU-25, it is *more than twice the U.S. value*. So, perhaps a strategy of convergence—involving such standbys of American policy as a unified pension scheme, a continental minimum wage, land-grant universities, and Richard Nixon's great program of General Revenue Sharing—might be more successful and effective than the repeated failure of labor market reform. (Einstein defined insanity as always doing the same thing and expecting a different result.)

Finally, taking a truly global and macroeconomic view, one can sense the necessity of examining the patterns of inequality not merely within and between countries that are part of defined regions, such as Europe or North America, but across the entire world. The task of the University of Texas Inequality Project (UTIP) has been to develop data of sufficient range and adequate quality to make this examination possible, and we have succeeded at this task. The UTIP data are now widely accepted and in increasingly wide research use. I hope the Post Keynesian community will begin to explore them as a resource, for they are fundamental to testing and demonstrating the Keynesian character of our globalized world.

In particular, it is a basic, almost unspoken, precept of neoclassical models of inequality and growth that each country chooses its own sound structure, economic institutions, and degree of inequality; the theories then examine the alleged consequences of this "choice." The precept of national choice is shared, unfortunately, by neoradical or neoinstitutionalist arguments on the left—the so-called varieties of capitalism (VOC) approach—which hold that there are "good" as well as "bad" routes to full employment, a belief that implicitly forces the abandonment of any systematic theory of unemployment.

My Global Keynesian perspective holds, of course, that there is only one route to full employment: a strategy of wage convergence fueled by permissive, endogenous growth of total demand and anchored, to avoid inflation, by administered stability of key prices, including oil and the interest rate. This coincides with policy choices often made by social democratic politics—hence my pragmatic alliance with the VOC approach—but the difference is that a Global Keynesianism can explain the outcome, whereas the VOC approach has no underlying theory.

Finally, the systematic investigation of patterns in global inequality exposes the broad fallacy that inequality is, for most countries, a policy choice. If it were, there would not exist precise common patterns in the worldwide movement of inequality. But such patterns do exist; not only that, they dominate the worldwide movement of inequality. Take them out and most of the movement goes away.

The broad pattern is this: 1963–70, stabilization; 1971–79, declining inequality; 1981–2000, a turnaround, and sharply rising inequality, almost everywhere in the world. The turning points correspond to the breakdown of the stabilizing global financial framework of Bretton Woods, which inaugurated a decade of rapid growth fueled by rising commodity prices and negative real interest rates, and the advent of global monetarism in 1981–82, which brought all of that to a screeching halt.

The presence of these turning points and their effects, which are plainly visible in the global pattern of relative wages and therefore of migration and unemployment, decisively establishes the nonneutrality of the global money rate of interest. For this reason, it ought to grab the attention of all followers of Keynes, but particularly those still concerned with mopping up after the rise and fall of NAIRU and the general debacle of the new classical economics. Keynes was right, and we now observe the paramountcy of monetary policy on the global scale. The interest rate emerges as a prime global redistributive force and, through this, as a prime lever on global unemployment.

Rich countries, in other words, control the movement of inequality. They control it at home, for better or worse, with policies affecting employment, minimum wages, and unionization. And they control it beyond their own frontiers, through the global financial system.

My father would not be surprised. In the days when he was battling Milton Friedman's monetarism, he often sought to clarify matters for the deeply obtuse by enunciating Galbraith's First Law of the interest rate. As a general rule, he would say, people who have money to lend have more money than people who do not have money to lend.

References

Blanchard, Olivier J. 2005. European unemployment: The evolution of facts and ideas. *MIT Department of Economics Working Paper* 05–24, October 20.

Galbraith, James K. 1996. Uneven development and the destabilization of the North. *International Review of Applied Economics* 10 (1): 107–20.

———. 2006. Maastricht 2042 and the fate of Europe: Toward convergence and full employment. *Levy Economics Institute Public Policy Brief* 87, November. Commissioned by the Friedrich Ebert Stiftung and published separately by its International Policy Analysis Unit, March 2007.

———. 2007. Global macroeconomics and global inequality. In *Global Inequality*, ed. David Held and Ayse Kaya. Ralph Miliband Lecture Series on Inequalities at the London School of Economics. Cambridge, UK: Polity Press.

Galbraith, James K., and William A. Darity Jr. 1994. *Macroeconomics*. Boston: Houghton-Mifflin.

Galbraith, James K., and Lu Jiaqing. 2000. Sustainable development and the open-door policy in China. Paper for the Project on Development, Trade and International Finance. New York: Council on Foreign Relations.

Harris, John R., and Michael P. Todaro. 1970. Migration, unemployment and development: A two-sector analysis. *American Economic Review* 60 (1): 126–42.

Project LINK: http://www.chass.utoronto.ca/link/.

University of Texas Inequality Project: http://utip.gov.utexas.edu.

Yotopoulos, Pan. 1996. *Exchange rate parity for trade and development: Theory, tests, and case studies*. Cambridge: Cambridge University Press.

CHAPTER 13

MONEY AND DEFAULT

C. A. E. GOODHART*

INTRODUCTION

IF EVERYONE ALWAYS PAID THEIR DEBTS IN FULL and at the due date, there would be little or no need for commercial banks. Everyone would then have the highest possible credit rating, would need no monitoring, and could borrow, or lend, at the default-free rate of interest. Although many formal macroeconomic models (implicitly) employ an assumption of a default-free system in their so-called transversality assumption, it is not, alas, a characteristic of the real world.

Indeed, the probability of default (PD) is a key concept in any analysis of financial fragility. It is, of course, central to the Basel II exercise. At the more formal level, modeling of default (following from the approach pioneered by Martin Shubik and his co-authors) is the crucial element for the analysis of financial fragility that I and my colleagues have been developing (see Tsomocos 2003a, 2003b; Goodhart, Sunirand, and Tsomocos 2004, 2005, 2006a, 2006b; Tsomocos and Zicchino 2005).

On the academic side, however, there was not, in the early years, the 1970s and '80s, much analysis being undertaken that could really help with modeling and resolving financial fragility issues. In these years, economic specialists in money and banking were strong on institutional and

* Parts of this chapter have been taken from my earlier paper, "What can academics contribute to the study of financial stability?" in *The Economic and Social Review*, 36 (3), Winter 2005–06. I am grateful to this journal for permission to reprint.

historical knowledge—names such as Richard Sayers, J. S. G. Wilson, and T. E. Gregory in the UK spring to mind. They had direct knowledge of the many historical cases of bank failures, of what had happened and why. But such (so-called) descriptive studies were being downgraded in professional esteem relative to more mathematically based models.

Then the economics profession took a large step along the road to analytical rigor via the Lucas revolution, whereby all acceptable macro-models are required, or supposed, to have optimizing microtheoretic foundations. But such models are quite hard to construct; indeed, that built-in complexity is one of the underlying reasons for their academic *éclat*. To reduce the dimensionality of the macromonetary economic problem, the standard assumptions are that the agents in each main sector, notably persons and companies, can be modeled via a homogeneous, infinitely lived representative agent, who *always* manages, in due course, to pay her debts. This latter is known technically as the "transversality condition."

Armed with these simplifications, much, perhaps most, macromonetary analysis in the recent decade has revolved around a three-equation model: an IS curve, a Phillips curve, and a Taylor-type reaction function. A typical example, taken from McCallum (2004) is:

$$(1)\quad y_t = b_0 + b_1(R_t - E_t\Delta p_{t+1}) + E_t y_{t+1} + v_t$$

$$(2)\quad \Delta pt = \beta E_t \Delta p_{t+1} + \kappa(y_t - \bar{y}_t) + u_t$$

$$(3)\quad R_t = (1 - \mu_3)[r + \Delta p_t + \mu_t(\Delta p_t - \pi^*) + \mu_2(y_t - \bar{y}_t)] + \mu_3 R_{t-1} + e_t$$

where y_t = log of output, $\bar{y}_t$ = log of natural-rate output, p_t = log of price level, R_t = one-period nominal interest rate, and v_t, u_t, e_t = stochastic shocks.

There are numerous problems and shortcomings in this three-equation model, some of which I have detailed elsewhere (2005, 2006), but the main one that I want to address now is this transversality condition. What this assumption effectively does is remove all default risk from private-sector borrowing. If so, *every* agent can borrow, or lend, at the safe rate of interest.

Indeed, if there is no default risk, it is not at all clear why there is any need for money! All that is needed is a recording system, showing people's current net debit-credit position. There is no basis for a cash-in-advance requirement, since any seller knows that she can rely absolutely on any buyer's IOU being fully honored and earning the riskless rate until it matures. Moreover, any seller can at any time immediately buy anything she wants, since her credit is always impeccable. By the same token and analysis, there is no logical basis for money in the utility function. Indeed, setting up a model that simultaneously incorporates transversality conditions *and* an essential role for money is tantamount to making a fundamental logical error. This is one reason why a few of us monetary economists have paid some attention to the apparently arcane question of whether, in a world without money, a central bank could, and would, still set nominal interest rates, relative to some, perhaps notional, *numeraire* (see Woodford 1998, 2000, 2003, chapter 2; Goodhart 2000).

What this implies is that the possibility of default is central to the analysis of any monetary world (without default we reenter the Arrow-Debreu-Hahn paradigm). Let me take a brief digression to consider the implications of this for the analysis of the nature, and evolution, of money itself. The main competing theories about the evolution of money are the transaction cost minimization theory of Menger, now updated by Kiyotaki and Wright, and the Cartalist, or credit, theory of money (see, for example, *Credit and State Theories of Money*, Wray, ed., 2004). Insofar as the possibility of default is the main factor causing us to require immediate payment in some generally acceptable medium of exchange, rather than accepting an IOU, then the normal means of payment will become the IOU of that agent in society whose probability of default is least; usually a low probability of default is correlated with holding considerable power in the socioeconomic system, as with temples and, above all, governments.

This is *not* to claim that commodity moneys do not exist, that all money is credit money. But let us consider the two best known types of commodity moneys. The first of these are the precious metals, gold and silver. Let me make several points. First, an unstamped quantity of gold or silver—that is, one not in the form of a coin—would be a poor transaction medium, because a transactor would need to know its metallic fineness (carats), and that is specialized information. These precious metals need the intervention of a mint to provide reliable information on quality, and that too brings one back to the likelihood of default and debasement. Second, gold and silver were so valuable, relative to normal market transaction needs, that they were rarely used in day-to-day purchases. For the latter, subsidiary (not full-bodied) coins, or tokens, or IOUs were more common (on this, see a forthcoming book by G. Selgin, *Good Money*, about the provision of copper coins to meet transaction needs in the UK's Industrial Revolution, 1780–1820). Third Gresham's Law meant that, if the market value of a metal rose above its prescribed monetary value, that previous metal would disappear from monetary circulation. Thus, market forces would tend to ensure that precious-metal moneys were, on average, overvalued relative to their commodity valuation.

The second type of commodity money—amongst the most common and best known in Western history—is cattle; we derive the word pecuniary, which means monetary, from the Latin root of *pecus*, meaning cow. If we think of a basis for cost-minimization in transactions, we tend to require the following qualities in our commodity moneys: standardized, durable, portable, divisible. How closely do cattle meet these requirements?

While commodity moneys have surely existed, nevertheless the essence of a monetary system is that it has become based on the IOUs of the most creditworthy agent in that system, the least likely to default, notably the government. The question of whether money was essentially a commodity or credit could be, and was, debated fiercely under the gold standard, but the move to fiat money systems should really have resolved that issue by now, in favor of the credit or Cartalist theories of money.

Without default, we do not need money; and we do not need financial intermediaries either. If all agents always repay their debts in full, what more information does a creditor need? (Note that this also implies a perfect resale market for all IOUs of any initial maturity.) Without default, all agents can themselves lend, or borrow, at the safe rate. Why is there any need for banks as financial intermediaries? Indeed, there is none. In my view, the foremost text currently available on monetary economics is *Interest and Prices*, by Woodford, 2003. In it, there is absolutely no reference to commercial banks, and there is no financial intermediation. In most theoretical macromonetary models, there is only a central bank, which supplies base money and sets interest rates on a short-term, safe, default-free asset. There are no commercial banks, so obviously no bank failures, no risky assets, and no risk premia on defaultable assets. It is remarkable that money/macro analysts have managed to construct such a massive theoretical, and indeed empirical, edifice on such sanitized and implausible foundations. But, whatever one may think about the macroeconomic analysis, it can provide no basis whatsoever for the study of financial fragility.

Moreover, the conditions that would be necessary to allow the transversality condition to hold in the midst of life's many uncertainties are impossibly demanding. They would require either perfect foresight, or *complete* and perfect markets, in which *all* eventualities can be hedged at the outset.

Under such circumstances, a Walrasian general equilibrium (GE) model without money would, of course, be correct, and almost all Keynesian (and Post Keynesian) insights (for example, the importance of animal spirits, confidence, market psychology) and constructs (for example, the consumption function, liquidity preference, et cetera), are patently incorrect and superfluous. Thus Post Keynesian economics must give a central role to default. While this is widely accepted as a generality (Hyman Minsky comes immediately to mind), the problem is that the profession at large will take notice only if default is incorporated into rigorous, mathematical models. That, in a nutshell, is the purpose of my own, and my colleagues', recent work.

Default

The implication of the above analysis is straightforward. If academic theorists are going to be able to provide much help in the analysis and modeling of financial fragility, then they are going to have to include default as a central element of their analysis and models.

There has been an understandable reluctance to do so, in some large part because modeling default is difficult. It is difficult because it is not a continuous process, such as is more easily handled mathematically. Instead, it is akin to an on off switch. Firms and persons are either declared bankrupt or are supposedly solvent. Moreover, the penalties for bankruptcy—to reputation, to self-esteem, to access to future credit, et cetera—are frequently non pecuniary, and it can be difficult, or impossible, to give a monetary equivalence to such penalties.

In my view, the best current approach to modeling default has been that developed by Martin Shubik and his colleagues (Shubik 1973; Shubik and Wilson 1977; Dubey, Geanakoplos, and Shubik 2000). They assume that agents assess the likelihood of future (economic) conditions occurring and then choose a policy that will have state-varying probabilities of default, that is, bankruptcy. Naturally, if a bad state occurs, given the initial policy choice, the likelihood of bankruptcy occurring is much higher than if a good state occurs.

Therefore, given the expectations about the future states of the world (expectations that are usually assumed to be rational), bankruptcy probabilities will be endogenously chosen, although the number that actually occurs will be contingent on what state of nature arrives. This endogenous choice of bankruptcy obviously depends on the costs of becoming bankrupt compared with the benefits of choosing a higher bankruptcy probability. These benefits are twofold: first, a riskier strategy (normally) offers a higher mean expected return; second, in the bankrupt state, you get to save on financial out-payments—as the Argentineans were pleased to discover.

Obviously, if the penalties on bankruptcy are zero, everyone defaults; but this is socially sub-optimal, since no one lends and there is no financial intermediation. On the other hand, if the penalty is infinite (for example, the whole family of a bankrupt is stoned to death), no one defaults; but this is equally sub-optimal, since no one would borrow. There must be an interior optimum, given bankruptcy costs, future economic expectations, and risk preferences. In the medium term, however, penalties attached to bankruptcy are not fixed but depend on a variety of factors, including social norms and the legal framework. Perhaps because macroeconomists have shied away from dealing with bankruptcy directly, not nearly enough academic economic research has been undertaken on the questions of the socially optimal framework for bankruptcy laws and on how to set penalties so as to provide the best balance between the interests of creditors and debtors and between excessive and insufficient risk-taking in the economy.

This approach leads to models of endogenous, state-dependent bankruptcy, with the non pecuniary costs of default entering into the objective function of agents. The particular way in which default is modeled in the Shubik approach is that an agent will decide a policy which, in state of the world *j*, will lead her to default on *x* percent of her borrowing. That, however, raises a problem. Because of reputational effects, cross-default clauses, et cetera, most borrowers, and especially banks vis-à-vis their depositors, default either simultaneously on all of their liabilities or on none. An agent cannot normally refuse to pay out anything on one *tranche* of borrowing and yet go on fully meeting the payment schedules on other *tranches*.

In what I hope will be an important paper in this field, two of my colleagues researching in this area (Dimitri Tsomocos and Lea Zicchino) are proposing the argument that there is an equivalence, an isomorphism, between deciding to default in state *j* on 5 percent of one's debts for sure and deciding to have a similar 5 percent probability of defaulting on *all* of one's debts simultaneously. If there are *enough* agents, so that idiosyncratic chance gets removed by the law of large numbers, then the situation in each case is indeed the same. But, if there are only a few large banks in the system, then a certain default rate of 5 percent of assets is *not* the same as a 5 percent probability of default on all assets. However, large banks are almost never closed and liquidated. Instead, they are quickly reconstituted, with depositors taking an often small, proportional loss; that, in effect, takes us back to a default rate of, say, 5 percent on all assets.

Particularly if default is modeled in terms of choosing a probability of default, *i*, in state of the world *j*, then it matters precisely who does default. The default of large agents or banks, or more interconnected agents or banks, has a greater impact on other agents and banks than in the case of a smaller defaulter. In any case, risk preferences, and expectations of future economic conditions, differ from agent to agent. So this approach naturally leads to the inclusion of heterogeneous agents or banks in our models. This causes another problem: A model containing both (endogenously chosen) default and heterogeneous agents is almost bound to have a much larger dimensionality, more variables, than the standard macromodels now in common use, and that makes such models less easily tractable, either mathematically or empirically.

After all of this, it will not come as a surprise that it is just such models, incorporating default as a central factor, and with heterogeneous agents, banks, and households, that I and my colleagues have been working on in the last few years.

Probability and Default

If default is the key feature of financial fragility, the probability of an agent defaulting becomes the key statistic for risk management. And, of course, PD, or the probability of default, lies at the heart of current credit-risk assessment, notably in Basel II. How can academic economists help in the estimation of PD? There are several ways.

First, a stylized fact is that the occurrence of nonperforming loans (NPLs) and of defaults (both for banks and non-banks), is not constant but is time and state varying. One relatively straightforward, and essentially empirical, exercise is to explore what variables Granger-cause the time series fluctuations in NPLs, or bankruptcies, in some class of borrowers. A particular version of such a method is to identify a set of specific crisis events and examine what common factors preceded them. There is a vast literature on this.

Such largely atheoretical work may suffer somewhat from the Lucas critique (or, indeed, Goodhart's Law); that is, if a stable, strong relationship were to be found between a prior set of variables and some kind of subsequent crisis, then agents and markets would come to anticipate the likelihood of that crisis and thereby forestall it. The main factor, however, that is currently found to explain NPLs and bank crises is excessively fast prior expansion in bank lending (and in broad money). This empirical work may be rescued from the Lucas critique by a combination of our inability to distinguish between trend and cycle looking forward and of the engagingly optimistic human trait of believing that each cyclical upswing is the start of a new and better trend: that, in the common parlance, we are entering a "new economy."[1]

Another atheoretical way of estimating PDs that economists have developed is to try to back out the implied default risk of an agent from market valuations, whether equity or bond prices, using either Merton-type models or yield spreads. I have certain reservations about the likely accuracy of such implied predictions, both because the market may itself be prone to excessive swings of optimism and pessimism and have insufficient information, as in the case of Enron, and because the method for backing out default risk may not be able to distinguish between variations in credit risk and other factors, such as liquidity risk. Nonetheless, empirical models of this kind are now an important part of the armory of economists and supervisors and regulators.

This approach has normally been used to estimate the PD of a single agent. Now, however, in a valuable and original step forward, some Austrian economists connected with the Austrian National Bank (Elsinger, Lehar, and Summer 2003) have applied the same Merton-type methodology to seek to assess the PD of a portfolio of banks. Thus, can we use such models to predict the likelihood of failure of bank *y* conditioned on the prior failure of bank *z*?

As noted earlier, defaults, whether of banks or bank borrowers, are not constant over time but tend to come bunched together. There are two main potential causes of such temporal bunching. The first is that a common external shock may be responsible; the second is that a failure of one agent may make a second agent more fragile because of positive interconnections between them. This second source of fragility is normally termed contagion.

It is important to be able to distinguish between the two causes of bunched defaults, because the appropriate regulatory remedies will differ. In particular, rescuing individual banks will appear much more sensible if the main cause of financial fragility is contagion rather than a common shock.

One of the most obvious channels of interconnectedness between banks, and hence of potential contagion, is the interbank market. Recently, considerable work has gone into the estimation of whether, conditioned on the failure of one bank, other banks would also fail as a result of interbank defaults. Examples of this genre include Wells 2002, Upper and Worms 2004, and Furfine 2003. In general, the results of this work are quite encouraging, especially when it is assumed that the failing bank can realize its assets *quickly* and thereby pay off creditors a significant proportion of its indebtedness.

This latter appreciation leads to three further issues. First, how quickly will reliable and credible information on the extent of the insolvency (of the initial failing bank) be available? Second, and conditional on the first issue, how far will agents withdraw funds from those other banks perceived most at risk (but not necessarily insolvent), just on the precautionary principle? And third, how far will asset sales, either by the initial insolvent bank or, much more likely, by those that perceive themselves at risk from secondary withdrawals (see the second issue, above), drive down asset prices and thereby weaken the solvency status of all of the remaining banks (besides adding to general fears)?

If these extra conditions are met, so that there is quick, reliable, credible information, few secondary withdrawals from other banks (on the precautionary principle), and not much panic selling of assets, then the generally favorable results from these studies—that there is little contagious risk from the interbank market—will stand; if not, they won't.

What this suggests, in other words, is that there are potentially multiple channels for contagion and that any one channel may, or may not, become serious, depending on prior conditions. This again makes it difficult to undertake any fully satisfactory analysis and modeling. Once again, however, we hope that the modeling strategy that we have been exploring may allow us to examine multiple, simultaneous channels of contagion. However, our work is, at best, only a start.

Conclusions

If economic theory and formal models are to provide analytical support and guidance for issues relating to financial fragility, they must make the modeling of default a central feature of their work. This is not an easy exercise, although the treatment of default as an endogenously chosen variable, which was pioneered by Martin Shubik, seems a good starting point.

In the meantime, of course, assessment of the probabilities of default lies at the heart of risk assessment in general and of Basel II in particular. Economists have made considerable advances in developing techniques for assessing PDs, notably Merton-type approaches. There does, however, remain a difficulty in distinguishing among the causes of bunched defaults, that is, financial crises, between the common effect of an adverse external shock and the contagious interactions between banks. In this latter field, much remains to be done.

Note

1. Ministers of finance are particularly prone to this delusion, since their job, their raison d'être, is to introduce reforms that will raise average productivity and lower the natural rate of unemployment. So, if productivity rises or unemployment falls, they see it not as a cyclical phenomenon but as a sign of the success of their policies. Thus, a fiscal rule that demands surpluses during economic upswings to offset deficits during downturns is almost bound to fail, since ministers will rarely see themselves as being in an above-trend state. Such above-trend periods are far easier to identify looking backward than looking forward.

   Complaints about past failures to seize on good economic conditions—for example, to reduce debt levels—are easy to make *after the event* but harder to put forward convincingly at the time, when forward-looking expectations about the future are (excessively) optimistic.

References

Dubey, P., J. Geanakoplos, and M. Shubik. 2000. Default in a general equilibrium model with incomplete markets. *Cowles Foundation Discussion Paper* 1247. Cowles Foundation for Research in Economics, Yale University.

Elsinger, H., A. Lehar, and M. Summer. 2003. Risk assessment for banking systems. Oesterreichische Nationalbank (Austrian National Bank), working paper 79.

Furfine, C. 2003. Interbank exposures: Quantifying the risk of contagion. *Journal of Money, Credit and Banking* 35:111–28.

Goodhart, C. 2000. Can central banking survive the IT revolution? In The future of monetary policy, ed. A. S. Posen. Special issue, *International Finance* 3 (2): 189–210.

———. 2005. The foundations of macroeconomics: Theoretical rigour versus empirical realism. Paper presented at Louvain-la-Neuve Conference on the History of Economic Thought, January 20–22.

———. 2005–06. What can academics contribute to the study of financial stability? *The Economic and Social Review* 36 (3): 189–203.

———. 2006. Monetary and social relationships. In *Money, financial instability and stabilization policy*, ed. L. Randall Wray and Mathew Forstater. Cheltenham, UK: Edward Elgar.

Goodhart, C., P. Sunirand, and D. Tsomocos. 2004. A model to analyse financial fragility: Applications. *Journal of Financial Stability* 1 (1): 1–30.

———. 2005. A risk assessment model for banks. *Annals of Finance* 1 (2): 197–224.

———. 2006a. A model to analyse financial fragility. *Economic Theory* 27:107–42.

———. 2006b. A time series analysis of financial fragility in the UK banking system. *Annals of Finance* 2 (1): 1–21.

Selgin, G. Forthcoming. *Good money: Birmingham, button-makers, the Royal Mint, and the beginnings of modern coinage, 1775–1821*. Ann Arbor, MI: University of Michigan Press.

Shubik, M. 1973. Commodity money, oligopoly, credit and bankruptcy in a general equilibrium model. *Western Economic Journal* 11:24–38.

Shubik, M., and C. Wilson. 1977. The optimal bankruptcy rule in a trading economy using fiat money. *Journal of Economics* 37:337–54.

Tsomocos, D. 2003a. Equilibrium analysis, banking and financial instability. *Journal of Mathematical Economics* 39 (5–6): 619–55.

———. 2003b. Equilibrium analysis, banking, contagion and financial fragility. *Bank of England Working Paper* 175.

Tsomocos, D., and L. Zicchino. 2005. On modelling endogenous default. *Financial Markets Group Discussion Paper* 548.

Upper, C., and A. Worms. 2004. Estimating bilateral exposures in the German interbank market: Is there a danger of contagion? *European Economic Review* 48:827–49.

Wells, S. 2002. UK interbank exposures: Systemic risk implications. *Financial Stability Review*, Bank of England, December: 175–82.

Woodford, M. 1998. Doing without money: Controlling inflation in a post-monetary world. *Review of Economic Dynamics* 1:173–219.

———. 2000. Monetary policy in a world without money. In The future of monetary policy, ed. A. S. Posen. Special issue, *International Finance* 3 (2): 261–72.

———. 2003. *Interest and prices*. Princeton, NJ: Princeton University Press.

Wray, L. R., ed. 2004. *Credit and state theories of money: The contributions of A. Mitchell Innes*. Cheltenham, UK: Edward Elgar.

Index